Partitioning Palestine

PARTITIONING PALESTINE

Legal Fundamentalism in the Palestinian–Israeli Conflict

John Strawson

PlutoPress
www.plutobooks.com

First published 2010 by Pluto Press
345 Archway Road, London N6 5AA and
175 Fifth Avenue, New York, NY 10010

www.plutobooks.com

Distributed in the United States of America exclusively by
Palgrave Macmillan, a division of St. Martin's Press LLC,
175 Fifth Avenue, New York, NY 10010

British Library Cataloguing in Publication Data
A catalogue record for this book is available from the British Library

ISBN   978 0 7453 2324 4   Hardback
ISBN   978 0 7453 2323 7   Paperback

Library of Congress Cataloging in Publication Data applied for

10   9   8   7   6   5   4   3   2   1

Designed and produced for Pluto Press by
Chase Publishing Services Ltd, 33 Livonia Road, Sidmouth, EX10 9JB, England
Typeset from disk by Stanford DTP Services, Northampton, England
Printed and bound in the European Union by
CPI Antony Rowe, Chippenham and Eastbourne

In memory of my mother
Shirley Brokus Joffe

Contents

Acknowledgments

I am indebted to many who have commented on the arguments contained in this book. I owe a special debt to the staff and students of the Institute of Law at Birzeit University who taught me so much on my teaching visits in Palestine between 1996 and 2006. I would like in particular to thank Camille Mansour, Ghassan Faramant and Murdar Kassis for their generosity and wisdom. I am also grateful for the probing questions and thoughtful insights of Ghassan Abdullah. Fouz Abdel Hadi has been a source of inspiration. I learned a great deal from the work of the international research collaboration on legal reform in Palestine which was an initiative of the Law and Society Association and financially supported by the association and the British Academy. Working closely with Asem Khalil, Mahmoud Fayyad and Kim van der Borght was especially productive. I have also been fortunate to benefit from many challenging discussions in Israel especially with Sheva Freidman, Avram Shamroni, Alon Herel, Assaf Likhovksi, Shai Lavi, Jock Falkson and Sharon Bacher. The Law School at the University of East London has been very supportive of this project, not least with sabbatical leave at a critical stage. The Dean of the School, Fiona Fairweather, has been energetic in ensuring an excellent research environment in which to work. Collaborative work with many colleagues in the School, in particular with Barry Collins and Chandra Sriram, has made an important contribution to my thoughts about international law and conflict resolution. I must also thank the many students at the University of East London who over the past few years have asked me searching questions and offered such incisive analyses on the Palestinian–Israeli conflict in my classes on international law and Middle East studies. Peter Fitzpatrick has been an important influence on my thoughts about law and postcolonialism. Beverley Brown has been constant with her advice and encouragement. Roshan de Silva Wijeyeratne has never let an argument about nationalism go unchallenged. Some of the ideas in this book have formed the basis of conference papers and I am grateful for the many useful comments and exchanges they have engendered. Engaging with Irus Braverman who has offered such a unique contribution to any understanding of the Palestinian–Israeli conflict, was for me one of the richest encounters of the conference circuit.

My daughters Kate Hartnell and Anna Hartnell have been unwaveringly supportive of my work but have also been a source of stern and productive criticism. Ahmed Mehdi has been there at every stage, tolerated much and offered more ideas than I can ever acknowledge.

Particular thanks go to Roger van Zwanenberg and the team at Pluto Press. Roger has demonstrated generosity and patience without which this book would not have appeared.

Introduction

International law has too often been used as a cheerleader in the Palestinian–Israeli conflict. For over a hundred years law has served the protagonists as a resource not only to justify their rights but also to dignify lurid threats and violent acts. This use of law has engendered a festering sense of justice amongst Palestinians and Israelis that has fostered conflict rather than offering a means for its resolution. Each side has become cocooned within a legal righteousness in which its own legitimacy is unimpeachable while that of the other is compromised. This has nourished the existential character of the conflict. As a consequence war, occupation, and defiance of the international community are justified as the exercise of legal rights. A cycle of law has sustained a cycle of violence.

For over a century law has hovered over the Palestinian–Israeli conflict. In many ways it has been a conflict forged by law. From 1897 the Jewish claim to a national home was to be achieved by "public law." Few national movements have been so conscious of the utility of international law in pursuing national freedom as Zionism. While the Zionist movement drew ideologically on a secular version of the Jewish history of homelessness its early leaders were uncannily aware that in themselves a long history, the miseries of the Diaspora and the longing for return did not constitute a sufficient basis for winning a national home. It was not the existence of Jewish national identity but its legal recognition that was central. This was to be achieved though an assiduous diplomatic strategy that began with the Great Powers of the nineteenth century and adapted to the changing international community that took shape in the League of Nations and the United Nations in the twentieth century. In its first 50 years of existence the Zionist movement adopted a pragmatic attitude toward international law. International law was seen very much as the expression of the will of the powerful. As a result great emphasis was placed on gaining formal recognition for national status through international legal instruments. The League of Nations Mandate for Palestine and the United Nations partition resolution were the result.

1

Palestinians during the same period were also experiencing the rise of national consciousness. Arab nationalism, however, projected a new order for the Arab people that was to be fashioned through unification on the basis of culture and language. This drive to unification encountered the decomposing Ottoman Empire and the arrival of European colonial powers in the region. Palestine as an entity was only to become important once the Ottomans were defeated in World War I and the European powers completed their domination of the Middle East. It was this that was to prove decisive in the creation of a new Middle East patterned in the strategic interests of the colonial powers. The rivalry between France and Britain ensured that Arab unity was thwarted as new boundaries were decreed. Palestine made its appearance not merely in the wake of Ottoman defeat but also just at the moment that France and Britain succeeded in crushing Arab nationalism in Syria. The apparent ease with which the European powers replaced the Ottomans and established the network of Middle East mandates appeared as a great injustice to the Arab world. Nonetheless the new order was established with careful legal steps under the authority of the League of Nations. Zionist diplomacy achieved its critical success in winning support for creating a Jewish national home in the Palestine mandate. Thus whereas the Zionists benefited from the new legal dispensation, the Arab world seemed to be the loser. As a consequence the legal narratives of Arab and Palestinian nationalism were crafted against the grain of the positive legal order and sought succor from an imagined natural law. It was at this point that political resistance to the Mandate became iron-clad in a fundamentalist view of international law.

International law is an elusive system. Its modern form was only taking shape in the late nineteenth and early twentieth centuries. As a consequence its doctrines and institutions were somewhat rudimentary. The object of international law is to create an international environment where states act in accordance with the rule of law. However, the very basis of this idea, the existence of states, reveals its problematic character. As with the Palestinian–Israeli conflict the critical question that international legal doctrine has never satisfactorily resolved is the conditions under which states come into being. This problem is compounded by the abstract nature of the rule of law which lacks any fixed content. As a consequence the criteria for creating states and the content of the rule of law are prey to the politics of the time. As international law emerged it was colonialism that was to determine both.

This should not imply that international legal doctrine does not have the possibility of developing in a relatively autonomous way from the political sphere. Unlike politics which is determined by ideologies and expediencies international law is formed through a discursive engagement with principles. These are contained in the sources of law. The dominant sources are and remain treaties and international custom; while treaties are the result of negotiations between states and custom grows out of state practice both require legal determination to be implemented. However, legal determination at an authoritative judicial level is rare. International law exists mostly as scholarly and professional discourse that is conducted in articles and books that circulate amongst specialists. Statements about international law are also regularly made in reports by human rights organizations and other international bodies. This body of literature contains arguments about what international law might be and cannot offer declarations of what the law is. Thus international legal literature is highly speculative or takes the form of debates on key questions. The existence and identification of the sources of law, including such foundational ones as the Covenant of the League of Nations or the United Nations Charter, offer only the raw material for legal argument rather than offering a clearly understood code. As a result international law remains highly indeterminate as there are many competing but often equally authoritative statements about the same principles. As Rosalyn Higgins has said this means that international law is not so much about finding rules as making choices about their interpretation.[1] Legal fundamentalism denies that there is a choice to make and, rather, asserts that legal principles are clearly fixed, categorical and imperative. It is behind this wall of rigidity that the Palestinians and Israelis have positioned themselves.

The most authoritative legal view of the Palestinian–Israeli conflict is contained in the advisory opinion of the International Court of Justice on the legal consequences of the Israeli wall in the West Bank.[2] As Rosalyn Higgins pointed out the General Assembly did not ask the court to determine whether or not the wall was legal but for an opinion on the consequences of illegal acts.[3] The resolution which initiated the proceedings entitled "Illegal Israeli actions in Occupied East Jerusalem and the rest of the Occupied Palestinian Territory" made clear that the Assembly had already taken the view that the wall was in breach of international humanitarian law.[4] Many would agree with this view but it is highly significant that the General Assembly would think it appropriate to pre-empt an authoritative legal determination by the International Court of Justice. This position was not supported by legal argument or evidence. It may have been this tinge of legal fundamentalism that resulted in the resolution only attracting the support of 90 states out of the 172 who voted. Nonetheless whatever the imperfections in the request for the opinion it was to be the first time that an international judicial view would be offered on any aspect of the conflict. When the opinion was handed down it became evident that it was a challenge to the dominant legal narratives of both Palestinians and Israelis.[5]

The Court did not confine itself to dealing only with the consequences of an illegal wall but sought to explain how that illegality arose. It approached its task by determining the status of the territory on which the wall was built. This meant mining the key legal instruments that have constituted Palestine and Israel and those which since 1967 have attempted to regulate relations between them. While the comments on these instruments were cryptic their mention was highly significant. The Court referred to: the League of Nations Mandate for Palestine (1922); the United Nations partition resolution (1947); the 1949 Armistice Agreements; UN Security Council resolution 242 (1967); the Oslo agreements (1993–99) and the roadmap for Middle East peace (2003). The court made a critical distinction between the territory which lay to the west of the 1949 Green Line and that which lay to its east. It regarded the land to the West as "the territory of Israel itself."[6] In analyzing the areas to the east, the court determined that "all these territories (including East Jerusalem) remain occupied territories and Israel has continued to have the status of occupying power."[7] This clear distinction between Israel and the occupied territories dealt a judicial blow to both Palestinian and Israeli legal narratives. Claims that threw doubt on Israel's legitimacy were rejected as were any arguments that Israel had any title to the occupied territories. The opinion ends with an appeal to the UN General Assembly to encourage, "on the basis of international law, a negotiated solution to the outstanding problems and the establishment of a Palestinian State, existing side by side with Israel." This unequivocal judicial approval for a two-state solution reflected the long-standing view of the international community.

Partitioning Palestine sets out to analyze the key legal instruments that the Court identifies as central to the conflict. The book revolves around a discussion of these instruments that define distinct legal moments: the League of Nations Mandate that created Palestine; the United Nations partition resolution that divides it; and the Oslo agreements that aimed to resolve the conflict. In each stage the legal texts have an existential quality which seeks to give shape to national claims. The purpose of the book is to track the way in which these legal texts themselves form a legal narrative about how these national claims are constituted. Legal texts themselves encode the values of the time which produced them. The principles that they contain cannot be understood only through a textual analysis but need to be placed within their context. While part of this context is the historical period in which texts were written, another important element is the way in which texts produce discursive imagery that structures the way we understand their content. This approach is influenced by Edward Said's work which emphasized the power of discursive images in texts but insisted on the significance of their political and cultural environment.[8]

Partitioning Palestine thus takes the texts themselves seriously but only as a point of departure for the discussion. The issue is not to see these authoritative legal instruments as dictating a singular meaning but rather to see what possibilities they offer us. In the process of analyzing the texts in this contextual manner some myths that have achieved the status of facts can be disposed of. The partition resolution is a case in point. The creation of a Jewish state in 1948 is now commonly regarded as a form of international compensation to the Jews for the Holocaust. It is regularly claimed that guilt, in particular "western guilt," led the international community to foist the Jews onto the innocent Palestinians, thus provoking the conflict. However, through a systematic reading of contemporary UN debates and the partition proposal contained in the report of the United Nations Special Committee on Palestine (UNSCOP) no such intention can be found. The Holocaust is rarely mentioned. There are certainly no expressions of guilt. Indeed the UNSCOP report in a sideways reference to the Holocaust explicitly says that its recommendations for partition are not intended as a solution to the "Jewish problem."[9] In reading the debates in particular I was struck by the callous manner in which the Holocaust was either ignored or sometimes referred to. I was also surprised to find that anti-Semitic remarks were common and never challenged. Nor was the intention of partition to dispossess the Palestinians as the proposals made clear that all civil rights and property rights were to be undisturbed. It is thus a myth that the source of the problem was a legal decision to hand over part of Palestine to the Jews at the expense of the Palestinians.

The categorical rejection of partition by the Palestinians and the Arab world – such a central part of the legal narrative after 1947 – does need, in my view, to be re-thought. This is not just a question of historical accuracy. The view that the United Nations perpetrated such a fundamental injustice against the Palestinian people informs current politics and attitudes towards possible solutions to the conflict. Too frequently the real injustices of the present – such as the 2008–09 Gaza war – are seen merely as a continuation of the assumed injustices of 1947–48. The legal arguments that were used to justify the war against partition ensure that the lethal relationship between law and violence became established. This became especially problematic when the war was posed in such existentialist terms. The problem that we face is that this history has a hold over Palestinians and Israelis today.

This hold can be seen in the Oslo peace process. The expectations of the parties for a just peace were framed by these experiences. Israel, by 1993 a colonial power in the West Bank and Gaza, entered the negotiations as if it were the threatened state of 1948. As a result instead of addressing the issue of decolonization it rather set about working out how little of Palestine could be passed to the Palestinians. Oslo offered an important opportunity to both parties to make progress. While there can be much criticism of the Palestinian negotiating stance the main responsibility for Oslo's failure lies with Israel. Israel's starting point was informed by a legal view of the results of 1948 and so worked on the assumption that it had title to the occupied territories. When the issue of a Palestinian state did arise, it was posed not in the context of the right to self-determination of Palestinians but as a concession conditional on Israel's security. Oslo did not focus on the speedy withdrawal from a colonial territory in order to achieve Palestinian liberation but rather on the convenience of the colonizing state. This might be dismissed as a self-serving legal interpretation except that Israel was able to convince the international community to see things in the same light. The roadmap encoded this view which imposed conditions on Palestinians, including the demand to effectively change its leadership, while leaving the Israeli occupation intact.

This book's concern with the past is motivated by the desire to break its spell. An effort is needed to break the cycle in the conflict whereby each party constantly refreshes its confidence in the legal justice of its case. It is also true that international law has been used by supporters of both sides in the same way. This has engendered an equally circular process where international law is deployed to prove that one side is right and the other is wrong. International law becomes used in a censorious way as a substitute for political assessment. In its most extreme form this approach to international law has something more in common with the world of Harry Potter than the one we inhabit. It is turned into a magical substance to ensure that good triumphs over evil. As a consequence international law is used to push the parties into the next round of fighting in the belief that their complete triumph is not merely possible but totally justified. This version of law requires that one side wins and the other loses.

This book will no doubt irritate many Palestinians and Israelis – and their supporters. That is its intention. We cannot afford any more complacent legal pronouncements that delay Palestinian freedom or justify threats to Israel's existence. Rather, we have to decide what we want to do with international law in the Palestinian–Israeli conflict. We need to eliminate the idea that international law sets a series of strict imperatives that must be followed. We have a choice which can press international law into service for both Palestinians and Israelis. If *Partitioning Palestine* has one message it is that law and justice cannot operate well without wisdom. International law needs to encode the wisdom of compromise that can aid both parties to attain their state on the basis of full equality and security. It is evident that the international community needs to resume its responsibilities to ensure that this happens. Palestinians and Israelis cannot afford any more sweeping victories or catastrophic defeats.

1
Making Palestine:
Mapping the Middle East

Palestine came into being as part of a grand imperial plan for the Middle East. The Ottoman provinces that were to form it were backwaters compared to the metropolitan centers of Baghdad, Damascus and Beirut. The British and French in refashioning the region were aware nonetheless that Palestine was richly endowed by the nationalist imagination of both Jews and Arabs. As nation replaced empire with the collapse of Ottoman rule this was neither the result of liberation nor the application of the principle of self-determination. As a consequence of World War I, Britain and France were able to defeat the Ottoman Empire and then divide its Middle Eastern territories between them. First by force of arms against the Turks and then in competition with each other the two Great Powers set about creating a new political geography that has largely survived ever since. In dismembering the old imperial order the new conquerors paid little attention to the existing administrative units or to the political aspirations of the people themselves. By the war's end, however, Britain had an agreement with the French on a new Middle Eastern dispensation and at the same time had aided both Arab and Jewish nationalism. The new world of nationalism in the Middle East was thus ushered in under the patronage of European colonial powers.

Britain in particular played a pivotal role in making the contemporary Middle East. By the early 1920s it had become a sponsor of both Arab nationalism and Zionism. Its strategic and financial support for the Arab Revolt in 1916 and its public expression of sympathy for Zionist aims in the Balfour Declaration of 1917 were evidence of a complicated new imperial entanglement. The alliance with the Arabs was aimed at defeating and supplanting Ottoman power in the region. The support for Zionism appeared at times more utopian than utilitarian. However, both commitments were to seal a relationship between Britain and the region that would prove fateful to all involved.

BRITAIN IN THE MIDDLE EAST

By 1914 the British were already well established in the Middle East. Since 1882 Britain had occupied Egypt. While the country was governed as if it were a colony, it remained formally part of the Ottoman Empire. Britain intervened in 1882 to restore order after the 'Urabi revolt[1] and to secure its financial interests. Egypt's strategic importance at the east of the Mediterranean had been enhanced with the opening of the Suez Canal in 1869, in which Britain had gained a major financial stake in 1875. Further east in the region the British had been systematically building a relationship with the Al-Sabah family in Kuwait since the middle of the eighteenth century. The control of Egypt and influence in the Gulf secured important lines of communication between different parts of the empire – especially between Britain and India. Up until 1914 Britain had thus seen the Middle East as important not so much in itself but as a gateway to the rest of the world. As Lord Palmerston[2] had aptly put it in supporting the legal status quo of Egypt at an earlier stage in the nineteenth century, "I want a well managed inn to serve as a half way house to my country place; but I do not want to buy the inn."[3] As the war broke out this relationship with the Middle East was about to change.

The end of World War I brought with it transformed international relations. The defeat and then collapse of Europe's traditional enemy, the Ottoman Empire, opened the entire Middle East to the victorious powers. The region was no longer just a secure resting place on the way to India but had gained a growing significance in itself both strategically and economically. The discovery of oil in Arabia and the conversion of the British fleet to the new fuel underlined its critical role. These factors undoubtedly influenced the British and French to plan for a post-war dispensation for the Middle East as early as January 1916. The secret deal by Mark Sykes[4] and Georges Picot[5] sought an orderly replacement of Ottoman rule with Britain and France dividing the region between them. Under the Sykes–Picot agreement some of what became Palestine would fall under the French but most under the British – although there was a provision that the area could come under international supervision.[6] The implementation of the agreement would remain a contentious issue between both powers during and after the war.

The collapse of the Ottoman and German empires left the victorious powers with the issue of dealing with their respective colonies in the Middle East, Africa and the Pacific. In previous wars such colonies would have been annexed by the victors but, even before the end of World War I that option had been ruled out. The new international prominence of the United States had given President Woodrow Wilson the opportunity to press for a different world order. It was not in the United States' political or economic interests to see the extension of European colonial control. As a result the Great Powers decided that there would be a new international regime which would oversee the fate of the colonial territories of the defeated nations. These territories would be passed to the control of one of the victorious powers but under a mandate system which would be subject to regulation by the new League of Nations. Thus a new international layer was to be added to the direct influence of Britain and France over the Middle East. As new boundaries were contoured the populations of each unit were assigned a distinct identity and were forced to engage with a new colonial regime.

ARAB NATIONALISM

The new order took shape in a region where three influences had been dominant: the Islamic civilization, the Arabic language and Ottoman political allegiance. As British and French administrators set about mapping the Middle East they had to contend with the rising Arab nationalist movement. Arab nationalism had its origins in the second half of the nineteenth century and projected an expansive view of Arab identity that was based primarily on the Arabic language. Territorially, Arab nationalism while appealing to the past was not confined to the Arabian peninsula but encompassed the lands conquered by the Arabs from the seventh century. As Arabic was spoken from the Atlantic to the Gulf the idea of the Arab nation necessarily crossed many borders and included many non-Arabs, in particular Berbers, Jews, Greeks, Armenians and Kurds. As a result it was heterogeneous movement which tended to emphasize cultural attachments rather than ethnic origin.

The movement established itself amongst intellectual circles.[7] Its form of organization was a loose network of societies, libraries and newspapers. The emphasis on culture nonetheless often had political implications, as the work of Adib Ishaq (1856–1885) illustrates. In his *Al Durar* (The Pearls) he writes, "there is no terra patria apart from freedom, and there is no terra patria where tyranny prevails."[8] These sentiments underline the influence that the European Enlightenment had on a section of the movement.

Nationalism meant more than the recovery of formal independence but was the vehicle for modernization and emancipation.

The themes of freedom and nation are taken up by Negib Azoury. His book, *Le Reveil de La Nation Arabe dans L'Asie Turque* (The Arab Revival in Turkish Asia) was published in French in 1905 although it probably had little currency in the region but it was influential amongst the Arab intelligentsia in Europe. Some of the argument was anti-Semitic and he was much concerned with the "universal Jewish peril." He wrote that "exactly at the same moment when Israel is so near to success, our movement comes in order to destroy its project of universal domination."[9] Such views may well have been the result of European anti-Semitism, which was endemic in France where he lived, rather than of any Arab anti-Semitism.[10] However, the argument is interesting for another reason as it draws attention to the early relationship between Arab and Jewish nationalism. The book did elicit an Arab response from Farid Kassab who not only argued in favor of the Ottoman Empire but who also denounced Azoury for anti-Semitism and even praised the Jewish contribution to Palestine.[11] Azoury's work nonetheless placed the concept of the Arab revival on the agenda.

The reaction to Azoury's book illustrates that political aims of Arab nationalism developed in the context of attitudes towards the Ottoman Empire. While some Arab nationalists argued for independence others sought to extend Arab influence in the empire. In contemporary writing while some authors portray the Arabs as a "subject people,"[12] others argued that they were partners with the Turks and if there was a specific Arab project it was to reform the empire not to break from it.[13]

Islam had a major influence on the formation of Arab nationalism. The great moments of the Arab past were closely entwined with Islamic history. The Qur'an's emergence as a book in the seventh century established critical rules of Arabic grammar and script. The spread of Islam from the Arabian peninsula also saw the establishment of Arab empires which created much of what we know today as the Arab world. The Umayyad and Abbasid dynasties produced great works of art, poetry and architecture, but also theology, philosophy, jurisprudence and science. Islam may have inspired these developments but they all developed within an Arabic cultural environment. Any reconstruction of Arab history inevitably entailed an engagement with Islamic history – and vice versa.

The Islamic revival movement particularly operated within the twin tracks of religion and nationalism. Its main leaders Jamal al-din

Al-Afghani[14] and Mohammad Abduh[15] argued that the strategic weakness of the Ottoman Empire was undermining the international influence of Islam. One solution to this problem was to remove the Caliphate from Turkish influence and to return it to Arab control. Another was to establish Arabic as the official language of the empire. Such proposals were posed, however, in religious rather than national terms. The revival movement was principally concerned to project Islam as a force in the modern world. It opposed colonialism and advocated the importance of education and science. Some of these issues even appealed to Sultan abd al-Hamid himself. However, the debates about Islam were to become the vehicle for critiques of Ottoman rule. While many opponents of the regime, such as Rashid Ridda, were genuinely motivated by religious ideas their critiques helped to blur the boundaries between religious and political views. This is most clearly seen in the work of Ridda's colleague Abd-al Rahman al-Kawakibi who was to write one of the most systematic analyses of the regime in his *Tab'i al Istibdad* (Traits of Despotism).[16] Al-Kawakibi's vision of a just society was based on a reconstruction of the political systems in Medina and Mecca during the Prophetic period. This society is portrayed as dynamic, open to consultation (*shura*) and with high levels of freedom of religion and freedom of expression, in contrast to the sclerotic character of the Ottoman system. It is striking how an apparent discussion of a religious narrative offers a modernist political program within an Arab national setting. Arab and Jewish nationalisms thus share a common approach in articulating the identity of a people through apparent references to religious history. In both cases it would be more accurate to see these histories as reflecting civilizations rather than theologies.

The Islamic revival thus opened an important space for the emergence of discussion groups among Arab intellectuals that combined national, religious, social and cultural issues. At the turn of the twentieth century groups like the "senior circle" and the "junior circle" in Damascus were becoming common. These emerged in the build up to the constitutional crisis of the empire which was to culminate in 1908 with the overthrow of Abd al-Hamid II and the rise to power of the Committee for Union and Progress (CUP). This organization was to lay the basis for the emergence of Turkish nationalism and the start of a process of Turkification within the empire which was compounded by the centralizing project of the CUP. This necessarily set the stage for a clash between implicit Arab nationalism seen within the Islamic revival and the newly emergent Turkish nationalism. Those Arabs who had placed their hopes in reforms were increasingly disappointed with the results of the new regime. Even so when the first Arab Congress met in Paris in 1913 the key objective remained autonomy within the empire. Despite the many Ottoman crises the empire seemed so entrenched and unmovable within the region. Yet it was as a result of this apparent solidity that Arab involvement in the CUP led to the politicization of officials and army officers and other layers of Arab society that far exceeded the small circles of Arab nationalist intellectuals. Disillusionment with Ottoman reform and the impact of World War I were to have profound effects on these strata within the Arab provinces.

   The debate about Arab identity and the future of the Ottoman Empire had an important influence on the non-Arab minorities in the Middle East. Palestinian Jews were much concerned with the issue. The 7th Congress of the Zionist movement in 1905 hotly debated the issue of whether to make an alliance with Ottoman reformists or with Arab nationalism. At the time the decision was made to side with the reformists. This was no doubt the reason why in 1908 when the first elections to the Turkish Parliament took place some leading Jews were active in the Jerusalem Committee for Union and Progress.[17] This political strategy largely consisted of attempting to deal with those who held power at the time. However as Arab nationalist sentiment grew, Zionist leaders began to change track. By 1914 contacts between the two movements were well advanced. A high level meeting between representatives planned in Lebanon was only abandoned due to the outbreak of war.[18]

   It was the same war that was to see the British solicit Arab support against the Ottomans. The British were already fully aware of the emergence of an Arab national movement. In April 1914 Abdullah, the second son of Hussein Ibn Ali, the Sherif of Mecca,[19] made an approach to the British in Cairo with a request for arms to "defend" themselves against the Turks. At the time both the High Commissioner in Egypt, Lord Kitchener, and his colleague Ronald Storrs,[20] rejected the request on the grounds that Britain had no interest in undermining a friendly power.[21] This was to prove a fateful overture for a more serious relationship once hostilities broke out. At that point it was the British who initiated contact through Lord Kitchener[22] who began an earnest correspondence with Sherif Hussein. These contacts matured and with the involvement of other British officials, in particular, Mark Sykes and Sir Henry McMahon,[23] the stage was set for an alliance.[24] It was in the course of these contacts that an understanding appeared to have been agreed that the British would support a new order in the Middle East, at the center of which would be a unified Arab state.[25] However, the extent of the territory of this projected state was subject to much dispute.

It was in this context that the British and the Sherif planned an uprising aimed at destroying Ottoman rule. Sherif Hussein's plan for the revolt centered on a rising in Mecca that would be the spark that would attract Arab defections from the Ottoman army. The British agreed with this view and financed the revolt with an investment of about $20 million, then a considerable amount. The British mobilized Egyptian troops to fight alongside Hussein's supporters. However, when the expected defections from the Ottoman army were not forthcoming, the British were forced to deploy the British army and navy so as to avoid the defeat of the revolt. In the event with the British support, including the efforts of the British officer T.E. Lawrence[26] ("Lawrence of Arabia"), the revolt did play a role in destabilizing Ottoman power. More importantly it became an iconic moment in the development of Arab nationalism. Grainy images of the revolt are still played daily on Jordanian television. It acted as the impetus for the modern movement of growing Arab national consciousness, and from then on the Arab voice would become an important aspect of international politics.

The Arab Revolt highlighted the contradictions of the new nationalist movement. The British alliance was with the Hijaz aristocracy who sought to acquire support for a united Arab Kingdom free from the Ottomans. That project ran counter to the liberal wing of Arab nationalism which saw the movement as an instrument for modernization that would both overthrow the Ottomans and the aristocratic elites and create not a traditional kingdom but the free republic that Adib Ishaq had written of. These divisions were further complicated by differences in the character of Arab nationalism itself. While there was broad agreement that the Arab nation was constituted through linguistic and cultural bonds there was greater controversy on the political form that the nation might take. Was its logic the creation of a single state or could Arab unity coexist alongside several states? The vast expanse of the Arab world also meant that its peoples were divided territorially and had been subject to the rule of different imperial powers. In the late nineteenth century this meant that the Arabs had experienced Ottoman, French and British rule each of which sought to foster distinct elites to ease their colonial governance. This produced specific political, bureaucratic and even cultural differences which created more local or regional attachments. This was not new to Arab history during which different cities and regions had competed for political and religious authority from the seventh century. The differing centers of Arab politics enmeshed traditional clan structures with local economic interests to form a rather decentralized phase of Arab nationalism. While liberal and radical trends of the movement established themselves ideologically it was the established elites who headed the movement in practice. It was a period that Yapp calls the "leadership of the notables."[27] However, the "notables" had to compete with the modernizing radical forces. This conflict between tradition and modernity was to become a feature of Arab nationalism for the century to come.

The end of World War I found the British and French in the Middle East wielding maps that neither related to the previous Ottoman territorial units nor to the growing aspirations of the Arab peoples. For both Great Powers their motivation was to divide territory in ways that ensured administrative convenience of their respective empires, while gaining as great a strategic advantage as possible. The end of 400 years of Ottoman Empire in the Middle East was to see the beginning of a short but decisive European colonial interlude.

ZIONISM

In the minds of progressives, nationalism was an instrument for achieving human freedom. The project was to achieve freedom from foreign domination and at the same time achieve emancipation within the nation. While Arab nationalism had developed in conflict with the Ottoman Empire, Jewish nationalism was honed in conflict with the Tsarist Empire. Whereas Arab emancipation was to be achieved on Arab soil, Jewish emancipation required the acquisition of Jewish territory.

When it was founded as a structured political movement in 1897 the Zionist Organization sought to "establish a home for the Jewish people in *Eretz-Israel* [land of Israel] secured under public law."[28] The latter phrase was to prove critical as the Zionist leadership placed great emphasis on a legal campaign to secure their objectives. This involved three quite different stages. First was to achieve the recognition of the Jewish people as constituting a legal entity in international law. Second was to establish a legal connection between the Jewish people and the historic land of

Israel (Palestine). Third, and this was the pre-condition for both objectives, was the recognition of the Zionist movement as the representative of the Jewish people. The Zionist movement was thus based on three propositions: (1) the Jews constituted a nation; (2) Jews had a historical connection to Palestine and; (3) Jews had a right to a national home.

Having established itself the Zionist movement was relatively successful in gaining a degree of recognition as a representative of the Jewish people, despite its tenuous support within the Jewish community. At this time tentative steps were taken to open discussions with representatives of the Ottoman Empire under which the provinces that constituted Palestine fell. However, the Zionist movement also understood that gaining any level of recognition from any of the Great Powers would add to their legitimacy and as we shall see it was in this connection that contacts with Britain were first established.

While the external activities of the movement sought to establish it as a presence in international affairs the Zionist movement simultaneously needed to position itself within the Jewish community as the agency of national consciousness. This meant an intervention into the life of the Jewish communities of Europe to build a political movement that could compete with religious orthodoxy which saw Judaism as the key signifier of Jewish identity and political ideologies which sought to attach Jews to national or class-based projects. Amongst the community there would have been widespread agreement that the Jews constituted a nation. Orthodox Judaism held this position but believed that divine intervention would redeem the nation. Many socialist currents, such as the Bund, would also have concurred with the view of Jews as a nation, although one which could maintain itself as such in the Diaspora.

While the Zionist Organization was not established until 1897, Zionism predated it.[29] Notions that Jewish nationhood should be recreated on a territorial basis were well established by the late nineteenth century. The origins of modern Zionism probably derive from the work of two rabbis, Yehudah Alkalai (1798–1878) from Sarajevo and Zvi Hersch Kalischer (1795–1874) from Poland. Both these rabbis reversed the existing religious orthodoxy that had long held that Jewish return to Israel would only be possible with the coming of the Messiah and argued instead that human intervention was justified and indeed necessary in establishing a center of Jewish life in historical Israel. Thus in this account human beings were to play a role in assisting divine redemption. Alkalai put some of these views forward in his booklet, *Hear, O Israel* published as early as 1834. Kalischer expressed support for Zionism at about the same time but it was in his book *Seeking Zion* published in 1862 that he developed his thesis theoretically. While framing their arguments in spiritual terms both emphasized the character of the Jews as a people with a connection to the land of Israel. As Alkalai put it: "we, as a people, are only properly called Israel in the land of Israel."[30] Alkalai proposed a planned return which was a radical break with most Orthodox thinking at the time. Kalischer advocated the establishment of agricultural settlements in Palestine which could be bought and sustained by financial collections amongst Jewish communities. The latter position is important to bear in mind as from the nineteenth century the Zionist project was based on the assumption that people already lived in the country and that the land was not vacant. Any question of acquiring land would therefore be subject to normal economic intercourse: it would have to be bought. The same year that Kalischer's work appeared, Moses Hess, the socialist associate of Marx and Engels up until 1848, published his classic book *Rome and Jerusalem*.[31] Hess famously observed: "as long as the Jew denies his nationality, as long as he lacks the character to acknowledge that he belongs to that unfortunate, persecuted, and maligned people, his false position must become ever more intolerable."[32] The publication of both books in the same year brought together two aspects of Zionism; its reliance on the long-standing spiritual affinity of Jews to Israel and a new modern secular inflection of this nationalism. This interplay between spirituality and secularism becomes the most enduring feature of Zionism. In the blurring of the lines between spirituality and politics a narrative could be created that ancient dispossession could be overcome through return. Jewish nationalism's politics of return from exile (*hagalut* in Hebrew) was not unique. The creation of Liberia, first as a colony in 1822 and then as an independent republic in 1847 by freed American slaves, was also premised on the idea that only return to a specific territory could create the basis for freedom.

It was in the Russian Empire that Zionism was to take root as an organized political current known as the "lovers of Zion" (*Hovevie Zion*). The movement promoted the idea of "national renewal" of the Jewish people at the spiritual, cultural, political and economic levels. Central to the notion of revival was the promotion of Hebrew as a living language. As a result Hebrew was wrenched from its then theological use and was set to work as a secular cultural force.

Hebrew clubs and Hebrew newspapers and magazines sprang up in Russia and other parts of Eastern Europe.

Widespread pogroms swept through the Russian Empire in 1881. These were orchestrated by the Court in revenge for the assassination of Tsar Alexander II by a Jew (Hessia Helfman was in fact part of the non-Jewish revolutionary group, the Peoples' Will). The pogroms were coordinated by the racist right-wing Black Hundreds movement. In the course of 1881–82 hundreds of Jews were killed and thousands driven from their homes. While many Jews found an immediate solution in emigration a minority sought a political response in Zionism. The most systematic literary response to the pogroms was Leo Pinsker's *Auto-Emancipation*,[33] published in 1882, which argued that they had proved the need for a national solution. While he argued that this required a territorial basis he did not insist on Israel as its location. For Pinsker the urgent need was for enough land that could productively sustain several million people. It was a project for a life-raft state. *Auto-Emancipation* was to be very influential although despite the intention of its author it focused attention on the issue of place and fostered the idea of return.

The development of Hebrew as a demotic language marked a critical stage developing a Jewish national consciousness. Within the Russian Empire and most other parts of Europe Jews spoke Yiddish, a language written in Hebrew script but based mainly on German. The language was seen by the growing nationalist circles as a symbol of exile and oppression and it was often referred to as a ghetto language. Hebrew by contrast was the language of a nation. Writing and speaking in Hebrew thus became a critical aspect of renewal and the symbol of shaking off the deforming effects of exile. The leading figure in this process was Eliezer Ben Yehudah[34] who settled in Jerusalem in 1881 and whose insistence on using Hebrew in Palestine was to prove decisive. Hebrew was also central to the development of the current known as cultural Zionism which was crystallized around Asher Zvi Ginsberg[35] who is better known by his Hebrew name Ahad Ha'am (One of the People).[36] Cultural Zionism emphasized the importance of spiritual renewal which required a new consciousness which preceded any return to the land. This was spiritual in the ethical not religious sense. It taught that merely taking the cultural baggage of the Diaspora to another territory would just reproduce it there. Thus the key was deepening Hebrew culture and values. To Ahad Ha'am the territorial aspect of Zionism remained important in that it could become a physical center that could sustain an intensity in schools, universities, theatres, art galleries, and publishing houses that could ensure that Jews everywhere, including those who did not live there would have an attractive national culture to identify with.

Various attempts were made to organize a coherent Jewish national movement. In 1884 for example a congress of the "Lovers of Zion" organizations was convened in Kattowitz. The congress supported practical steps to create Jewish communities in Palestine. It adopted policies to assist the wave of Jewish immigrants that had begun in 1881 (and was to continue until 1903) known as the "First Aliyah."[37] During this period some 30,000 Jews arrived in Palestine and established some 23 agricultural communities and also reinforced the Jewish urban population in Jerusalem, Jaffa and Haifa. Organizations such as the "Lovers of Zion" facilitated migration to Palestine and collected money to buy land. This was very much the tactical phase of Zionism. It was only with the founding of the Zionist Organization in 1897 that the movement acquired the strategy that could sustain it. The agricultural settlements ceased to be romantic experiments and would become part of the Jewish national home.

HERZL AND THE ZIONIST MOVEMENT

If it was the Jews of the Russian Empire who pioneered modern Zionism it was to be the Jews of central and Western Europe who provided it with its political program. Theodor Herzl[38] was to become the pivotal figure in generating a vision of Jewish emancipation. The Viennese journalist Herzl had little contact with Zionism or Judaism until the mid 1890s. While he had encountered anti-Semitism while as a student at Vienna University it was his coverage of the Dreyfus trial[39] that brought him face-to-face with its political manifestation. In attempting to get to grips with the meaning of the trial he wrote *Der Judenstaat* which was published in 1896.[40] The title can be variously translated as "the Jewish State" or "the State of the Jews." His starting point was that the Jewish question was not essentially religious or social but national and that Jews were a people, "one people," who had a common origin in Israel. The book describes what Jewish life would be like without anti-Semitism in a society where Jewish culture freely develops. The book was an extraordinary mixture of utopian vision and mundane practicalities. It is based on the assumption that anti-Semitism was endemic, in his words "the world resounds with clamor against the

Jews." As a consequence Jews would only be free of anti-Semitism once they had a state of their own. He argued for "a portion of the globe" over which Jewish sovereignty could be exercised. Herzl did not envisage an instant movement of Jews to the Jewish state but rather that this would be a process that could take many decades. He proposed that a "Society of Jews" would be established that would decide political details of the state. He also envisaged a Jewish company that would be responsible for the economic and financial aspects of the relocation of Jews to the new state. As to the location of the new state he was open minded and mused that the open spaces of Argentina could be as suitable as Palestine. On central questions such as the language and law of the new state he held curious views. The language question he assumed could be modeled on multi-lingual Switzerland. However, he was concerned that there would be so many different languages that translators would be needed so that communication could be ensured. He was rather dismissive of the possible use of Hebrew, asking "who amongst us has sufficient acquaintance with Hebrew to ask for a railway ticket in that language?"[41] His ideas on a legal system were equally problematic as he proposed that the main legal systems of Europe could be used for about 20 years simultaneously and then a commission of jurists could select whichever was best.

It was a work which underlined the fact that Herzl was not part of the existing Zionist movement as he seemed insensitive to Hebrew and indeed to the centrality of Israel. It was in some ways extraordinary that the publication of this book was to have such an impact. An explanation could well be that it was precisely the combination of utopian vision and practical detail that appealed. He was the first Zionist to attempt to deal with the many practical objections to the re-creation of a Jewish territorial state. He addressed head-on the mechanics of mass migration, the issue of Jewish property in the Diaspora and the absorption capacity of the projected state. Even his views on language and law demonstrated that he did not shy away from problems and had answers to them. The book did appeal to many Jews. Herzl's rather unsentimental and detached view of Jewish nationalism would prove to be the basis for its transformation into a professional and modern project. As a result it played a key role in drawing 197 delegates from 16 countries to attend the First Zionist Congress in Basel in 1897.

Under Herzl's influence the Zionist Organization was to become a force that could intervene in the high politics of Europe. Herzl played a major role in normalizing Jewish nationalism, so that it would become no less marginal than Italian or Czech nationalism. His attention to the details of the future Jewish commonwealth was equaled by his determination to gain international recognition for its creation. On one detail he was to be proved decisively wrong. Hebrew would become the nation's language. Even so the Zionist Organization was not to adopt Hebrew as its official language until 1907, three years after his death.

The Zionist movement was thus forged on two fronts, within the Jewish community and in the general political arena. A critical part of the former was in Palestine itself, and although only about half of Palestinian Jews were imbued with Zionist ideals in 1897 the community did offer an exemplar of nation-building. The existence of the Palestinian Jewish settlements created a relationship between the country and European Jews which was consolidated by visits and fundraising. Although the development of Jewish-Zionist projects in Palestine was small in scale it was through them that a vision of the new nation could be glimpsed by Diaspora Jewry. The agricultural communities laid the basis for a new image of the Jew which was free from the confines of both religious authorities and anti-Semites. The physical labor of redeeming the land also transformed Jews into physically powerful people which became a motif of the Zionist project. Whereas the Diaspora was synonymous with weakness, Palestine became the site of strength. Whether this reflected the reality on the ground is another matter, as early Zionist pioneers were frequently to experience agricultural failure and illness that left many disillusioned by the hardships. Nonetheless the Zionist movement was able to mobilize around the idea of a liberating nationalism that was nourished through contact with the land itself.

The Zionist movement was not alone in fighting for allegiance of the Jews. The established centers of religious Orthodoxy guarded their positions jealously. Socialism and the trade union movement were also powerful forces amongst Jews in urban areas. In Western Europe there were also strong assimilationist trends among successful and professional Jews. While the latter group was to prove problematic, Zionism was remarkably successful in offering a program that was able to draw on religious symbols and at the same time address the need for a radical transformation of the Jewish condition. As a result the Zionist movement established itself as a significant although not majority current amongst Jews by the beginning of World War I. It had organized eleven Congresses and had established organizations in most parts of the Jewish world, not just in Europe but also in the Arab countries and other parts of Asia.

EAST AFRICA

While the Zionist movement had some degree of success in projecting its vision of national renewal within the Jewish community its great success in its early years was the impact of its considerable diplomatic skills on the international arena. The movement never missed an opportunity to make its case, however apparently insignificant the occasion was. While within Zionism there were many controversies over the character of the project and the policies that should be adopted there was complete unity on the principle that the Zionist movement was the sole representative of Jews at the political level. While there were attempts to hold talks with Ottoman officials the most important breakthrough came with an approach from the British. In 1902 Joseph Chamberlain,[42] the Colonial Secretary, suggested to Theodor Herzl that he might like to consider the creation of a Jewish colony in British East Africa (in what is now Kenya – but at that time was referred to as Uganda). At the time the Zionist movement had been attempting to negotiate with the British Colonial Office to obtain a portion of the Egyptian Sinai. It appears that when these talks failed, Chamberlain offered some of East Africa.

Chamberlain's idea was seized on by Herzl and the negotiations between the Colonial Office and the Zionist movement were pursued seriously.[43] The project was to create a self-governing Jewish community although securely under British colonial rule. The Colonial Office had been seeking a migrant community to colonize some of the richest agricultural soil in Kenya for some time and had investigated the possibility of attracting Finns and Indians before the Jews were to come to mind.[44] On August 14, 1903 a Colonial Office official, Sir Clement Hill formally communicated the plan for consideration to the Zionist Congress. The document was remarkable for its detail in creating Jewish self-governing institutions. Needless to say the indigenous inhabitants were not consulted. It was interesting that the proposal created intense opposition from the British white settlers, who led by Lord Delamere campaigned against the "Zionist invasion."[45] It was also controversial amongst Zionists, most of whom were solely concerned with establishing the national link with Palestine. Some, however, thought that the East African plan could be a transitional one until Jews could gain access to Palestine itself. The idea of a "temporary national home" was already in circulation as the discussions on Sinai illustrate – another much talked about destination was Cyprus. Herzl's enthusiasm for Chamberlain's proposal lay more in the official recognition that the negotiation process accorded to the Zionist movement than with the plan itself. As Chaim Weizmann,[46] an opponent of the East Africa project said, it re-established "the legal personality of the Jewish people."[47] The Zionist Congress rejected the British offer but Weizmann's view was prescient. It was not only that the Jewish people had been accorded a significant degree of legal personality by a Great Power but that the Zionist movement had become the organized expression of it.

There has been much speculation as to the motives of the British government in making this offer. Some have suggested that this was an early sign of Zionism acting in alliance with imperialism. A particular allegation has been made that the offer was linked to the developments in South Africa in the wake of the Anglo-South African War (known by the British as the Boer War, 1899–1902). Stevens, for example argues that Chamberlain was eager for Jewish support for the reconstruction of the country:

> A recent visitor to South Africa, Chamberlain realized that the ultimate success of his white conciliation policy in the post-Boer War era might turn on whether he received Jewish support. Faced with crushing financial burdens in the war's aftermath, the Colonial Secretary was aware that only the great industrial and mineral wealth of the Rand could bring about the reconstruction of South Africa. Yet of all the British Dominions, South Africa was the one in which Jews and Jewish capital were most deeply interested. As Julian Amery, Chamberlain's biographer noted, "the Rand, in particular, was mainly in Jewish hands, and…it was upon its prosperity that Chamberlain and Milner counted for the reconstruction and future progress of South Africa."[48]

This comment is revealing as it suggests that Jews had the power to help or hinder the British Empire's plans for South Africa. Stevens, writing in the 1970s, recycles the arch imperialist Amery's views about the Jews although in a context that is allegedly anti-colonialist. While there was a relatively large Jewish community in South Africa in 1905 – possibly 40,000 – most were poor refugees from the Baltic who worked in the trades or were itinerant salesmen.[49] The idea that there was a preponderance of Jewish financiers in the

Rand has little truth, although there was one, Max Mangermann.[50]
This is an early example of the idea that Jews had the capacity
to manipulate world powers to achieve a national home. It also
assumes that Jews constitute an organized homogeneous group
that would be able to consider such a deal. Like all versions of
conspiracy theories this one is quite contradictory. It would seem
odd that if the Jews were so critical in South Africa that the British
would propose a project that might divert Jewish investment from
South Africa to the projected Jewish East African colony. The more
prosaic truth is that Chamberlain thought that Britain could use
Jewish nationalism to help develop a British colonial enterprise.

The East Africa affair demonstrated the success the Zionist
movement had achieved as the recognized representative of the
Jewish people. The debate at the 6th Zionist Congress on the question
also demonstrated the pragmatic character of the movement. While
most delegates were opposed to the proposal they also realized the
importance of the British gesture. Instead of rejecting it outright
the Congress set up a commission of enquiry to consider it. In May
1905 it reported against the project, which disappointed a minority
who wanted to proceed with it. However as Solokow commented,
the incident "raised Zionism to the rank of a political movement
of international importance, and demonstrated the interest of the
British Government in the solution of the Jewish problem."[51]

PALESTINE

In its first decade the Zionist movement had thus considered the
possibility of establishing a Jewish home in Argentina, Egypt,
Cyprus and East Africa. After 1905 the territorial focus returned
to Palestine, the founding principle of the Basle Congress. As a
result the movement confronted two related tasks. The first was
the diplomatic campaign which sought to achieve legal recognition
of the Jewish national presence in the country. The second was to
safeguard and expand the Palestinian Jewish community.

The geographical term "Palestine" was somewhat ambivalent
before 1918. There was no administrative area of that name in
the Ottoman Empire. What was to become Palestine under British
rule was divided under Ottoman rule into three different *sanjaqs*
or provinces (Acre covering the north, Nablus in the center and
Jerusalem, with greater administrative independence covering
some of what became the south of Palestine).[52] However, even

these areas were not exactly coterminous with the boundaries of British Palestine.

Palestine may not have existed on the map or figured in the Ottoman bureaucratic schedule but the idea of Palestine as a place with its own history and culture did exist. As Kimmerling and Migdal point out such distinctiveness was born out of experiences such as the uprising against invasion of the area by the Egyptian leader Mohammad Ali in 1834 which can be seen as a critical moment in the forming of a national consciousness.[53] This rebellious attitude towards Egyptian rule, however, was shared with Syria and could be understood as a Levantine phenomenon. It was the growth of Arab nationalism that was to forge new notions of identity that would challenge Ottoman hegemony. As in other parts of the Arab world it was to be intellectuals and professionals who through the establishment of libraries, schools, clubs, journals and other cultural organizations would give expression to it.[54] Within Arab nationalist discourse Khalidi notes increasing references to "Palestine" as a distinctive geographical place. Publication of the daily paper *Falastin* (Palestine) from 1911 was a highly symbolic example of this process.[55] Palestine gained significance as a place although the people who lived in the territory were not to regard themselves as "Palestinians" until the second half of the twentieth century. A national consciousness was emerging amongst the Arab population which embraced a wider Arab identity while potentially nourishing a narrower Palestinian coloration.

The Jewish population of Palestine thought of the country in historical terms as the land of Israel. Nonetheless Palestinian Jews and the Zionist movement did not entertain illusions that modern Palestine was unpopulated or that the Arab people were anything other than the preponderant population. It was also striking that it was the Jewish community that would refer to Palestine in many of their political and cultural institutions. As a result in the 1920s and 1930s the term "Palestinian" was often used to refer to Jews.

In assessing the Palestinian population and its ethnic composition in the critical years 1914 to 1922 we are faced with several difficulties. Ottoman statistics while available are problematic on two main grounds. First the Ottoman districts were not coterminous with mandate Palestine. Second the Ottomans only included persons in the census with a fixed address and excluded foreign citizens. As a result Bedouin Arabs and foreign Jews were not recorded. As the census was used for taxation and military conscription it is also likely that evasion was common. Palestinians and Israelis have long used statistics as an extension of the conflict with each side attempting to bolster its case by maximizing its population while minimizing the other's.

With these factors in mind it is only possible to assess the Palestinian population by taking into account a range of sources. Justin McCarthy's thorough study of the Palestinian population[56] proceeds on this basis. In addition to the factors mentioned above, he suggests that many women and children were often not included in official statistics. He used the Ottoman figures as a base line and attempted to make a calculated estimate. He projects a population of nearly 800,000 by 1914, of whom some 60,000 were Jews (7.6 percent). In 1914 Arthur Ruppin of the Palestine Zionist Office used the same sources to suggest a total population of nearly 700,000 with Jews comprising 85,000 (12 percent).[57] In 1922 the British-held census recorded the population at 752,000 with 83,790 Jews. The British figures probably suggest that the likely population in 1914 was somewhere between McCarthy's and Ruppin's estimates. The Arab population included a significant Christian population which is likely in 1914 to have been about the same size as the Jewish population, 70,000 or thereabouts. In the 1922 census the figure was just over 71,000. World War I had a major impact on the demography of Palestine through the combined effect of the hardship of the conflict itself and an authoritarian regime. It has been estimated that some 18,000 Jews left the country in the course of this war.[58] The latter figure would suggest that the Jewish population was about 55,000 in 1918 compared to 73,000 at the outset of the war.[59]

The Palestinian population was overwhelmingly agricultural, although there were significant urban centers in Jaffa, Haifa, Nablus, Hebron and Jerusalem. The Christian population tended to be more urban than the Muslim. The Arab population had, like the Jews, suffered during the last period of Ottoman rule under the Damascus-based authoritarian regime of Jamal Pasha. The war had been particularly hard as the Ottomans had made high demands for soldiers through conscription[60] and requisitioned food for its armed forces. Some estimates suggest that the Palestinian population as a whole declined by 6 percent during World War I.[61]

The Jewish population in the period 1917–18 was thus much smaller than it had been before the war. The city of Jerusalem suffered the most drastic decline, from a total population of about 80,000 in 1914 to about 50,000 four years later. In the same period the Jewish population fell from 45,000 to 27,000. The Jewish population in Palestine was composed of three main groups. Jewish religious communities, particularly in Jerusalem, Safed, Tiberius and Hebron, had been well established for centuries. To these had been added Zionist Jews arriving in the late nineteenth century particularly in the period 1882–1903 (often known as the First Aliyah) and then supplemented by the more radical and socialist immigrants of the Second Aliyah (from 1904 to 1914). Both waves of migrants had come from Eastern Europe, most from Russia and Romania. Although the Zionist Jewish community was associated with agricultural projects and had established 43 communities by 1917, most Jews lived in the towns and cities. In 1914 it is likely that some 60 percent lived in Jerusalem alone. Jews owned 2 percent of the land. This statistic is much more reliable than those for population figures due to the careful records necessitated by the Ottoman Land Code of 1858. By 1914 the balance between the religious Jewish community and the Zionists had swung in favor of the latter with about two out of three Jews being in the latter camp. Few amongst the religious communities probably supported the aims of Zionism.

There were great differences amongst the Zionist Jews on their attitudes to the national project. The immigrants of the Second Aliyah were much more ideological emphasizing their commitment to socialism and self-reliance and they had often clashed with immigrants of the First Aliyah especially over issues of Jewish Labor and Jewish self-defense. Amongst the Second Aliyah immigrants was David Ben-Gurion,[62] later to be the founding Prime Minister of Israel, who looked askance at what he thought was the too comfortable life of the earlier Zionists.[63] Amongst Zionist Jews in Palestine there were many shades of opinion as to the characteristics of the nation and indeed the stage at which nation-building had reached. This had produced a lively pluralist political scene, although increasingly dominated by socialist ideology. Trade unions and cultural organizations also played a central role in etching national identity. The creation of a teachers' union to promote Hebrew-medium instruction in 1903 was a good example of the consolidation of politics and culture. The founding of Tel Aviv in 1909 as the first new Jewish town for two millennia added to this sense of nationhood. By 1914 Palestine had acquired a small but distinctive Jewish national community.

TOWARD THE BALFOUR DECLARATION

While World War I had a serious impact on the Palestinian Jews, the defeat of the Ottomans would ultimately secure their position. The war in the Middle East turned in favor of the Allies in 1917. In March the British achieved a great success with the occupation of Baghdad. As the year progressed the military campaign in the Sinai and Palestine was also to produce important British gains. It was against this background that the Zionist movement increased its campaign for a Great Power to issue a public statement supporting its aims. Although the movement was active in a number of countries it was in Britain that the Zionists had been most successful in developing relations with the political establishment, including at the highest level. Herbert Samuel who served as the first Jewish member of a British cabinet (1910–16) had circulated a paper in 1914 advocating support for Zionism in Palestine under British patronage. This paper provoked much discussion, mostly of a mildly favorable character. He had left the cabinet but proved a useful point of contact between the Zionists and the government. Lloyd George, the Prime Minister, was known to be sympathetic and another energetic supporter of Zionism was the South African, Jan Smuts. The Foreign Secretary at the time was Arthur Balfour[64] who had been Prime Minister during the East Africa project and had remained sympathetic towards the idea of a Jewish national home.

In January 1917 the Zionist movement made an unofficial approach to the British government by submitting a memorandum to Mark Sykes, the Cabinet Secretary. The heart of the document was the request that "the Jewish population of Palestine...shall be officially recognized...as the Jewish Nation and shall enjoy in that country full civic, national and political rights."[65] Shortly after the submission of the memorandum a meeting took place which Chaim Weizmann described as "the first full dress conference leading to the Balfour Declaration."[66] The meeting took place in a private house and was attended by many leading Zionists including James de Rothschild, Herbert Bentwich and Nahum Sokolow but also Herbert Samuel and more significantly Mark Sykes. The latter's presence was said to be "in his personal capacity."[67] This, however, did not prevent him from presenting a detailed account of the international situation and his assessment of the attitude of allied governments to Zionism and especially the policies of the French. He also discussed the positions of the Arabs and Weizmann records him as saying, "within a generation...the [Arab national] movement would come into its own, for the Arabs had intelligence, vitality and linguistic unity," but they "would come to terms with us – particularly if they received Jewish support in other matters."[68] Contact between the British government officials and the Zionist movement continued including a significant meeting between Balfour and Weizmann to iron out outstanding differences.

As the discussion became more concrete there were stirrings of opposition amongst a small but influential group of anti-Zionist Jews. The most prominent amongst these was the Secretary of State for India Edwin Montagu who began to make public protests against government support for Zionism through the pages of *The Times*. This not only unsettled the Zionists but also complicated the task of their supporters in the government. Nonetheless the Zionists were asked to propose a formal draft of the statement they would like to see the British government support. This was submitted in July 1917 and included the statement that the British government should "accept the principle of recognizing Palestine as the national home for the Jewish people." It should be seen "as essential for the realization of this principle the grant of internal autonomy to the Jewish nationality in Palestine, freedom of immigration for Jews and the creation of a Jewish National Colonizing Corporation."[69]

There were differences between the Zionist leaders on what was possible and desirable. The draft was mainly the work of Nahum Sokolow,[70] who thought that "if we want too much we shall get nothing: on the other hand if we get some sympathetic declaration, I hope we can get more and more."[71] Others wanted to use the term "Jewish State" and Harry Sacher proposed that the statement should read "that one of its [Britain's] essential war aims is the reconstitution of Palestine as a Jewish State and as the national home for the Jewish people."[72] Many were wary of such precise formulations such as Herbert Sidebotham who suggested, "not a state of which membership is restricted to Jews but a state whose dominant national character...will be Jewish."[73] Sokolow carefully avoided use of the term "state" and remained faithful to the term used at the founding Zionist congress and thus requested a "national home for the Jewish people." The draft that was submitted contained two substantive points. The first was that there should be "a national home" for the Jews, the second that Palestine should be reconstituted as such. The statement contains no reference to the status of the majority of the inhabitants of the country.

After much debate through the summer Balfour was able to give Weizmann a text that the Foreign Office was going to submit to the cabinet. It read:

1. His Majesty's government accepts the principle that Palestine should be reconstituted as the national home for the Jewish People.
2. His Majesty's government will use its best endeavours to secure the achievement of this object and will discuss the necessary methods with the Zionist Organization.[74]

This was far less detailed than the draft submitted by the Zionists but it did contain the main object. It also represented the first official acceptance by the Foreign Office of the Jewish national home policy.

Within the Zionist movement there had been much debate on the meaning of the term "national home." In the year before the Foreign Office endorsed the concept several leading Zionists had attempted to give it a clearer content. Chaim Weizmann argued that:

To find a home for the Jewish people does not mean to congregate all Jews together in one place. That is obviously impossible, even if it were desirable. ...millions of Jews in Eastern Europe could not be transplanted by the wave of a wand to a Jewish land... The Political and economic problems of the Jews of Eastern Europe must be settled, for the great mass of them, in the countries where they live.[75]

The purpose of Zionism was rather to create in Palestine "the home of the Jewish people, not because it will contain all Jews of the world, but because it is the only place in the world where Jews will be masters of their destiny." He continues that it would be "the national centre to which all Jews will look [to] as home."[76] He compares the Jewish relationship to the envisaged national home to that which existed at the time between Irish people and Ireland. Most Irish people did not live in Ireland but nonetheless viewed it as their national center which guaranteed their sense of identity. A Jewish national home could act in the same way for the Jews. Thus for Weizmann as for many other Zionists, ending the conditions of Jewish exile did not mean necessarily the return of all Jews to Palestine but rather that a national home in and of itself would act to transform the position of Jews everywhere.

Norman Bentwich,[77] the future Attorney-General of Palestine, wrote at the same time that the "interests of the present and future population in fact coincide, and it should be within the powers of a just administration to secure a good understanding and cooperation between the two elements that are in origin akin."[78] Bentwich's use of the present and future tense in describing the populations of Palestine is instructive as is his view that Jews and Palestinians had similar origins. In his opinion the complementary relations between the two peoples was marked by a particular assessment of the position that Jews occupied between the East and the West. As he explained:

Experience of the past warrants the expectation that Western Knowledge and Western methods will be introduced into the towns and fields of Palestine…by Jews who will come with the determination of building up a fresh national life, and who will here not have to assimilate a strange culture, but to emulate a civilization they have left. For nearly a thousand years the majority of Jews have lived in Europe; though it should be remembered that the Jewry of Spain was geographically in Europe but intellectually in the East, while Russia, which has long been home to the chief community of Jews, is only a very recent accession to intellectual Europe. In a real sense, therefore, right down to our time the Jews have been a link between Europe and Asia, and they return to Palestine adapted to perform this function with far greater efficiency.[79]

Bentwich rejected the idea that the image of the new Jewish life was to be found in the "Ghettos of Jerusalem or Safed" as these were "obsolete survivals of the old outlook." It was rather to be found in the "streets and schools of Tel Aviv…and the democratic organization of the Jewish colonies."[80] Bentwich was in no doubt that Palestine had a current population but he was at pains to suggest that the future Jewish population would not threaten it as the Jews would act as mediators between Palestine and the western modern world. Nor would the Jewish population-to-come be like the Jews who had traditionally lived in the religious communities of Jerusalem or Safed. The Palestinian population would benefit from the new Jewish way of life as exemplified by the modern city of Tel Aviv and democratic modes of organization. The future Jewish population was to become the agency of modernization for all inhabitants. In stressing common ethnic origins, Bentwich underlined his view that there was no intention to harm the Palestinian population as the Jewish population was another part of the Palestinian self. Bentwich represented a common view amongst Zionists at the time that the project of a Jewish national home was not antagonistic to Palestinian interests. Jewish nationalism was to be seen as complementary to Arab nationalism and indeed could bring many economic and social benefits to Palestine.

Both Weizmann and Bentwich offer a useful insight into Zionist thinking but also indicate something of the arguments that they would have been putting to the British during this crucial period. The relative modesty of Weizmann's conception of the Jewish national home and the practicality of his arguments neatly mesh with Bentwich's stance that this proposal is not aimed at undermining the rights of the Palestinian Arab population. The conception of the national home that they advocated meant that the Jewish presence had to be accommodated with the existing Palestinian Arab population.

Some accounts of Zionism have sometimes stressed the view that the movement saw Palestine as a "land without a people for a people without a land."[81] However, many readings of Zionist writing make it clear that there was an acute awareness of the existence of an Arab population settled in Palestine. The political project for a Jewish national home was not premised on the removal of that population. Relations with the Arabs in Palestine and the Arab world generally were a constant theme of Zionist discourse. The Jewish national home was to be seen as complementary to Arab emancipation. As can be seen there could be a rather romantic aspect to these views, as exemplified by Bentwich whose writings exuded sentiments of cooperation and mutual benefit. Bentwich was also noteworthy for his emphasis on the national character of Palestinian Arabs. He was perhaps equivocal as to whether the nation in question was the Arab nation or a Palestinian one. However, his equivocation would have been one expressed by many Arabs at the time. Nonetheless, significantly he understood the need to engage with the established Arab population in Palestine and with its national characteristics. Some of the Israeli new historians in attempting to address the post-1967 occupation have far too often attempted to trace the sins of the occupation regime to an essential Zionist blindness of the Arabs in Palestine.[82] It is difficult to sustain this argument in the face of the evidence.

THE BALFOUR DECLARATION

The British government having exchanged the draft statements with the informal group of Zionists then sought to establish the extent to which it truly represented the views of the Zionist movement. As a result the services of Mark Sykes were called upon once more. He held yet another meeting with the Zionists and reported to the cabinet. This time he was acting in his official capacity as Cabinet Secretary. His report consisted of a short note that reduced the aims to a list of what Zionists did and did not want. His note records:

> What the Zionists do not want:
> I. To have any special political hold on the old city of Jerusalem itself or control over any Christian or Moslem Holy Places.
> II. To set up a Jewish Republic or any other form of state in Palestine or in any part of Palestine.
> III. To enjoy any special rights not enjoyed by other inhabitants of Palestine.
>
> On the other hand the Zionists do want:
> I. Recognition of the Jewish inhabitants of Palestine as a national unit, federated with (other?) national units in Palestine.
> II. The recognition of [the] rights of bona fide Jewish settlers to be included in the Jewish national unit in Palestine.[83]

This note is of significance as it reinforced the view that the Zionists negotiating with the British were maintaining the moderate conception of Weizmann's published positions. The question mark after "other" national units accurately indicated the differences amongst Zionists on the question. The thrust of the text was clear; the Zionist movement did not possess aggressive intentions towards the existing population but did want the legal entitlement of Jews to be in Palestine as a constituent nation of the country.

The British war cabinet subsequently considered various drafts for a statement on the issue during the late summer and early autumn. In so doing it decided to consult the British Jewish community on the content of versions drawn up by Milner[84] and Amery.[85] As we have noted a group of British anti-Zionist Jews were already voicing public opposition to any support for Zionism. This campaign became more acute when the then only Jewish member of the cabinet, Edwin Montagu,[86] circulated a document provocatively entitled "The Anti-Semitism of the Present Government." It argued that Zionism was a "foreign theory developed by an Austrian and organized from Berlin,"[87] words which written in the midst of a war with both countries are endowed with more than the standard xenophobic rhetoric. He was also concerned that once Jews were allocated a national home their British citizenship would be at risk. Indeed he argued that, "every country will immediately desire to get rid of its Jewish citizens."[88]

We have obtained a greater share of the country's goods and opportunities than we are numerically entitled to. We reach on the whole maturity earlier, and therefore compete with people of our own age unfairly. Many of us have exclusive friendships and are intolerant in our attitude and I can understand that many a non-Jew in England wants to get rid of us.[89]

Despite the tone of the document concerns raised at such a high level made more consultation with the Jewish community necessary. While the Chief Rabbi and the President of the Board of Deputies of British Jews supported the draft there was opposition from the Member of Parliament Philip Mangus and the Chair of the Anglo-Jewish Association, Claude Montifiore. The latter wrote, "I would subordinate my Jewish feelings, wishes and interests to the interests of England and the British Empire."[90] It is noteworthy that the Jewish opponents of Zionism framed their arguments in terms of commitment to the British nation and empire. It perhaps signifies the tenuous sense of identity that Jews had acquired in the Britain of that time. It also indicates the power of the imperial age. And it sheds another light on the view that Zionism was from its origins either a colonial movement or one that acted in the interests of colonialism. As can be seen, opposition to Zionism was argued precisely in such terms. While some Zionist leaders did attempt to appeal to imperial self-interest in order to win support for their claims, on the whole this was opportunism. Imperial powers and certainly Britain did not need lessons on colonialism – and would have gained control of Palestine irrespective of Zionist politics.

While consultation with the Jewish community was taking place the British were also engaged in soliciting support for their position with their allies, particularly the United States. As a result President Wilson gave his agreement to the declaration.[91] This was not just a diplomatic nicety as a result of the United States' entry to the war in April 1917 but also due to the interest that Wilson had in the post-war world order. In a series of lectures and speeches he had attempted to spell out an open democratic world in place of the secret diplomacy and imperial rivalries that had marked the past. Securing his agreement to Britain's Middle East policy was thus useful. This early US support for the Jewish national home also indicated that the future of Palestine was already an international concern by 1917.

The Declaration was published in the form of a letter from the Foreign Secretary, Arthur Balfour, to Lord Rothschild[92] on November 2, 1917. It reads in full:

> I have much pleasure in conveying to you, on behalf of His Majesty's Government, the following declaration of sympathy with Jewish Zionist aspirations which has been submitted to and approved by, the Cabinet.
>
> "His Majesty's Government view with favour the establishment in Palestine of a national home for the Jewish people, and will use their best endeavours to facilitate the achievement of that object, it being clearly understood that nothing shall be done which may prejudice the civil and religious rights of the existing non-Jewish communities in Palestine, or the rights and political status enjoyed by Jews in any other country."
>
> I should be grateful if you bring this declaration to the knowledge of the Zionist Federation.

The statement reflected the discussion both between the British government and the Zionist movement and within the British government itself. It was carefully phrased and took into account two issues that the original draft proposed by the Zionists did not: the position of the "existing non-Jewish communities" in Palestine and the legal status of Jews outside of Palestine. The final version thus addressed one of the fears raised by Montagu about the status of Jews in the Diaspora. While he had lost on the principle of Zionism at least his British title and English country estates were to be secure.

The statement was described as a "declaration," however it was issued in a low-key political way as a letter sent to a prominent individual asking him to bring its contents to the knowledge of a civil society organization. This is not a statement issued by the Foreign Secretary in Parliament or a policy issued in a white paper, but a letter. In itself it would be difficult to attach much legal significance to it. However, subsequent statements of the British government did indicate that they felt bound by its terms. This became clear once the war ended and Winston Churchill as Colonial Secretary described the Balfour Declaration as constituting an obligation or pledge that was non-negotiable. Although in November 1917 Britain did not control the territory and the British had only promised to favor a policy and use their "best endeavours" to facilitate it, the British government did see the Balfour Declaration as more than a mere political statement.

The declaration followed quite closely the list of Zionist aims that Sykes had noted. It was carefully drafted to avoid any reference to a Jewish state and thus avoided any specific commitment on the part of Britain to a particular outcome. It made clear that the national home would be created "in" Palestine rather than that Palestine itself would become the national home. As a result of this formulation the fact that there was no juridical unit called Palestine at the time is less significant than it might appear.[93]

The declaration did use the term "Jewish people" in connection to acquiring a national home and thus was faithful to the Sykes position that the Jews wanted to establish national rights in Palestine. The character of a national home was not defined and we shall come to the debate about this issue later. The term "national home," it should be stressed, was used as if it had legal significance although it was unknown in international law or in political discourse.

The ambiguity on the identity of the majority of Palestine's population was striking with the Palestinian Arabs being designated as the "existing non-Jewish communities." The formulation avoids any description of the positive identity of the majority of the "existing" population, constructing them only negatively as non-Jews. The British government was well aware of Arab nationalism and had close relations with many Arab leaders. The Arab Bureau which was the arm of military intelligence in Egypt carried regular surveillance of Arab political sentiments and its work would have been well known in the Foreign Office. While the exact national character of the majority of Palestine's population might have been in question, that there was a national issue would have been evident. The effect of the formulation was to have devastating impact on the conflict as it could be read to imply that the non-Jewish Palestinian population did not possess national rights. This was compounded by the use of the plural in "communities." This reference to the Muslim and Christian religious communities suggested that these would be the primary identities of Palestinians. Whereas Jewish rights are posed in national terms, Palestinians are conceived as possessing rights as individuals – civil and religious. The Balfour Declaration clarified the national rights of the Jewish people while apparently questioning national rights for the Palestinians.

WAR AND CONQUEST

The declaration was published on November 2, 1917, but its portent was overshadowed by the Bolshevik revolution which took place in Russia just days later. Thus international reaction to it was somewhat muted at the time. However, significant British military advances against the Ottomans in Palestine resulted in the capture of Jerusalem some six weeks later. General Allenby's entrance to the city was more than the arrival of the triumphal power but of a power with a policy for the conquered land. The declaration's political and legal significance was about to be unleashed.

The entry of the United States into World War I introduced a new factor into international politics. The old European Great Powers were no longer able to shape their imperial domains alone. As we have seen, the British government saw US approval for the Balfour Declaration as important and this symbolized the changing relations between Europe and America. The emergence of the United States as a world power necessarily brought it into competition with the old imperial powers and their strategic and economic position. In seeking to secure its newfound power the United States sought to establish a new framework for international relations. It was within this new framework that Palestine was destined to be fashioned.

The idea for the League of Nations had been much discussed during the last two years of the war. While the United States and President Woodrow Wilson were much associated with the plan, another of its main proponents was the South African statesman and member of the British war cabinet, Jan Smuts. He was strongly in favor of the idea that the League of Nations should be given powers over colonial territories of the defeated powers. While he opposed annexation of these territories by the victors he nonetheless wanted to avoid granting independence to peoples who he regarded as unready for self-government.[94] Before the end of the war he was arguing:

> The peoples left behind by the decomposition of Russia, Austria and Turkey are mostly untrained politically; many of them are either incapable of or deficient in the power of self government;

they are mostly destitute and will require much nursing towards economic and political independence.[95]

Smuts' concern was thus how to deal with the "untrained" peoples that the dissolution of empire would potentially let loose upon the world. They posed a threat of great disorder. The League should establish a mandate system to ensure their effective regulation. At the same time the organization would play a role in mediating relations between the victorious imperial powers. Smuts, who had begun his political career fighting against the British Empire in the Anglo-South African War (1899–1902), had made the complete transition to a supporter and indeed leader of it, symbolized by his membership of the British war cabinet. Smuts was therefore in a pivotal position to assume the role of imperial modernizer, which he did with enthusiasm. He in particular understood that conquest alone was no longer in itself legitimate and that colonialism had to be brought within international regulation. This would both achieve the subjection of the colonial peoples to "advanced nations" while also avoiding an unseemly struggle between the victors over the spoils of war. He was quite frank that the peoples of any of these colonies were unlikely to obtain immediate independence as "it will probably be found that they are as yet deficient in the qualities of statehood."[96] Smuts' description of the inhabitants of the German colonies in the Pacific and Africa as "barbarians...to whom it would be impractical to apply any ideas of political self-determination in the European sense,"[97] is shockingly redolent of the times. It also indicated the racialized character of the principle of self-determination which was to inform the League of Nations; self-determination was not to be extended to the "uncivilized." The League was to reflect the view that global order was maintained on the basis of a notional civilization which was to be defined by the dominant powers. International law also rested on this principle and thus only those entities which were civilized could possess sovereign rights or indeed could shoulder obligations. It was thus within this order that existing states would determine when societies had reached the stage of civilization and could be admitted to the international community. The mandate system was to provide the route through which Turkish and German colonies could acquire civilization.

The distinctive part of Smuts' proposals was that the purpose of the mandate system was to bring about self-determination for the colonies concerned. This was innovative in that the mandate system for some colonies was to provide a school for self-government, a goal not contemplated for most such territories. This position was not inconsistent with colonialism and as Anghie has observed it provided that "the new international law…could embark on its next step of the civilizing process of preparing non-European states for independence."[98] This was to be a highly conditional policy and provided no time-frame for its achievement. In some situations the mandate system would encounter more complex issues, as Smuts was keen to point out:

> there will be cases where owing chiefly to the heterogeneous character of the population and their incapacity for administrative co-operation, autonomy in a real sense would be out of the question, and administration would have to be undertaken to a very large degree by an external authority. This would be the case, at any rate for some time to come, in Palestine where the administrative cooperation of the Jewish minority and the Arab majority would not be forthcoming.[99]

Smuts' view that the "heterogeneous" populations by their character could not be left alone without an "external authority" was noteworthy in itself but as applied to Palestine foreshadowed the terms of the mandate that was to be adopted four years later. The central thrust of the mandate was to determine the relations between Jews and Arabs in Palestine mediated by the British presence.

When the war ended, the international peace conference at Versailles amongst other matters established the League of Nations and its covenant came into force on January 10, 1920. Although established by this formal means the structure and powers of the League were worked out through intense discussions between the British and the Americans during 1918 and 1919. This involved drafts by the jurist Lord Phillimore[100] at the time working on behalf of the British Foreign Office and another by Colonel House,[101] President Wilson's key advisor. In addition Smuts finessed his proposals on the structure of the League. He was insistent that the Council should have powers so it could act on behalf of the organization. He also wanted to draft the specifications for the mandate system.

As a result of this activity by the beginning of February 1919 a joint British–US draft covenant was submitted to the peace conference.[102] The League was to have three main bodies: an assembly representing all members, a council with a combination of permanent and non-permanent members, and a secretariat. The permanent members of the Council were originally to have been the United States, Britain, France, Italy and Japan. The covenant also provided for the creation of a Permanent Court of International Justice to encourage the resolution of conflicts through judicial means. While a commission representing 19 states was set up to consider a covenant, the British–US proposals were agreed within days due in part to Wilson's chairing of the commission. The peace conference adopted this text by the end of April 1919 with very few changes. This underlined the close relationship between political power and the creation of international legal institutions. The League of Nations was the product of Great Power bargaining and ensured that those same Great Powers had a privileged place within it as permanent members of the Council. The United States was not to take up these advantages, however, when the Senate did not ratify the covenant.

The mandate system was dealt with in article 22 of the League of Nations Covenant which applied to:

> those colonies and territories which as a consequence of the late war have ceased to be under the sovereignty of the states which formerly governed them and which are inhabited by peoples not able to stand by themselves under the strenuous conditions of the modern world.

However, the peoples of these territories had the right to "well-being and development" which should be seen as "a sacred trust of civilization." It was noteworthy that the covenant did not refer to self-determination but to "well-being and development." As if to make this quite clear article 22 explained that the best way to achieve these objectives was that "the tutelage of such peoples should be entrusted to advanced nations." The imperial order was also maintained as the character of the mandates would depend on the "stage of development of the peoples, the geographical situation of the territory, its economic conditions and other similar circumstances." The territories were then broken into three categories on the basis of these criteria: the former Turkish territories, those in Central Africa, and those in South West Africa and the Pacific. While the last two categories were given no hope of independence, the former Turkish territories were said to have reached "a stage of development where their existence as independent nations can be provisionally recognized subject to the rendering of administrative advice and assistance by a Mandatory until such time as they are able to stand alone." It appeared that it was into this category that Palestine would fall.

The article was ambiguous as to the exact legal status of the territories. They were at once constructed as "independent nations" but they could only be "provisionally recognized" as such. Recognition was critically dependent on the "administrative advice and assistance" that the Mandatory would provide. Until that "advice and assistance" had been acted upon to the satisfaction of that power the territory would not be able to "stand alone." Some of the leaders of the territories under discussion, including in Palestine, were understandably keen to emphasize the phrase "independent nations." However, the circumlocutions of the article ensured that any decision as to the status of mandated territories would be decided by the League of Nations once the Mandatory power was satisfied by the behavior of their charges. This was after all the purpose of placing these peoples under "tutelage" of an "advanced nation." The League of Nations was not about the overthrow of the existing international order but rather offered a new lease of life to its colonial character.[103] Thus the stress should be placed on the "provisional" rather than the "independent" character of the nation. Article 22 was to prove critical in international legal debates about the Palestinian–Israeli conflict in which the legal status of the mandate was to be hotly disputed.

2
Mandate Palestine

When the war ended in November 1918 the British were in control of a vast swath of the Middle East. Palestine, Jordan and Iraq were added to Egypt as the British sphere of influence. Britain had also emerged from the conflict with an alliance with the Hashemite dynasty who had led the Arab revolt, with commitments to the Zionists and a Middle East pact with the French. The Versailles peace conference became the main forum in which Britain had to juggle these competing interests. It was at the conference that Palestine was designated within defined borders and allocated to the British as the Mandatory power. In this chapter we shall focus attention on the key legal instruments that effected these arrangements: the League of Nations Mandate for Palestine and the British Order-in-Council.

In the mandate, the League of Nations stipulated the terms under which Britain would administer Palestine. The Order-in-Council for Palestine contained the administrative structure and specified the legal system that the British would use in implementing the terms of the mandate. Orders-in-Council are in effect decrees that are issued by the Privy Council, a somewhat feudal body that still exists in the British constitutional system. The drafting of the mandate and Order-in-Council began in 1919 but neither was published in full until the summer of 1922.

Within Britain responsibility for Palestine had passed from the Foreign Office to the Colonial Office in 1921 coinciding with the arrival of Winston Churchill as Colonial Secretary. Officials from both ministries had been involved in drafting both texts. However, when they were published it was the Colonial Office alone that had the task of dealing with representations from interested parties. The Colonial Office had established an Arab Affairs Department which was to prove useful both in dealing with Arab interests and in briefing officials.

JEWS AND ARABS IN PALESTINE

In Palestine itself the Zionist movement moved quickly after the British conquest and had established a Palestine Executive which had the task of organizing the Jewish community to take advantage of the national home policy. Jewish immigration in the period 1919–22 was considerable with 28,000 entering the country. However, due to emigration particularly between 1917 and 1919 the Jewish population was still only 83,790 by the time of the 1922 British census. According to the census the Palestinian Arab population was 668,258 of whom some 71,000 were Christian.

The Palestinian Arab population had begun to organize politically.[1] As with other Arab nationalists in the region the main political goal was the creation of a united Arab state. This project was conceived of in stages and the first was the formation of such a state with Damascus at its center which would unite most of the lands of the Levant. This objective provided the main political focus for the General Syrian Congress which was the main Arab nationalist organization with branches in all the territories concerned including Palestine. However, the British control of Palestine created the necessity for its Arab inhabitants to establish organizations that could provide them with specific representation in dealings with the new colonial authorities. Muslim–Christian Societies were founded immediately after the war although on a local basis. In January 1919 through these societies the first Arab Congress was held which was the first Palestine-wide Arab political movement. The Congress was firmly in the greater Syrian camp.

Meanwhile at the Versailles peace conference Prince Faisal (the Hashemite heir) was not only making the case for the creation of the unified Arab state but was also in contact with the Zionist delegation. These contacts produced an agreement signed with Chaim Weizmann that supported the Balfour Declaration and thus endorsed the creation of a Jewish national home in Palestine. This agreement was conditional on the establishment of the unified Arab state. Its territory, in some accounts, would extend from the Arabian peninsula to Iraq, including Syria and Lebanon although excluding Palestine. The Jewish role in Palestine was not defined. This agreement indicated that there was no common view of Zionism amongst Arab nationalists at the time. Most significantly this incident demonstrated that from that point onwards Palestine was to be seen in the context of Arab nationalism and would be subject to its political rhythms.

Faisal had been installed as the titular ruler of Syria with British support in 1918 partially in an effort to weaken French influence. Faisal found himself simultaneously at the helm in Syria and the Arab world's representative at the peace conference. In Syria itself the ousting of the Ottomans had produced a particularly strong nationalist reaction and the most organized national movement in the General Syrian Congress. The Congress sought the recognition of a state in the *bilad al sham*, the entire Levant (what is today, Syria, Lebanon, Palestine, Israel and Jordan). This was seen as the center of the Arab world around which the future united Arab state would take shape. The movement rejected any idea of a mandate and attempted to pre-empt the League of Nations through a declaration of independence in March 1920. The cautious Faisal was at first wary about antagonizing the Great Powers and had attempted to negotiate with the French to gain some attributes of statehood if not outright independence. When this failed he was unable to resist the nationalist wave and so he agreed to be crowned King.[2]

The declaration of independence was a momentous event which challenged the new colonial order. It was a rare moment of serious political challenge to empire. The British and French also understood that the stakes were very high – and would have implications not just for the Middle East but for their colonies beyond. Immediately they settled their rivalry and set about cooperating to defeat the revolt. Both countries carefully coordinated a military response and by July 1920 General Gouraud occupied Damascus and the uprising and the plan for a Greater Syria were defeated. The French immediately created Lebanon as a separate territory with boundaries extending from Mount Lebanon along the Mediterranean coast. Faisal was spirited away by the British to their other mandate, Iraq, where he was installed as King and where his branch of the Hashemite dynasty was to rule until the 1958 revolution.

The Palestinian participation in the Syrian events was an important experience and represented a widespread view that Palestine was a constituent part of the Arab nation. However, the sharp reversal of the independence bid through the decisive action of the French and British was perhaps a lesson that the Great Powers were intent on imposing their new order on the Middle East. This reality confronted the Palestinians with a major issue of how to define their identity in relations with the British. As a result Palestinian representatives began to focus, at least in the medium term, on a Palestinian horizon. This meant turning attention to the details of the mandate and the plan for British administration of Palestine. In December 1920 the third Arab Congress had to grapple with the new situation. It attempted to maintain the perspective of greater Syria but demanded that the Arab Executive (elected by the congress) should be recognized by the British as representing the people of Palestine. The congress also opposed Zionism and demanded a halt to all Jewish immigration and to the Jewish acquisition of land. Palestine was now to be seen as a stage on the route to Arab unity and independence. As the prominent nationalist leader Musa Kazim Pasha Al-Husseini[3] was to observe, "after the recent events in Damascus we have to effect a complete change in our plans here. South Syria no longer exists. We must defend Palestine."[4] Thus as a result of the failure of one national Arab project a new distinctive Palestinian one began to emerge.

The British and French, having resolved their differences over Syria, then set about implementing their common plan for dominating the Middle East. The Syrian events also forced both countries to agree the delimitation of their areas of control and it was in this manner that borders between the countries of the region were established. Palestine's northern border along Lebanon and Syria dates from these discussions. The process of formalizing these arrangements took place in a number of international conferences early in the 1920s, and meetings at San Remo (April 1920) and Sèvres (August 1920) were to prove critical in confirming that Great Britain would be accorded the Palestine mandate. These conferences were also decisive in providing international endorsement for inclusion of the Balfour Declaration in the mandate. For most states this was not a new policy; France formally endorsed the declaration in February 1918 and the Italians had followed suit in May of the same year. The Americans, as we noted, under Woodrow Wilson had consented in advance to its terms. This was formalized under his successor when a joint resolution of Congress adopted the policy in 1922 and President Harding duly signed the resolution.

Before publication of the Mandate or the Order-in Council the British addressed the exact areas to be allocated for the Jewish national home. The area designated for the mandate encompassed what are today Israel, the Palestinian territories and Jordan. For several reasons the British wanted to divide this territory into two administrative units at the River Jordan. This was formally accomplished at the Cairo Conference in March 1922 which created Transjordan to the east of the river and Palestine to its west. By 1920 this arrangement had already been effected. At the time Abdullah, brother of Prince Faisal, had been gathering a military force to aid his brother's efforts in Syria. In an act of inspired imperial politics his military force was intercepted as it passed through Transjordan and he was offered the title of Emir of the region. He agreed although only initially for six months. The job, like the country, became permanent and his great-great grandson, of the same name, still rules the Hashemite kingdom. This territorial change created a new entity in the Middle East as well as limiting the area for the Jewish national home to the west of the Jordan. The latter principle was to be included in article 25 of the mandate.

THE MANDATE

The adoption of the text of the Mandate for Palestine[5] represented a major victory for the Zionists in that the Jewish national home assumes the central place in the text. The second clause of the preamble reads:

> the Principal Allied Powers have agreed that...the Mandatory should be responsible for putting into effect the declaration originally made on November 2nd 1917 [by the British government] and adopted by the said powers, in favour of the establishment in Palestine of a national home for the Jewish people, it being clearly understood that nothing should be done which might prejudice the civil and religious rights of existing non-Jewish communities in Palestine or the rights and political status enjoyed by Jews in any other country.

The preamble continues: "recognition has thereby been given to the historical connection of the Jewish people with Palestine and to the grounds for reconstituting their national home in Palestine." This proposition went beyond the terms of the Balfour Declaration which had been silent on any historical connection between the Jews and Palestine. The League of Nations was to show no such reticence and thus endorsed a basic tenet of Zionism. However, this was not just a political position, but its incorporation in the mandate gave it a legal character. Thus within a quarter of a century the Zionist movement had won international legal recognition for the establishment of the Jewish national home in Palestine. The mandate placed obligations on the British to realize the objective as outlined in article 2:

> The mandatory shall be responsible for placing the country under such political, administrative and economic conditions as will secure the establishment of the Jewish national home, as laid down in the preamble, and the development of self-governing

institutions, and also for safeguarding the civil and religious rights of all the inhabitants of Palestine, irrespective of race and religion.

The ordering is significant: first the Jewish national home, then self-governing institutions for the country and then civil and religious rights for its citizens. The priorities of the mandate are thus neatly set out. This was underlined by article 4 which provides for the establishment of a "Jewish Agency" which will be:

recognized as a public body for the purpose of advising and co-operating with the Administration of Palestine in such economic, social and other matters as may affect the establishment of the Jewish national home and the interests of the Jewish population in Palestine and subject always to the control of the Administration, to assist and take part in the development of the country.

The second clause of article 4 names the "Zionist Organization" as the recognized Jewish Agency, which it says will "take steps in consultation with His Britannic Majesty's Government to secure the co-operation of all Jews who are willing to assist in the establishment of the Jewish national home." Article 4 thus granted to the Zionist movement an officially recognized role in Palestine. This role, it should be stressed, was not only to represent the interests of Palestinian Jews but to be the organizing center to "secure the co-operation of all Jews." This concretized the implications of according international legal personality to the Jewish people. The Palestine-based Jewish Agency would thus have functions within the existing Jewish community in Palestine but would simultane-ously involve Jews world-wide in the creation of the national home. This recalled the manner in which Bentwich had earlier formulated the difference between the present and future populations of the country. The Jewish Agency became the pivotal legal and political institution of the Jewish national project. Its transnational character was reflected in its subsequent composition which brought together leaders of the *Yishuv* (the settlement or the Palestinian Jewish community) with those of the Zionist movement in the Diaspora. Its functions were to provide an administrative structure for the national home while at the same time coordinating the efforts to assemble its population.

The assembling of the Jewish population raised the critical question of immigration. As article 6 of the mandate puts it, the administration

> while ensuring that the rights and position of other sections of the population are not prejudiced shall facilitate Jewish immigration under suitable conditions and shall encourage in cooperation with the Jewish agency...close settlement by Jews on the land...

These two principles, Jewish immigration and Jewish acquisition of land, were to be the two most controversial issues that would divide Palestinians and Jews and would bedevil the British authorities throughout the mandate period. The way that this article was phrased provided the Mandatory powers with a great deal of discretion in assessing what "suitable conditions" for immigration might be as well as evaluating the extent to which immigration would prejudice the rights of the Palestinians. The mandate is silent on any criteria that might be used to judge either. Immigrants would be able to acquire citizenship relatively easily as article 7 provided for a nationality law that would be "framed so as to facilitate the acquisition of Palestinian citizenship by Jews who take up permanent residence."

The powers of the Jewish Agency were referred to again in article 11 where it was given powers to be able to "construct or operate, upon fair and equitable terms, any public works, services and utilities, and to develop any of the natural resources of the country." This was subject to the proviso that the administration itself was not carrying out these activities. This underlined the important role that was being assigned to the Jewish Agency. In effect it was gaining elements of political authority over areas normally assigned to a government. The Zionist Organization had thus succeeded in acquiring a significant role in Palestine while retaining its international reach.

The creation of the Jewish national home as the central aim of the Mandate was not just contained in its institutional clauses but also in the repetition of the Balfour Declaration's marginalization of the Palestinian Arab population. As in the declaration, Palestinian Arabs are characterized by not being Jews. The text of the mandate referred variously to the "existing non-Jewish communities," "other sections of the population" and the "inhabitants." At no time is the Palestinian Arab population described with the attributes of any national identity. The Arab character of Palestine was only alluded to in article 22 which designated three official languages: English, Arabic and Hebrew. The mandate did enshrine the principle of non-discrimination on the basis of race, religion or language and the freedom of conscience and religion (article 15). These rights provided only for individual protection and were not couched in collective terms. The Palestinian Arabs are not designated as a people. The provisions for the creation of representative institutions, it could be argued, might allow for the emergence of collective national identity in due course.

ORDER-IN-COUNCIL

The simultaneous drafting of the Order-in-Council was in an effort to ensure that the British administration would be consistent with the terms of the mandate. The order was formally adopted shortly after the mandate in August 1922. The text incorporated terms of the Balfour Declaration and then set about to create a legal and adminis-trative structure for Palestine. The Order-in-Council was not drafted in a vacuum as Britain had been in control of Palestine since 1917 and had already established an elaborate system of administration. The country had been run at first as an occupied territory according to the provisions of The Hague Conventions (1899 and 1907). During the war Palestine was under the command of the Egyptian Expeditionary Force which was replaced by the Occupied Enemy Territory Administration. In July 1920 this military government was replaced by a civil government headed by Herbert Samuel[6] as High Commissioner. As a result of these previous regimes the Order-in-Council had to ensure that the laws passed during these periods were consistent with the new dispensation.

The Order-in-Council created the main government institutions. The Executive comprised of the High Commissioner and a Council appointed by him. A legislative Council was envisioned to comprise of ten standing members (essentially the heads of the executive departments) and twelve indirectly elected members, presided over by the High Commissioner. The powers of the Legislative Council were circumscribed in several ways and in particular the Council could not adopt any law that was contrary to the provisions of the mandate. In addition the High Commissioner could refuse to give his assent to laws or request the opinion of the Secretary of State for the Colonies whose decision was final. Only the High Commissioner could initiate financial legislation.

The twelve members of the legislature not chosen by the High Commissioner were to be selected in two rounds of voting. Males of 25 and over could vote in the first round but only to choose secondary voters who would form electoral colleges on a confessional basis. Eight colleges were to be for Muslims and two each for Christians and Jews. Indirect voting was quite common at the time especially in colonial situations. This highly confessional form of representation replicated the manner in which the Balfour Declaration characterized Palestinian society.

The Order-in-Council created a supreme court and integrated Palestine into the colonial legal system which meant that appeals on points of law would go to the Judicial Committee of the Privy Council in London – in reality the supreme court of the empire. The sources of law that the courts were to implement, with the exception of ordinances introduced by the High Commissioner, were complex. According to article 46 an entire menu of law appeared to be on offer for civil courts, including Ottoman Law and the common law and equity of England. This was in addition to laws introduced by the British since 1917. However, the clause ended by stating that the common law and doctrines of equity "shall be in force in Palestine so far as only the circumstances of Palestine and its inhabitants and the limits of His Majesty's jurisdiction permit and subject to such qualification as local circumstances render necessary." This granted major discretion to the courts as to what law would be applied in any given case. This synthetic legal system which combined "local" law with law of the colonial power was the pattern of the British Empire. It was modeled on the system adopted in Bengal in the second half of the eighteenth century. It gave the appearance of granting legitimacy to the law and customs of the colonized country although in practice the latter were ensnared within the imperial legal institutions which became adept at choosing which law to apply. The judiciary thus became experts in making expedient judgments based on their own discretion, often much to the advantage of the colonial administration. It should be stressed that this provision only applied to civil law and did not apply to criminal law which appeared to be entirely in the hands of the administration. Personal status laws (marriage, divorce, inheritance and religious endowments) remained in the hands of the religious courts. The High Commissioner was also empowered to establish customary courts provided they dispensed justice in a way that was not "repugnant" to the colonial regime.

The provisions creating the legal system demonstrated conclusively that Palestine was now in effect a British colony.

VOICES FROM PALESTINE

In the period between drafting and publication of both the Mandate and the Order-in-Council the British Colonial Office engaged in consultations with Palestinians and the Zionist Organization. This was recorded in correspondence that was published in June 1922.[7] The Palestinian Arab delegation was led by the President of the Arab Executive Musa Kazim Al Husseini and Shibly Jamal who served as secretary.

Musa Kazim Al Husseini was at the time the leader of the national movement in Palestine. He came from a leading Jerusalem family whose members had held office under the Ottomans in various roles including as Mufti of Jerusalem. The British had appointed him Mayor of Jerusalem on the death of his brother in 1918. His office as mayor was rather brief due to his alleged involvement in the first major inter-communal violence in 1920. In April of that year three religious festivals of Jews, Muslims and Christians coincided: Pesach, Nabi Musa (Prophet Moses) and Easter. The festivals also took place against the background of the Syrian bid for independence and so Arab national feeling was high. The Nabi Musa festival included a demonstration that began with a nationalist rally held outside the Arab Club. The mayor spoke, as did the editor of the main paper *Suriyya al-Janubiyya* ("South Syria"). According to Tom Segev's account the crowd shouted slogans such as "Independence! Independence!" and "Palestine is our Land, the Jews are our Dogs."[8] This rhetoric triggered two days of disturbances which left five Jews and four Arabs dead, with over 200 Jews and 20 Arabs injured – and several incidents of rape. The Governor of Jerusalem, Ronald Storrs held Husseini responsible for inciting the crowd and dismissed him as mayor. His relative, Amin al Husseini, who was to play such a crucial role in Palestinian politics, was prosecuted for his part in the events. The British selected Regheb al-Nashashibi as the new mayor, which was a mischievous appointment as he came from a rival family.

Musa Kazim Al Husseini's position did not depend on being the mayor. By 1920 he was well established in a nationalist leadership role and had regularly made representations to the British administration against Zionism and in particular in opposition to Jewish immigration. In 1921 he was to meet Churchill in Jerusalem and personally attempted to persuade him to abandon the national home policy and to halt Jewish immigration. Churchill rebuffed him. While the Husseini family had lost the mayor's office they were to gain the prized Mufti of Jerusalem post which Herbert Samuel, acting on advice from an anti-Zionist British official, gave to the youthful rebel of the Nabi Musa events, Haj Amin Al Husseini.[9]

Musa Kazim Al Husseini headed the Palestinian Arab delegation to London in 1921 and 1922 to lobby for the rescinding of the Balfour Declaration and the creation of Palestinian government. The delegation's negotiations with the British came soon after the collapse of the Syrian project and thus offer a critical insight into the fashioning of Palestinian nationalism at an early stage.

A flavor of the character of Palestinian opposition to Zionism can be gained in the first letter addressed to Colonial Secretary Winston Churchill. The delegation accused Britain of using its power "to impose on the people against their wishes a great immigration of alien Jews, many of them of a Bolshevik revolutionary type."[10] The two images of the Jews as aliens and as Bolsheviks were to prove recurring ones in the Palestinian and Arab discourse of the conflict. Jews were thus constructed as disruptive revolutionaries and alien interlopers in contrast to the natural and traditional authentic Arab inhabitants. These images coined in the 1920s have remained in currency ever since.[11]

The idea that Jews in Palestine, or at least some of them, were communist trouble-makers was well established by the time of the delegation's letter. For example a year earlier in the United States the Arab Palestine Congress had warned that "Jewish immigrants are introducing and spreading in Palestine the spirit and principles of Bolshevism."[12] This was written in the wake of the May 1921 Jaffa riots which killed 95 people and had been sparked by May Day demonstrations organized by Jewish socialists and communists.[13] A member of the British military administration, Captain C.D. Brunton had been of the same opinion and assessed the riots as the responsibility of "Bolshevist Jews," claiming that "the outbreaks of today may become a revolution tomorrow."[14] It was likely the Palestinian delegation would have assessed that, given the British military support for the anti-communist forces in the Russian civil war, anti-Bolshevik sentiments would find some resonance amongst British officials. This would certainly have been the case with Churchill himself who was well known for his staunchly anti-communist views. What was of significance is that the delegation did not object to Zionism on the grounds that it was a British plan to colonize Palestine but rather that it was a revolutionary doctrine that threatened both Palestine and the British Empire. The Bolshevik menace was to figure in the Arab discourse in the campaign against the United Nations plan for Palestine in 1947.[15]

The delegation objected to the draft Order-in-Council on several grounds. While these were grounded in opposition to the Balfour Declaration there was also some astonishment at the transformation of Palestine into a British colony. The mundane reality that the grand language of the League of Nations translated mandates into old-style colonial rule had not been foreseen. The delegation was thus faced with two battles, one against Zionism and the other against British colonial rule. An attempt was made to link the two by focusing on the way in which the structure of colonial governance would advance Zionism.

> It is thus apparent that too much power is given to a High Commissioner whom we will suppose is impartial. But when, as is the case with the present High Commissioner, he is a Zionist, i.e. a member of the Organization which is prompting the flood of alien Jew immigration into Palestine, whose officials as well as those members appointed by him must, naturally, carry out his policy, and when one or two of the 12 elected members will most probably be Zionists, then the Zionist policy of the government will be carried out under a constitutional guise, whereas at present it is illegal, against the wishes of the people, and maintained by force of arms alone.[16]

As can be seen the delegation assumed that Zionism was illegal but was concerned that the Order-in-Council would change that situation. No arguments were advanced as to why Zionism would be illegal; it was merely asserted and this became an approach that is to characterize much of the Palestinian legal narrative. International law was at that time in a critical stage of its evolution but it remained a system of institutions and doctrines imprinted with its colonial origin.[17] The delegation seemed to assume that a pure and just international law existed beyond the realm of the actual international society which was creating Palestine at that very moment. The implicit legal narrative imagined an international law based on values and doctrines that were in accord with a Palestinian perspective. It was early evidence of legal fundamentalism and confused the international legal doctrine that the Palestinians wished to see in place with the doctrines that were in place. This was to be a view of law that was to wrong-foot Palestinians on many occasions.

The argument that the High Commissioner could not be trusted because he was a Zionist and as a result he would pack the Legislative Council with Zionist appointees was more understandable. Samuel might have seen an extraordinary appointment to the delegation given his known Zionist views. However, Samuel was above all a British politician whose loyalty was to the British Empire. There was to be little evidence that his appointments were made on narrow political grounds. Many of his officials were seen as unsympathetic to Zionism. He was widely criticized in Zionist circles for many of his policies. However, the issue was not the personality of the High Commissioner but the basis and form of British rule. The delegation in focusing on the personality of the High Commissioner ignored the greater legal issue that they would need to address; that the policy of the Jewish national home was no longer a British peculiarity but had become an international one.

While the letter requested that the British establish representative institutions the delegation tended to put the argument more in anti-Zionist rather than pro-Palestinian terms. A representative legislative council was seen as a barrier to Zionism rather than as a step towards Palestinian emancipation. The tone very much reflected Husseini's view that the Arab national task was to defend Palestine. Palestinian nationalism thus emerged as a defensive movement.

John Shuckburgh,[18] Churchill's senior official, answered on Churchill's behalf. He was at pains to point out that the Colonial Secretary regarded the discussion as informal as "he is not in a position to negotiate officially" with the delegation or "with any other body which claims to represent the whole, or part of the people of Palestine, since no official machinery for representation has as yet been constituted."[19] This made it quite clear that it was Britain who would decide who would represent Palestine. It was ironic that the delegation's challenge to British plans for Palestinian representation was met by a challenge to the legitimacy of the Palestinians who raised the issue. Nonetheless as the reply continued it appeared that the British were taking the substantive issues raised by the delegation quite seriously.

In addressing the Balfour Declaration, the Colonial Office was straightforward; it had "no intention" of repudiating it. The delegation had stated that it was a contravention of article 22 of the League Covenant to treat Palestine differently from the other Arab mandates. On this Shuckburgh referred to the different ways in which the Treaty of Sèvres dealt with Syria and Iraq designating them "provisionally independent" whereas Palestine was not mentioned in the same context. In any event, he continued, the government was "bound by a pledge which is antecedent to the Covenant of the League of Nations," and "they cannot allow a constitutional position to develop in a country for which they have accepted responsibility to the Principal Allied Powers which would make it impractical to carry into effect" a "solemn undertaking."[20] This statement rather neatly demonstrates the interplay between national policy and international law. In this case the British explained that they were bound by the Balfour Declaration as it was an obligation imposed on them by the "Principal Allied Powers." Thus while the British were the authors of the declaration it had been removed from the provincialism of British politics and had become dignified as an international obligation. The Balfour Declaration was an international legally binding commitment which pre-dated the League Covenant. Subsequent agreements such as the Treaty of Sèvres had also reinforced this legal position. Accordingly Britain was unable to negotiate with the Palestinians over the terms of the Balfour Declaration as it constituted a prior obligation and one which has received widespread recognition internationally. From both of these national and international angles the terms of the declaration are deeply embedded in international law and as such could not be subject to political negotiation. As a consequence "it is quite clear that the creation at this stage of a national government would preclude the fulfillment of the pledge made by the British government to the Jewish people."[21] As if to underline further the hierarchy of international norms already referred to, the letter continues to explain that the allies "concerned as they were to ensure the fulfillment of a policy adopted before the Covenant was drafted, were well advised in applying to Palestine a somewhat different interpretation of paragraph 4 of Article 22 of the Covenant than was applied to the neighbouring countries."[22]

THE NATIONAL HOME

In the second round of letters the Palestinian delegation attempted to make two rather contradictory arguments. The first was to suggest that the British had made a pledge to Emir Hussein of Hejaz to recognize a unified Arab state once the Ottoman Empire had been defeated. This it was argued was contained in the famous Hussein–McMahon correspondence of 1915.[23] However, the content of the correspondence was highly speculative and there was much disagreement by both the British and Hussein as to the exact territory of such a state – in particular it was disputed whether Lebanon or Palestine would be included. Whatever the true facts of those ill-fated discussions the delegation's approach was to use a similar argument as the British and to create a hierarchy of chronological legal obligations. According to this logic the Hussein–McMahon correspondence should take precedence over the Balfour Declaration as the former pre-dates the latter. However, the second argument undermined this approach as it reminded the British government that article 20 of the covenant was "accepted as abrogating all obligations or understandings *inter se* which are inconsistent with the terms thereof."[24] Article 20 of the covenant provided that the principles of the League would take precedence over any other international obligations of its members. The delegation assumed that the commitments to the Zionists were "not in keeping with the Covenant." This position was rather weak as the British had already offered a more sophisticated understanding of the way in which the obligations to the Zionists had arisen as both a prior commitment and as one which was consistent with the covenant. This position gained some authority due to the way in which the mandate system was designed with the question of Palestine and the Jewish national home in mind. The British were careful not just to refer to their commitment to the Jewish national home as being superior to other international obligations, but at the same time to make great play of their duties to implement the will of the international community represented as the "Principal Allied Powers." Shuckburgh made it clear that for the British government the Balfour Declaration provided "first for the establishment of a national home for the Jews in Palestine; and, secondly for the preservation of the rights and interests of the non-Jewish population."[25] This underlined the terms of the declaration in allocating priorities to the two principles. This interpretation emphasized that the legal marginalization of the Palestinians went beyond their lack of any collective national identity but also suggested that their rights were to be secondary to the creation of the Jewish national home.

This brought the discussion centrally to what the content of British obligations constituted. What did the British understand by the term "the Jewish national home"? In addressing this issue Shuckburgh referred to the definition offered by Samuel who as High Commissioner had explained:

These words (national home) mean that the Jews, who are a people scattered throughout the world, but whose hearts are turned to Palestine should be enabled to found here their home, and that some amongst them, within the limits fixed by numbers and the interests of the present population, should come to Palestine in order to help by their resources and efforts to develop the country to the advantage of all its inhabitants.[26]

This was not so much a definition as a description of a process which left many critical issues open to question. It did not explain what the political or legal parameters were for the national home. It avoided commenting on what its jurisdiction would be in Palestine or whether it would possess any degree of international legal personality. Nor was there any elaboration of how terms like "the interests of the present population" and "to the advantage of all its inhabitants" were to be assessed. The failure by the British or indeed the Zionist movement to spell out details of the national home gave rise on the part of the Palestinians to a suspicion that a plan existed but was being hidden from them.

In the early 1920s, the British appeared to have had no particular plan of their own for the national home. At its most precise they envisaged a larger Jewish community which would be facilitated by immigration. The legal status of that community remained unclear. The British placed great reliance on official positions of the Zionist movement itself. While the final form of the national home remained somewhat ambivalent in Zionist thought, there were three constant elements: Jewish immigration to Palestine was an absolute right; Jews should have autonomy over their affairs in Palestine; and the Jewish national home was to be complementary to the existing Arab population. While the British had been dubious as to the character of Palestinian Arabs, in the 1920s the Zionist movement was much clearer: Palestinian Arabs constituted a national community. This was a position that the British found helpful. In its publication "British Policy in Palestine"[27] the government was able to quote from the 12th Zionist Congress (held in September 1921) that had resolved "the determination of the Jewish people to live with the Arab people on terms of unity and mutual respect, and together with them to make the common home into a flourishing community, the upbuilding of which may assure to each of the peoples an undisturbed national development."[28] This two-nations position allowed the Colonial Office to argue that Jewish nationalism was not a threat to Palestine.

The British devoted much attention in attempting to allay Palestinian Arabs' fears of Zionism. In the correspondence the delegation was assured that the national home was not to be all of Palestine but "in Palestine." This latter point was quite crucial and although it was being addressed to the Palestinians it was also intended to remind the Zionists of the limited geographical character of the national home. In addition to a limited area for the national home the British insisted that the Palestine Zionist Executive (to become the Jewish Agency under the mandate) "has not desired to possess, and does not possess, any share in the general administration of the country."[29] From this point of view the image that emerged was of a confined geographical area which would have room for a finite number of new Jewish immigrants which would constitute a polity with no jurisdiction over the country as a whole. The Colonial Office drew this picture of the national home:

> During the last two or three generations the Jews have recreated in Palestine a community, now numbering 80,000, of whom one-fourth are farmers or workers upon the land. This community has its own political organs: an elected assembly for the direction of its domestic concerns; elected councils in the towns and an organization for the control of its schools. It has its elected Chief Rabbinate and a Rabbinical Council for the direction of its religious affairs. Its business is conducted in Hebrew as a vernacular language, and a Hebrew press that serves its needs. It has its distinctive intellectual life and displays considerable economic activity. This community, then, with its town and country population, its political, religious and social organizations, its own language, its own customs, its own life, has in fact "national" characteristics. When it is asked what is meant by the development of the Jewish National Home in Palestine, it may be answered that it is not the imposition of a Jewish nationality upon the inhabitants of Palestine as a whole but the further development of the existing Jewish community; with the assistance of Jews in other parts of the world, in order that it may become a centre in which the Jewish people as a whole may take, on grounds of religion and race, an interest and a pride. But in order that this community should have the best prospect of free development and provide a full opportunity for the Jewish people to display its capacities, it is essential that it should know that it is in Palestine as a right and not on sufferance. That is the reason why it is necessary that the existence of a Jewish

National Home in Palestine should be internationally guaranteed, and that it should be formally recognized to rest upon ancient historic connection.[30]

In this account the existing Jewish community was portrayed with national characteristics although in miniature. It was the nucleus around which the national home would take shape. The reference to its "internationally guaranteed" status could well be a clue that the British envisaged the legal model of a community with minority rights – although somewhat enhanced. The rights of minorities had been a concern at the Versailles peace conference which was followed by a series of treaties aimed at protecting national minorities within states. Beginning with Poland in 1919 some 15 states were obliged to protect their national minorities.[31] Such treaties provided rights for the minorities to control language, schools, the press and culture generally. The statement suggested that the national home might go beyond this and would have a high degree of political autonomy although stopping short of becoming an independent state.

The British were less forthcoming about how progress towards the national home would be assessed and indeed at what point it could be announced that the national home had been created. The failure to be concrete and to outline the ultimate destination of the policy was to have serious consequences for the British as it nourished suspicions amongst Palestinians and raised expectations amongst the Zionists. Without a clear picture of what the Jewish national home meant the British were to adopt radically inconsistent policies during its administration. Each shift would be seen as acting against the interests of one side or the other. The result was that during the mandate both Arabs and Jews would regard the British as acting in bad faith. The main example of the zigzag policy was on the question of Jewish immigration.

IMMIGRATION

The British government formulated the question of immigration in a highly elliptical manner. Having accepted that immigration was the only way in which it could fulfill its commitment on the national home, it stated that it

cannot be so great in volume as to exceed whatever may be the economic capacity of the country at the time to absorb new arrivals. It is essential to ensure that the immigrants should not be a burden upon the people of Palestine as a whole, and that they should not deprive any section of the present population of their employment.[32]

This policy was based on an assumption that there were fixed economic laws which regulated immigration flows and that there was an objective test which could evaluate the absorption of new immigrants. However, this was a dubious assumption. Immigration it could be argued can have a positive impact on the economy as it stimulates economic growth due to the influx of new labor and capital. That had been the experience of the United States, for example. In Palestine rising Jewish immigration as it turned out was to have an equally positive effect on the economy. However, the British in their efforts to address the fears of Palestinians assumed that there was an absolute absorption capacity. In the early 1920s the British administration had not fully grasped that the Zionist project would lead to parallel economies in Palestine.[33] As the Jewish economy grew its need for more labor, capital and enterprise would intensify. Its capacity would be determined by the pace of investment, house-building, land acquisition and the development of public services. Yet those factors would in turn be influenced by the rate of Jewish immigration. As a result the Jewish community would regard limitations on immigration as undermining its ability for economic sustainability. The Palestinians on the other hand were concerned that immigration could undermine the economic balance of the country.

It was, however, the political and social consequences of Jewish immigration that was uppermost in the minds of the Palestinians. On this the British had great difficulty in giving assurances due to their policy that Jews were in Palestine "as of right and not on sufferance." This meant that once Jews arrived in Palestine they were able to gain residence and citizenship relatively easily. This was not quite as expansive a right as the Zionists wished, as these rights could only be gained on arrival in Palestine. Immigration was not a right but subject to British control. The Jews thought the commitment to the national home obligated the British to allow free immigration. The Palestinians objected to any policies that facilitated any Jewish immigration and settlement.

As we have seen, for the Palestinians the immigrants were seen as foreigners, they were "alien Jews." As such they were seen as disruptive, bringing alien political ideas (Bolshevism) and generally threatening the country's peace. For the delegation, "public security in Palestine has been greatly disturbed by those Jews who have been admitted into the country from Poland and Russia, that arms are continually being smuggled in by them and that their economic competition with the Arabs is very keen."[34] Thus the lines of the confrontation on immigration are clearly marked. For the Jews immigration was essential in order to build the national home, but for the Palestinians this was a threat to their society.

In the early days of British rule the Jewish population increased rapidly due to returning Jews, who had left during the war, as well as new immigrants. Some 28,000 Jews were recorded as arriving in the years 1920–22. This increase brought the Jewish population by the time of the 1922 census to just over 83,000 which was probably about 10,000 more than the pre-war population, and thus while an increase it was not substantial. Palestinians, however, described this increase as a "flood." This was a somewhat problematic description as the overall rise of the Jewish population had been modest. However, from this moment onward the view that Jewish immigration constituted a danger was to become a central element of the Palestinian narrative.

THE "EXISTING NON-JEWISH COMMUNITIES"

It was only after five months of correspondence that the Palestinian delegation addressed the question of national identity. This was framed as a challenge to the British position that the Jewish community had "national characteristics." While the delegation wrote "we would here remark that all these outward signs of 'national' existence are also possessed by the other communities in Palestine,"[35] it chose not to elaborate the case for Palestinian national identity but rather to argue that the Jews did not constitute a nation. The starting point was that, "the Arabs should be confirmed in their national home as against all intruders."[36] As far as the Jews were concerned the institutional and cultural features noted by the British were incorrect. "There was no trace of these Political Organs," it was claimed, "but they appeared after the Armistice, when the Balfour Declaration came out. The Hebrew language is not universally used by the community as a vernacular." It was true that the Jewish community did not have any country-wide representative institutions until the end of the war – the first elections took place in 1920. However, there were well-established organizations coordinating activity in agriculture and education as well as political and cultural groups. There were also the courts which dealt with personal status issues. The argument about Hebrew was particularly weak as it had been a medium taught in Jewish schools for over two decades. Indeed by 1919 some 10,000 children were attending such schools. It was also significant that in 1919 the Hebrew daily paper *Haaretz* was established; incidentally the same year that the main Arabic Palestinian daily *Suriyya al-Janubiyya* began publication.

The argument about the Jewish lack of national characteristics before 1917 drew on a narrative of good Arab–Jewish relations in Ottoman times. Jews were portrayed as a quiet religious community which "never agitated for the Declaration of 1917." That was the work of "Zionists outside Palestine." The view that Jews and Arabs lived harmonious lives in Palestine during Ottoman times and that only outsider Zionists undermined these relations has become common in many descriptions of the conflict. However, this picture was inaccurate. Zionist activity was as we have seen well underway before 1917 and involved increasing numbers from the Palestinian Jewish community. The Zionist Organization had many offices in the country and did indeed campaign for a Jewish national home in Palestine. Nor was this done in secret or within the confines of the Jewish community itself. For example Nissim Malul, a Jew of Tunisian origin, was assiduous in replying to all anti-Zionist articles in the Arabic press in the period before the war. He also established a paper in Arabic *Sawt al-Uthmaniyah* (Voice of the Ottoman) to make the case for Zionism – and to argue for Jewish–Arab cooperation. Like many Jews, Malul was deported during the war but interestingly on his return to post-war Palestine he established more Arabic papers to put the Zionist case, first *Al-Akhbar* (The News) and then *Al-Salam* (Peace).[37]

The delegation frequently returned to the narrative of the disruptive Jew who had arrived from foreign lands as an interloper. This required a particular reading of history, as this passage illustrates:

> We have shown over and over again that the supposed historic connection of the Jews to Palestine rests on very slender historic data. The historic rights of the Arabs are far stronger than those of the Jews. Palestine had a native population before the Jews even went there, and this population has persisted all down the ages and never assimilated with the Jewish tribes, who were always a people to themselves. The Arabs on the other hand have been

settled on the land for more than 1,500 years, and are the present owners of the soil.

Further, Christians as well as Moslems look upon Palestine as a sacred land, and make yearly pilgrimages to it in a spirit of devotion and prayer. Any religious sentiment, therefore which the Jews might cherish for Palestine is exceeded by Christian and Moslem sentiment for that country.[38]

In this account it is noticeable how the Jews were constructed as consistently "other." The Jews had been in Palestine but alone amongst the waves of inhabitants had "never assimilated," unlike the Arabs who "have settled on the land." The reason for the Jewish lack of "assimilation" is that they "were always a people to themselves." The latter phrase was drawn from the stock of stereotype images of Jews amongst which exclusivity is a common one. The use of the term "Jewish tribe" is also of note. Its use can hardly have been unintentional when addressed to the British Colonial Secretary.

The argument that Jews had little connection to Palestine was an early version of a theme that recurs in each stage of the conflict. As can be seen here the claim was made that Jews or "Jewish tribes" even in antiquity were transient residents of the country. As a result even Jewish religious attachments are less significant than those of Christians and Muslims. This insistence that Jews had neither connection to Palestine nor any national status was, it should be noted, critical in making the case for Palestinian national claims. Jewish nationalism was constructed as essentially bogus which is contrasted with the genuine Palestinian variety. It was almost as if the effort to prove the aberration of the one normalized the other.

BRITISH CONTROL

With the publication of the Mandate and the Order-in-Council in the summer of 1922, the period of consultation on the terms of British rule came to an end. The mandate formally came into effect in 1923 but for the population the system of government was undisturbed. The objections of the Palestinians both to the terms of reference of the Legislative Council and to its composition meant that the council was never established and Palestine was governed by the High Commissioner, the heads of department and advisors. As Norman Bentwich was to write of this time:

It was recognized by Great Britain and the Council of the League that, on account of the special purpose of facilitating the establishment of the Jewish National Home, there could not be at once democratic self-government but the process must here be developed in stages. The mandatory therefore directed to secure the development of self-governing institutions and to encourage local autonomy. But the Arab majority could not be allowed uncontrolled legislative power to prevent the fulfillment of the Mandate in relation to the minority Jewish population.[39]

At the beginning of the mandate, Bentwich was the Attorney-General and as such was primarily responsible for the implementation of the Order-in-Council. As can be seen from his comments above, the brief that the Colonial Office had given him left him no room to modify the system of governance. The commitment to the Jewish national home was seen as prior to other objectives and effectively acted as a veto to the development of country-wide representative institutions. As a result Bentwich abandoned the attempt to create the elected part of legislative council. Of this situation he was later to comment: "the government of Palestine, as in most countries is divided between central and local authorities. In its central aspect it is a benevolent autocracy. In its local aspect it includes representative and self-governing bodies subject to a certain control and supervision."[40] We might wonder about the benevolence of the rule but the term "autocracy" does seem apposite.

Bentwich's opinion must be taken in the context of the time when democratic government was a rather limited concept and did not mean what it does today. Colonial rule was the norm for most of the territories of the globe and where this was the exception the right to vote in the 1920s was rarely extended to women. Discrimination against women and ethnic and racial groups was common and usually lawful. Bentwich's comments on Palestine were instructive but also represented views that could have been found amongst most colonial administrators at the time. The one difference was that the British view of Palestine was fashioned by its commitment to the Jewish national home. In this narrative self-government was not opposed, as such, but rather delayed until the existing majority would be no longer able to veto the self-government of what Bentwich had referred to earlier as a "future population." In the history of colonialism playing one section of the population against another was quite normal – and the British had become adept at that in India for example – the difference here was that divide and rule was based on temporal conditions: dividing and ruling the present against the future.

As the British set about governing Palestine questions about the legal implications of the terms of mandate were both of practical and theoretical concern. The new rulers were aware of the importance of law and at an early stage appointed Frederic Goadby as the advisor on Legal Education and in November 1920 he established the Jerusalem Law Classes, a law school that was to be a permanent feature of the British period. Goadby had been based in Cairo since 1906 where he had taught at the Khedival law school and no doubt knew Bentwich when he worked as an official in the Egyptian Ministry of Justice. Goadby's particular role was to introduce the study of English common law to the students whose study centered on a French-based civil law system. His lectures became the basis of his influential book *Introduction to the Study of Law: A Handbook for the use of Egyptian Students*[41] in which he contrasted the English common law system and the codified French system with what he termed Mohammedan Law. Once in Palestine he adapted his text for Palestinian students in 1921.[42] The Jerusalem law classes attracted both Palestinian and Jewish students and lectures were held in what became the three official languages: Arabic, Hebrew and English. For the British the establishment of a law school even before the mandate came into force reflected their experience of colonial rule. Legal education produced not only lawyers but also officials and judges. These lawyers, judges and officials played an important role in legitimizing the regime in the eyes of the population. In India the British had realized the importance of this at an early stage when they had established Fort William College at the beginning of the nineteenth century – and after the India rebellion of 1857 when Indian legal education was modernized. In Palestine it was important for lawyers and judges to understand the complex character of the mixed sources of law that were available to the civil courts which, as we have seen, could refer to Ottoman Law as well as to the English common law. As Goadby's book indicated, the task of legal education was to draw the colonized legal profession onto the terrain of the colonial regime.[43] This was perhaps particularly vital in Palestine given the legal disagreements over the terms of British rule. Law was central to legitimating British rule. The law school attracted almost equal numbers of Arabs and Jews throughout the period and within its class rooms there was little conflict.[44] Whatever the arguments about the mandate, the British understood that law, the courts and the legal profession could play an important role in bringing Arabs and Jews to a common loyalty. Although this policy ultimately failed it did nonetheless provide a degree of common discourse between the communities.

ARGUMENTS ABOUT THE MANDATE

The legal arguments about the mandate were conducted in Palestine and beyond. Jacob Stoyanovsky's book *The Mandate for Palestine*[45] offers a contemporary full-length study of the legal issues. Stoyanovsky devoted great attention to the Arab assertion that the Palestinian Mandate was contrary to the League of Nations Covenant. He writes:

> it has been said that the Mandate for Palestine, in its present form is incompatible with Article XXII of the Covenant, because the mandates system as contemplated in that Article is instituted in the interests of the actual inhabitants of the mandated territories, while the Palestine mandate contemplates the interests of a people actually outside the territory. This criticism is thus concerned with the underlying principles of the mandates system as applied to Palestine. But the main objective of the system is to guide towards independence and self-government those races, peoples or communities who for various reasons are not able to stand alone. This is the very object of the national home policy, which aims at giving the Jewish people the necessary assistance to form in Palestine an independent and self-governing community. The underlying principles not only of the mandates system but of the Covenant as a whole, are thus given effect in the national home policy.

> Thus the principle upon which the Palestine mandate – including the national home provision – is based appears to be the very same as that which underlies the other mandates, namely the well-being and development of the peoples not yet able to stand alone form a sacred trust of civilization. The peculiarity of the national home policy seems to be the extension of this principle so as to include the Jewish people in the category of above peoples. The reason why the Jewish people is as yet not able to stand alone matters but little from the point of view of the mandate, although it may be said that the incapacity is mainly due to its dispersion and not, as in other cases to a more or less low degrees of development.[46]

In Stoyanovsky's account the mandate was consistent with the covenant as the Jews were categorized amongst those peoples who "cannot stand alone." This was not because the Jews were in the same position as the other peoples of Turkey's erstwhile empire. The Jews could not exercise self-government in Palestine because of their Diaspora status. The mandate thus acted to rectify this status and to provide the means through which the national home could be nurtured. In Stoyanovsky's view it was not administrative assistance that the Jews required from the international community but the conditions to return to Palestine. This argument rested on the assumption that historic rights have the capacity to be transformed into legal rights. It was precisely to oppose such a conclusion that the Palestinians had argued earlier that the Jews did not have such legitimate historical rights. This argument that connects historical claims to contemporary legal rights anticipated many battles that indigenous peoples were to fight in the Americas and Australasia in the latter part of the twentieth century. Moreover, historical claims including the right to return which Stoyanovsky applied to Jews were to become central in Palestinian legal narratives after the establishment of Israel in 1948.

Stoyanovsky's defense of the legality of the mandate was the dominant view of the period. A year after the publication of his book, Norman Bentwich was selected to give the prestigious annual lectures at The Hague Academy of International Law. Bentwich's topic "The Mandates System" should leave in little doubt that the mandates were regarded as part of international law and an appropriate topic for the lecture series. In due course, as was the practice, the book of the lectures was published. Angus McNair, in introducing the volume commented that Bentwich was "one of the few international lawyers to whose lot it has fallen to be intimately responsible for the actual working of a mandate."[47] McNair explains the purpose of the mandate system as

> introducing a new code of mixed law and morality into the dealings of the colonising Powers with the peoples inhabiting their dependent possessions. It has also introduced into the colonial administration a defined objective, namely, the gradual preparation of dependent peoples for the independent management of their own affairs and for their ultimate growth into statehood.[48]

This was a useful insight into the way in which international lawyers saw the mandate system and its operation within the framework of the League of Nations. The new form of regulation of colonialism was marked by an educational phase for the colonized. This confirmed not only imperial power but also the imperial role in international law. Bentwich offered a clear view of the objectives of mandates:

1. A system of national responsibility for the government of a country under the control of an international body.
2. A system of guardianship of peoples, similar to the guardianship by individuals of minor persons.[49]

These statements well indicate the character of international legal discourse of the time. The binary division of peoples into guardians and minors was a given and no further explanation was provided as it would have been regarded as uncontroversial by his audience. This is not to suggest that there were no anti-colonial movements at the time, which there were, but that such voices were not really heard amongst international legal circles. Bentwich continued by explaining that the Palestine mandate had special features and was in a "class by itself" as the Arab peoples "were opposed to the basic idea of the mandate."[50] He, however, offered the view that:

> Of the Palestine Mandate it may be said that, if the Mandate system had not been evolved for other purposes, it would have had to be created for the government of this little land… For Palestine, by its history, its geography, its population and its destiny is an international country, and its well-being and development form in the nature of things, a sacred trust of civilization.[51]

This echoes the political views that Smuts held before the end of the war when he proposed the mandate system. Bentwich's contribution was to explain the manner in which such politics have been brought into the orbit of international law. He was keen to underline that the mandate "recognizes the historical connection of the Jewish People with the territory as giving a national right to which the Mandatory in the first place, and the League of Nations, ultimately, has pledged itself to give effect. It is the application in law of the idea that 'memory also gives a right.'"[52] Bentwich was on safe ground in arguing that the mandate does give legal recognition to the Jewish historical claim although his deployment of memory as underlying the legal recognition was probably more controversial – and if consistently applied would have been inimical to colonialism. It is doubtful whether he would have applied the same test to indigenous peoples. His point was no doubt to rebuff the Arab position that Jews had little historical connection to Palestine.

In the lectures Bentwich outlined his view that there are two "national selves" in Palestine and that the majority cannot be allowed to use its position to deny the minority its national rights. The Palestinians would have argued that the real problem of the mandate was that the Jews were acting a veto on their national rights. He did not address that point. Nor did he outline any ideas on how the Palestinian "national self" can exercise its rights either under the mandate or once the Jewish national home had been established. However, it is interesting that he assumed that Palestinians had national rights no less equal to those of the Jews.

The content of The Hague Academy lectures did not in itself add much that was new. Their importance rather lies in that they were given and that the views expressed were necessarily endowed with great authority. Through the lectures and then the book the interpretations of the League of Nations Covenant, the mandates system and the Palestine mandate would enter international legal discourse. These ideas would have been circulated amongst government officials, legal advisors, academics and students. The decision to invite Bentwich to give the lectures (while still Palestine Attorney-General) indicates the status in which he was held at the time internationally and the significance of the mandate system to the international legal order.

As we have seen, Palestinian representatives had challenged the legality of the mandate at its inception. However, the first systematic legal challenge had to wait until the 1930s with the publication of the book by the Palestinian lawyer Wissam Boustany.[53] His argument essentially elaborated the original view of the Palestinian delegation that the terms of the Palestine mandate were inconsistent with the provisions of the League of Nations Covenant, and thus it was "ultra vires." His argument did not take into account that the mandate system was essentially international legal regulation of a colonial project as Bentwich had explained. Boustany assumed that the principle of the "well-being" of the community and the "development of the people of the mandated area" necessarily excluded the Jews.[54] Or as he later argued the Mandate should not offer "a legalization" of an infringement of the League Covenant to make "the special exception of a policy in favour of 12–16 million Jews in the presence of hundreds of millions of Muslims and Christians."[55] There were both legal and political curiosities about these statements.

Boustany's term "legalization" when referring to the relationship of the Palestine Mandate and the League Covenant was especially significant. This comment appeared as a major concession given his general argument that the League of Nations had acted beyond the law. It implies that the League indeed "legalized" the very result he objected to. If that was correct then Boustany appeared to have accepted that the Jewish national home was a lawful project. In effect he tied himself in a knot of his own making as he tried to claim simultaneously that the League of Nations was acting both illegally and legally at the same time. It suggests that he underestimated the jurisprudence whereby international organizations define their own competence and thus interpret their own powers independently. Nor did Boustany comment on the regular reaffirmation of the legality of the mandate by the League organs.

His political characterization of the conflict as one between all Arabs and Jews was highly significant. Palestine he was accepting was an international conflict. The intersection of Palestinian identity and Arab nationalism was to remain the enduring feature in subsequent developments. Palestine was to become a symbol of Arab unity which was to be portrayed as being threatened by Zionism. Boustany anticipated the manner in which the fate of Palestine was to become increasingly bound up in Arab politics. Legal rights in Palestine were to be seen as affecting the legal rights of all Arabs.

While a small circle was involved in the details of these legal debates the broad principles had great resonance amongst the Jewish and Arab publics. Both sides sought legitimacy for their case in the belief that law sustained it. Political leaders were to draw heavily on legal justifications when elaborating their policies. The appeal to law was to be woven into the political fabric of each side.

The British mandate was to be a short but dramatic interlude in the region's history. Palestine had been constituted but its identity was to be fought over. It was to see rebellions by both Arabs and Jews as both doubted British intentions. During the 30 years of British rule the demography of Palestine was to change dramatically as the Arab population doubled in size and the number of Jews rose from 83,000 to over 600,000. British Palestine was to be bordered by two world wars. While the first gave Palestine to Britain, the second was to see its control dissolve. As the Palestine question was to move from the League of Nations to the United Nations, the arguments about the mandate were to intensify.

3
The United Nations Partition Plan

On November 29, 1947, the United Nations General Assembly adopted resolution 181 which partitioned Palestine into three entities: a Jewish state, an Arab state, and an international zone around Jerusalem but all within an economic union. The United Nations had been handed the issue of the future of Palestine by the British government in February of that year. In passing the matter to the United Nations the British government broke new ground as it abandoned its imperial role and pushed the new international organization into deciding the political and legal future of a colonial territory. This chapter will focus on the way the United Nations responded to this challenge through a reading of the contemporary debates and the partition plan itself.

The Attlee Labour government which had been formed in July 1945 had inherited the previous British policies toward Palestine that had been contained in the 1939 White Paper.[1] This had envisioned an independent unitary Palestine within ten years and set strict limits on Jewish immigration. Despite the Labour Party's recent Zionist sympathies and its support for a Jewish state at its 1944 conference,[2] once in power the government continued the policies of the White Paper although with a slight liberalization of the immigration quotas. While the war-time coalition government had rejected making a decision on Palestine's future, the new government had empirically adopted a policy of creating a unitary state with some concessions to the Jewish minority. Limitations on Jewish immigration remained critical in an effort to calm the fears of the Arab world about Britain's intentions. However, this policy was to provoke violent Jewish resistance to British rule. Violence, however, escalated even after the United Nations became involved leading the British to announce in September 1947 that, whatever the decision of the organization, they would abandon the Mandate.

British policy toward Palestine was not helped by the conflicting policies of the three government departments that were responsible for it: the Colonial Office, the War Office and the Foreign Office. As Elizabeth Monroe comments, "the first wanted to save some of its handiwork from ruin, the second wanted to extricate its men and materiel; the third wanted to keep up the British position in the rest of the Arab world."[3] These fissures undoubtedly affected British policy-making at the time. It should also be pointed out that Palestine was not the main issue the government faced. Much more central at the time were the financial consequences of World War II, the rising strategic threat of the Soviet Union and Indian independence. The uncharacteristic decision to involve the United Nations and then to announce the unilateral end of the Mandate has to be seen in this context. In Palestine itself the British were caught between Arab aspirations for independence and Jewish demands for a state.

The war had transformed the international situation and Palestine's place within world politics. The emergence of the Soviet Union as a world power and its alliance with Britain and the United States through the creation of the United Nations in 1942[4] was the defining feature of this new period. For the Jewish people this new international situation took place in the context of the genocide against Europe's Jews. The Holocaust had intensified the Zionist argument for the necessity of a Jewish homeland. While Nazi Germany had carried out the mass murder of 6 million Jews during the war, with the full knowledge of the Allies, no action had been taken to prevent it. The Jews had been trapped in Nazi-controlled Europe and appeared to have been abandoned. An array of international and national measures had placed restrictions on Jewish migration, including to Palestine. For the Zionist movement this experience underlined the need for Jews to have free access to their national home and the realization that the fate of the Jewish people was in their hands alone.

It was against the background of the news of ghettos and concentration camps that Zionist policy on the national home was replaced with the demand that Palestine should be "established as a Jewish commonwealth." This change was adopted at the Biltmore conference held in New York in May 1942.[5] Although the conference had been organized by the American Zionist movement its policy became the official Zionist line. The resolution adopted at the conference envisaged the liberation of Europe's Jews as the full extent of the Nazi extermination program was then unknown. The Jewish commonwealth was conceived of as a place of refuge, as a life-boat state at a time of extreme danger. However, this Jewish commonwealth was still seen as complementary to "the economic, agricultural and national development of the Arab peoples and states." The resolution also elegantly linked its creation to "the struggle against the forces of aggression and tyranny" and sought for the commonwealth to be "integrated into the structure of the new democratic world."

After the war when the extent of the Holocaust became widely known the objective of a Jewish state became more insistent. While within the Zionist movement this was not a universal position and some groups still argued for bi-nationalism, Jewish support for a state was now broadly established. As we shall see even David Ben-Gurion was prepared, in private, to investigate alternatives to a Jewish state but in public he held resolutely to the official policy. In 1945 the Zionist movement had to engage with a new international situation where British power was much diminished and that of the United States and the Soviet Union was in the ascendancy. While the Zionists fought for a Jewish state to become part of this new world order it had to confront Britain's old policies on the ground.

The Arab world had been somewhat sheltered from World War II's political impact through its colonial position. This was somewhat fortuitous given the sympathy that existed within the Arab world for Berlin.[6] To some extent the support for Nazism by some movements, such as Young Egypt, could be explained by the adage that "my enemy's enemy, is my friend." It was hoped that a German victory would end British and French dominance in North Africa and the Middle East. However, it has to be said that some Arab support for Nazism went beyond such tactical considerations and was ideological – and sometimes practical.[7] French collaborationist regimes in Morocco, Tunisia and Algeria did impose anti-Semitic laws modeled on the Third Reich which were generally supported. It should not be forgotten that Jews in these North African territories (and Italian Libya) suffered forced labor and concentration camps and were sometimes sent to camps in Europe.[8]

The Palestinian political leadership contained several figures who were active supporters of Nazism. Mufti Haj Amin Al Husseini was the most prominent amongst them. Al Husseini participated in the short-lived pro-Nazi rising in Iraq and then spent the rest of the war in Berlin actively collaborating with the Nazi regime. He was responsible for broadcasting to the Middle East and made many appearances himself. The six radio stations which he favored (Berlin, Zeissen, Bari, Rome, Tokyo and Athens) were renowned for their vitriolic anti-Semitic propaganda.[9] He also played a major role in the recruitment of Muslims to Waffen SS divisions in the

Balkans, especially in Bosnia. Al Husseini went to great lengths to stress the similarities between Nazism and Islam, arguing that the Bosnian SS division was a "visible and practical expression of both ideologies."[10] This similarity was attired in anti-imperialist rhetoric:

> Many common interests exist between the Islamic world and Greater Germany, and those make cooperation a matter of course. The Reich is fighting against the same enemies who robbed the Moslems of their countries and suppressed their faith in Asia, Africa and Europe. Germany is the only Great Power which has never attacked any Islamic country. Further, National Socialist Germany is fighting against world Jewry. The Koran says: "You will find that the Jews are worst enemies of Moslems." There are also considerable similarities between Islamic principles and those of national-socialism...[11]

Despite these activities the Palestinian leadership was to defend the Mufti after the war. In the debate which established the United Nations Special Committee on Palestine (UNSCOP) Moshe Shertok speaking for the Jewish Agency referred to his record of being "directly involved during the war in the Nazi policy of the extermination of European Jews."[12] Emile Ghouri representing the Higher Arab Committee mounted an aggressive defense of Al Husseini: "we have been victimized by Anti-Arab propaganda,"[13] he said. As for the Mufti, his flight to Nazi Germany was an act of self-defense, "a stand that any threatened nation would have taken in order to protect itself. He had to escape to Europe to avoid arrest by the British as a result of Zionist propaganda... His sole crime was that he has stood in the way of Zionist aims."[14] That the image of refuge from Zionism being sought in Nazi Germany in the early 1940s so seriously argued at the United Nations within two years of the end of World War II is extraordinary. Lest listeners were in doubt about the anti-Semitic content of this intervention, Ghouri concluded his oration:

> The question of the Mufti was raised this morning by the spokesman of the Jewish Agency. The Jews are questioning the record of an Arab spiritual leader. Does this properly come from the mouth of a people who have crucified the founder of Christianity?[15]

These comments rather accurately reflect the way in which trends within Arab nationalism had become compromised with Nazism and mainstream European anti-Semitism in the 1930s and 1940s. They also illustrate a reckless lack of diplomatic skill in presenting the Arab case. It would have been wise to distance the Palestinian cause from the Mufti's activities on behalf of Berlin and the short-lived pro-Nazi regimes in Syria and Iraq.[16] The latter while portraying themselves as nationalist enterprises had also excelled in copying Nazi activities. During the *farhoud* (pogrom) in Baghdad in 1941 between 180 and 400 Jews were massacred in the wake of the pro-Nazi coup attempt led by Rashid Ali.[17]

The subordinate position of the Arab world meant that actual alliances between Arab sovereign states and the Axis powers were never more than fleeting. As a result independent Arab states were able to take their place in the new United Nations system untainted by any formal connection with the defeated powers. The establishment of the Arab League in March 1945 ensured Arab participation in the post-war world order. Little discussion took place in the Arab world about the flirtation with Nazism and as a result no balance sheet was made. This has had detrimental consequences for Arab politics and diplomacy.[18]

During World War II the mainstream Zionist movement led by David Ben-Gurion had continued to oppose the 1939 White Paper but also cooperated with Britain against the Nazis. The slogan "to fight the White paper as if there was no war and to fight the war as if there was no White paper" on the whole was to Britain's advantage. Once the war was over this restraint was lifted and Ben-Gurion and other leaders came under pressure from the more radical Zionist fringe (the Irgun[19] led by Menachem Begin and the Lehi[20] of Avraham Stern), which advocated a much more militant stance. Armed resistance to British rule became widespread, especially against the restrictions on immigration. The Haganah[21] and the other organizations took direct action to facilitate Jewish immigration. In order to carry out these actions the militias needed a constant supply of arms. Defiance of the British immigration rules and the buying (and smuggling) of arms brought all wings of the Zionist movement into conflict with the British.[22]

Immigration was necessarily linked to the question of territory on which the migrants would settle. The Biltmore program in calling for a Jewish commonwealth had been carefully ambiguous on the territorial question.[23] It had been assumed that an area would be needed that could accommodate hundreds of thousands and possibly millions. In the early 1940s a population of 2 million had been projected by the Zionist movement.[24] Since the 1939 White Paper the British had permitted little Jewish immigration to Palestine. According to British figures 55,486 Jews had been admitted as legal immigrants between 1939 and 1945.[25] This was even fewer than envisaged by the White Paper which had provided for 75,000 in the five years from 1939. Overturning these restrictions and providing room for the survivors of the Holocaust meant concretely addressing the territorial question.

The issue of how much land was required for a significant population was open to question. At the time Jews occupied and owned a small amount of land. Most Jews lived in three cities, Tel Aviv, Haifa and Jerusalem, and the rural population was a minority. During the mandate period while the Jewish population rose tenfold the area of Jewish-owned land increased only threefold, amounting to less than 6 percent of Palestine by 1947. The Jewish urban population was thus highly concentrated in small areas whereas the Jewish countryside was widely scattered with often isolated communities living in the densely populated Arab rural areas. This population distribution taxed the Zionist leadership in developing a coherent territorial policy.

Until the Biltmore program dominant Zionist thinking had been in favor of some form of federal solution which would cover all of Palestine but with a distinct Jewish area. One such proposal had been advanced in 1940 by a special committee of the Jewish Agency Executive which proposed a federal Palestine based on parity autonomy between Jews and Arabs. The committee chaired by Shlomo Kaplansky had been set up in the wake of the 1939 Zionist Congress which had adopted resolution XXI calling for a definitive policy on the "Arab question."[26] Under the Kaplansky plan the federal government would be weak with most powers to be devolved to the Arab and Jewish states – including immigration. This had been one of the options that Weizmann had suggested in the 1939 Congress debate where he had identified three possibilities: a parity regime under the British mandate, partition of Palestine into two independent states, or a federal system with Jews controlling immigration into the Jewish area.[27]

The main objective was to acquire sufficient land for Jewish settlement. The political arrangements were subordinate to that, with the proviso that Jewish immigration would be unrestricted. In 1946 even after the Biltmore decisions Ben-Gurion floated a proposal to some members of the Zionist Executive for a loose bi-national federation to be formed by re-dividing Palestine and Jordan. While the Arab and Jewish states would both be formally sovereign they would cooperate over the economy and their security would be internationally guaranteed.[28] This kite flying was to come to nothing particularly as it would have involved opening the unpopulated areas of Jordan to Jewish settlement. Removing the Arab population from any area of Palestine was not considered an option. Ben-Gurion's proposal illustrates how fluid the Zionist thinking was about the character of the Jewish state – and the form that relations with Arabs in Palestine and the region could take.

Some groupings within the Zionist movement did continue to advance bi-national solutions. Hashomer Hatzair whose political party Mapam was to gain the second largest number of seats in the first Israeli Knesset, was its most prominent advocate. However, the adoption of the partition resolution effectively ended any significant support amongst the Jewish community for anything less than an independent Jewish state.

The political outlook of the Palestinian Arabs was complex. The Mufti remained the titular head of the national movement but he remained exiled from Palestine and spent much of the period after the war eluding arrest for collusion with the Nazis. He had not been in Palestine since 1937 and thus was rather removed from the tempo of events. While there were other prominent nationalist leaders in Palestine the movement was highly fragmented. In these circumstances the Arab League was to acquire a central position in Palestinian politics. One of the League's early decisions had been to implement a boycott of Jewish goods from Palestine (in December 1945). The League then reconstituted the Arab Higher Committee (AHC) in Palestine with the Mufti at its head but with Jamal Al Husseini actually responsible for it in Palestine. This Arab dimension to Palestinian politics which had been so much a feature of the formative period in the 1920s was to become formalized through the League. The Arab League and Palestinian politicians invested much hope in the new United Nations system which was apparently based on the principle of self-determination. The League hoped that what it regarded as an error of the League of Nations would be rectified and a way would be opened for an independent Palestinian state.

What the Palestinian and Arab leaderships had not grasped was the character of the shift in world politics during the war. The lack of Arab participation on the side of the Allies weakened the Arab voice. Moreover the Arab League states (Egypt, Iraq, Syria, Lebanon, Saudi Arabia, Jordan and Yemen) were in practice tied to their former colonial powers, and had undemocratic and often corrupt governments. With the possible exception of Jordan, none of them had any military clout. What was perhaps more significant was that no Arab government had good relations with the Soviet Union or, with the exception of Saudi Arabia, with the United States. Indeed both the USA and the USSR viewed the Arab world as being far too much under the sway of the old imperial powers Britain and France. This was to have important consequences for Arab diplomacy.

ESTABLISHING THE UNITED NATIONS SPECIAL COMMITTEE

In May 1947 the United Nations decided to establish the Special Committee on Palestine (UNSCOP) with the task of making proposals for a solution on the future of the country. It was to be chaired by the Swedish judge Emile Sandstrom and was composed of representatives from Australia, Czechoslovakia, Guatemala, India, Iran, the Netherlands, Peru, Uruguay and Yugoslavia. The wide terms of reference for the committee were "to submit such proposals as it may consider appropriate for the solution to the problem of Palestine."[29]

In the debate on creating the committee and its terms of reference the main lines of political and legal confrontation between Palestinian Arabs and Jews were drawn. These voices could be expressed directly as the United Nations General Assembly had invited the Jewish Agency and the Arab Higher Committee to participate in its deliberations. The Jewish Agency was represented by a high level delegation including Ben-Gurion, Moshe Shertok and Abba Silver. The Arab Higher Committee was represented by its secretary Emile Ghouri and the lawyer Henry Cattan.

The first main controversy was to center on the exact terms of reference for the committee and in particular whether it would have any remit to consider factors outside Palestine, including Jewish displaced persons in Europe. The AHC and the Arab states wanted to exclude such considerations. The final resolution was to be a defeat for the Arab perspective as the critical clause read:

The Special Committee shall conduct investigations in Palestine and, wherever it may deem useful, receive and examine written or oral testimony, whichever it may consider appropriate in each case, from the mandatory Power, from representatives of the population of Palestine, from governments and from such organizations as it may deem necessary.[30]

As a result the committee could work anywhere and consult whom it chose. The resolution was adopted by a wide margin for 45 votes to 7. The five Arab members were only joined by Afghanistan and Turkey, indicating their relatively isolated position. The Arab starting point had been that there was only one legal and just solution to the Palestinian problem: immediate independence as a single state on the basis of permanent Arab majority rule. While the Arab representatives attempted to argue that such a result was the only possible interpretation of the United Nations Charter, clearly a large majority of the organization thought that other options could be legitimately considered.

The Arab case had not been skillfully argued. The position that the League of Nations mandate had been illegal and invalid was endlessly repeated to representatives of the very same states who had voted for the mandate in 1922. Such questionable legal arguments were then embellished with rather bizarre accounts of religious and political history. Syrian representative El-Khouri went so far as to compare contemporary Jewish demands for a state with the Exodus story. He suggested that the lesson of the Exodus was that Jews had long cherished political ambitions to dominate the region.[31] He argued that the Jews had purposely made life difficult for Pharaoh. As a result he had been forced to release them from Egypt, at which point the Jews could cause havoc in the entire region.

> Under the guidance of Moses, and afterwards, under the guidance of Joshua and the other judges and kings, they started to invade Palestine and occupy certain portions of it with the policy of exterminating everyone there – men, women, children, old and young, even the animals – in order not to leave a trace of the living population of that country; and the places which they succeeded in conquering were so dealt with to utter destruction and extermination.[32]

El-Khouri assured his audience this account was not derived from "any human historical source. It is all in the Bible." One assumes that his message was that if the United Nations succumbed to the modern political designs of the Jews, it would merely force on the Middle East the same disaster that befell the region in antiquity.

He continued his speech with a potted history of the Jews, apparently approving of the Roman dispersal and Titus' decree that no Jew could enter Jerusalem – and that this decree was kept in place after the Arab conquest of the city. After the arrival of the Ottomans, "a few Jews did sneak into Jerusalem."[33] He continued that later in the Ottoman period the Jews attempted to bribe Caliph Abdul Hamid to gain access to Palestine but the Caliph was dismissive, "let the Jews keep their millions for themselves."[34] The story then became even more convoluted as El-Khouri unmasked the Jews who tried to bribe the Caliph as not Jews at all but Mongols who had converted to Judaism and set up the Khazar dynasty in southern Russia between the seventh and tenth centuries. This was an attempt to suggest that European Jews were their descendants and not at all connected to the Jews of the Middle East or to Palestine.[35] Whether these people had acquired the unattractive traits of the early Jews we were not told.

It is difficult to imagine the circumstances in which Arab diplomats would have thought that framing such problematic arguments would have been persuasive let alone principled. The anti-Semitic subtext became unmistakable and could sometimes have a particularly callous element given recent history. For example, in discussing the Jewish displaced people El-Khouri attempted to persuade the United Nations of the economic advantages they would accrue by remaining in Europe:

> We understand that a great percentage of the Jews were massacred in eastern Europe. Well, the survivors, who are a small percentage under the ruling democracies of eastern Europe, could go back and take into their possession the properties of all the Jews who were there before, and each of them would be seven or eight times as rich as they used to be before.[36]

Such arguments would not advance the Arab case. The five permanent members of the Security Council all lined up behind the resolution as did India and Iran. However, the implications of this did not seem to register with the Arab missions and their line of argument was to remain the same. The Arab misjudgment of the international political situation was also clear when it came to their relations with the Soviet Union and the new socialist camp. The most vigorous intervention on behalf of the Jewish case had come from the USSR's Andrei Gromyko. His speech set out the parameters for the discussion: "it is essential to bear in mind," he said, "the indisputable fact that the population of Palestine consists of two peoples, the Arabs and the Jews. Both have historical roots in Palestine. Palestine has become the homeland of both these peoples."[37] Thus for the Soviet Union, "an equitable solution can be reached only if sufficient consideration is given to the legitimate interests of both peoples."[38] His preferred option was for what he described as an "independent, dual, democratic, homogeneous Arab-Jewish state."[39] However, if this proved to be impossible he was in favor of partition into two states. The Soviet Union and the other socialist states had clearly taken a decision that Jewish nationalism was a legitimate force in Palestine. The reaction of the Arab missions was to return to the 1920s argument that Zionism was a means of communist penetration into the Arab world.

UNSCOP quickly established itself and set about its task. In the course of its work the committee visited Palestine, Lebanon, Syria, Jordan and displaced peoples' camps in Germany and Austria. It held public and private sessions and took evidence from 37 people representing both Arab states and Jewish organizations. While the Palestinian Arab Higher Committee boycotted the UNSCOP and refused to give evidence this was not the policy of the Arab states. The Foreign Minister of Lebanon, Hamid Frangie, presented the views of most of the Arab League. The committee then paid a separate visit to the Jordanian King Abdullah to hear his opinion.[40] Thus while it is true that the Palestinian Arabs did not directly make representations the views of the Arab world as a whole were strongly put to the committee. The formal reason for the separate meeting with Jordan was that it was not yet independent. This conveniently permitted differences in outlook within the Arab world on Palestine to be put to the committee. Some historians have argued that there was in fact a prior agreement between Jordan and the Zionist movement over the division of Palestine so that Jordan would acquire the West Bank.[41] However, this is much disputed on all sides.[42] There was also some evidence to suggest that boycott by the AHC was associated with levels of intimidation against Palestinian Arabs who wanted to give evidence to the committee. According to the Guatemalan representative to the United Nations the AHC "ordered its affiliated organizations to refuse to cooperate with the committee and to threaten and intimidate all Arabs who seemed to favour conciliation."[43]

The UNSCOP was charged with publishing its report at the beginning of September 1947. The committee had begun proceedings at the end of May and so had carried out all its work within three months. Despite the speed of operations it was significant that the report adopted an extremely calm and methodical tone. It was a measured and systematic account of the conflict despite the time pressure and the drama of the events which surrounded its drafting.

It explained the technical details of how the report was drafted and then turned to the history of Palestine during the mandate period. It also described the geography, demography and the economic factors of Palestine. These were thought a necessary context to evaluate the Jewish and Arab conflicting claims. The core of the report, its recommendations, were divided into (a) unanimous recommenda-tions, (b) recommendations by a substantial majority and (c) the majority plan for the partition of Palestine into a Jewish state, an Arab state and an internationalized zone for Jerusalem within an economic union. Before turning to the detailed proposals it is instructive to reflect on the manner in which the report records the situation in Palestine.

The conditions prevailing in Palestine were described as "one of profound tension...in many respects the country is living under a military regime. In the streets of Jerusalem and other key areas barbed wire defences, road blocks, machine-gun posts and constant armoured car patrols are routine measures."[44] The report continued to explain that the high levels of security meant that detention for an unlimited period and even expulsion from Palestine were measures frequently invoked at the discretion of the High Commissioner. Of the 820 people detained in July 1947 all were Jewish except for four Arabs. A further 17,873 illegal immigrants were also being detained at the time.[45]

The British administration had explained to the committee that the necessity for these measures was due to the Jewish community's use of force to gain its "political ends" through "an organized campaign of lawlessness, murder and sabotage."[46] However, as the report quite subtly makes clear, Jewish activities were mainly aimed at the policies contained in the 1939 White Paper and in particular the restrictions on Jewish immigration. In the period after 1945 most militant Jewish activity had been conducted by two small groups, the Irgun and Lehi, outside of the control of the Jewish Agency and usually acting against its policies. However, the *Yishuv* and all the organizations were opposed to the rigid and often brutally enforced immigration controls. Legal immigration was limited to 1,500 per month. Given the consequences of the Holocaust and existence of several hundred thousand Jews in displaced peoples' camps, these restrictions were seen as particularly cruel. As a result there were organized attempts to bring Jewish immigrants to Palestine by any means, all of which involved challenging the British blockade. The success of this campaign can be seen ironically in the large number of British-detained illegal immigrants. It was noteworthy that the 18,000 in detention was equivalent to an entire years' legal immigration quota. Members of the UNSCOP committee had seen for themselves one failed attempt to bring such immigrants ashore at Haifa from the ship *Exodus 1947*.[47] On this occasion British ill-treatment of immigrants and their subsequent expulsion (to Germany of all places) had taken place under the eyes of UNSCOP and the world's press. The report astutely records:

> in this, as in similar incidents, the committee has noted the persistence of the attempts to bring Jewish immigrants to Palestine irrespective of the determined preventative measures on the part of the Administration, and also the far-reaching support which such attempts receive from the Jewish community in Palestine and abroad. The unremitting struggle to admit further Jews into Palestine, irrespective of the quota permitted by the Administration, is a measure of the rift which has developed between the Jewish Agency and the Jewish community, on the one hand and the Administration on the other. In the present state of tension, little practicable basis exists for the discharge by the Jewish Agency of its function under the Mandate of "advising and cooperating" with the Administration in matters affecting the interests of the Jewish community.[48]

This is a striking comment on Jewish–British relations and is telling in that the committee looked at these relations in a legal framework. Such comments also indicate that the committee used the dominant interpretation of the legal issues connected with the mandate which was far more in accord with the Jewish than the Palestinian view.

In turning to the attitude of the Palestinian Arab community, the report neutrally states that the "committee has had less opportunity of ascertaining its attitude in detail" due to the AHC's boycott.[49] However, the report does include reference to an authoritative statement of the Arab League on Palestine which it takes as the "Arab assessment." This included a passage which is quoted in the report:

> "Zionism…does not content itself with mere propaganda in favour of the fulfillment of its expansionist projects at the expense of the Arab countries. Its plan involves recourse to terrorism, both in Palestine and in other countries. It is known that a secret army has been formed with a view to creating an atmosphere of tension and unrest by making attempts on the lives of the representatives

of the governing authority and by destroying public buildings... This aggressive attitude, resulting from the mandatory Power's weakness in dealing with them, will not fail to give rise in turn to the creation of similar organizations by the Arabs. The responsibility for the disturbances that might result therefrom throughout the Middle East will rest solely with the Zionist organizations, as having been the first to use these violent tactics." It was declared at the same meeting that "against a state established by violence, the Arab states will be obliged to use violence; that is a legitimate right of self-defence."[50]

The passage is not only interesting in itself but it is also significant that the committee included it in the report. The statement carefully hones a key segment of the Palestinian legal narrative. In this account Zionists were essentially expansionist, they initiated violence and constituted a threat not just to Palestine but to the entire region. Any violence by Arabs – and not just Palestinian Arabs – was a legitimate response and indeed constituted "self-defence." The statement does not refer to the military organizations created by the Palestinians under the auspices of the Arab Higher Committee in the 1936 Arab revolt, nor to the re-creation of at least one of them by 1946. Indeed by 1947 the Arab League had already taken the step of establishing the Arab Liberation Army.[51] Nonetheless the content of the statement is clear: the Arab League was threatening to use force if a Jewish state were to be created. The decision to include this position in the report appears to be a coded reference to the fact that the committee would need to take into account the threat to use force if it were to propose partition.

It is perhaps significant that immediately after this selected quotation from the Arab League, the report then turns to discuss the Arab economic boycott adopted in 1945. According to UNSCOP amongst the League's evidence was to suggest that the boycott would "prove effective due to the dependence of Jewish industry on the market of Arab countries."[52] The report does not dwell on this or make an assessment of its veracity but rather highlights the boycott's impact on the Palestinian Arab community. It quotes a speech given by Jamal Al Husseini in July 1947 who spoke of the necessity "of strengthening the boycott in order to pull down Zionist existence," and warned Arab merchants who did not observe the boycott that they would be regarded as "traitors," since "the nation cannot keep patient over humiliation."[53] The inclusion of this passage certainly conveys something of the political atmosphere and indicates the way in which the boycott was used not just as a weapon against the Jews but also as a disciplinary device within the Arab community.

In concluding this part of the report the committee reflects on the comment of the British Foreign Secretary in November 1945 that "since the introduction of the mandate it has been impossible to find common grounds between the Arabs and the Jews."[54] While accepting that this had indeed become the case the report comments that "one cannot ignore the belief of those responsible for the Balfour Declaration and the Mandate that the obligations towards to the Arabs and Jews respectively would not seriously conflict."[55] Again we should note the manner in which the mandate – or in this case its authors – are treated as acting in good faith. It is also interesting that the report is keen to stress that despite "the constant pressure exerted by Arab and Jewish political leaders to maintain and advance their respective national interests...there are those, both Arab and Jew, who believe in the possibility of mutually advantageous understanding, and, as circumstances permit, seek its promotion."[56] It then gives some examples of such cooperation as joint Jewish–Arab strikes, the General Agricultural Board and the Citrus Marketing Board. It accepts that these instances of cooperation were limited and in any case subject to political contingencies.

The report then turns to the substantive claims of Jews and Arabs. For each side the report first sets out the main argument put by the protagonists and then makes an assessment of them. In commenting on the Jewish case there is only one oblique reference to the Holocaust. It refers to "Jewish immigrants who are clamoring to come to Palestine from the displaced person camps and from other places in Europe, North Africa and the Near East where their present plight is difficult."[57] The mass murder of European Jews is never mentioned. As we shall see, with few exceptions, this would remain the case in the United Nations debate on the report. Contemporary arguments that the international community decided to create a Jewish state in a wave of guilt for the Holocaust is not borne out by reading UN documents. There were no expressions of guilt nor was there any public opposition to anti-Semitic statements expressed in the debates.

UNSCOP narrated the Jewish case through a discussion of the Balfour Declaration and the Mandate. It stated that the main Jewish claim was to a recognized legal right to a national home in Palestine. In the words of the report:

They regard the pledges to the Jews in the Balfour Declaration and the Mandate by the international community not to the Jews of Palestine alone, who were at the time only a small community, but to the Jewish people as a whole, who are now often described as the "Jewish nation".[58]

This accurate summary of the Jewish case illustrates the success that the Zionist movement had had in achieving its original aim of establishing the national home by "public law." UNSCOP was faced with deciding how to deal with the established legal right of the Jews to the national home as a central element in proposing Palestine's future. The committee set about assessing how the international pledges could be best discharged.

As a result the committee had first to address the issue of what a legal entitlement to a Jewish national home might mean. It needed to establish its character and scope. A particular concern was whether or not the use of the term "national home" necessarily implied the creation of a Jewish state. The committee viewed its use in both the Balfour Declaration and Mandate as not accidental as it "seems to be inescapable that the vagueness of the wording in both instruments was intentional. The fact the term 'National Home' was employed instead of the word 'state' or 'commonwealth' would indicate that the intention was to place a restrictive construction on the national home from its very inception."[59] Nonetheless that did not "preclude the eventual creation of a Jewish State."[60] This was a fine legal point. The mandate created an international obligation to facilitate a Jewish national home but that did not preclude the possibility of an eventual state. Nor could the vagueness of the term imply any prohibition on such a state.

The committee then turned to the significance of the obligation being addressed to the "Jewish people as a whole."[61] That commitment the report continued "would imply that all Jews in the world who wish to go to Palestine have the right to do so."[62] This was interesting as the legal personality acquired by the Jewish people was understood by the committee to confer rights on Jews as individuals. The Jewish people have the right to the national home and individual Jews "who wish to" have the right to move there. There was some speculation as to whether or not that was practical given the small size of the country and the questionable sustainability of the economy. In its commentary the committee appeared to have accepted that while these factors were to be taken into account they could not become insuperable barriers to the collective and individual rights which Jews had acquired. Given that these were legal entitlements the committee was concerned that no political solution should be advocated that would undermine them. In particular it accepted the argument that a sovereign state might be the only way that the Jewish national home could be "safeguarded from Arab domination."

In summarizing the Arab case the committee relied on statements issued by the Arab League and the Arab Higher Committee. From these sources it outlined the Arab view that Palestine should become independent immediately as a unitary state as the Arab majority had both "natural and acquired rights" to the country. The former arose from centuries of inhabiting Palestine[63] while the latter was the result of "promises and pledges officially made to the Arab people in the course of the First World War."[64] Evidence of such promises was contained for example in the McMahon–Hussein correspondence of 1915–16, the Anglo-French Declaration of 1918 as well as a series of other statements by or on behalf of the Allied Powers at the time. These were interpreted as guaranteeing the independence of the Arab world at the end of World War I – of which Palestine would be a part. The committee then summarized the now familiar argument that the Mandate was inconsistent with the League of Nations Covenant and that it was "illegal and invalid."[65] It was for that reason that the Arab states argued that Jewish immigrants had "no legal right to enter the country during the period of the mandate." Despite this illegality, as a concession, the Jewish community that existed in 1947 would be permitted to remain in the future Palestine.

The committee concluded that "the Arabs of Palestine consider themselves as having a "natural" right to the country although they have not been in possession of it as a sovereign nation."[66] It commented that "the desire of the Arab people of Palestine to safeguard their national existence is a very natural desire. However, Palestinian nationalism, as distinct from Arab nationalism, is itself a relatively new phenomenon." In evaluating any legal rights contained in the McMahon correspondence the committee decided that it is "beyond its scope to express an opinion."[67] Nevertheless the committee was able to offer opinions on related matters. It appeared to view favorably Emir Faisal's 1919 statement at the Versailles peace conference that as to relations between Arabs and Jews "there is no conflict of character between the two races."[68] It also noted the Faisal–Weizmann agreement in support of the Balfour Declaration. It then concluded this section with a quotation from the Peel Commission: "there was a time when Arab statesmen were willing to consider giving Palestine to the Jews, providing the rest of Arab Asia was free. That condition was not fulfilled, but it is now on the eve of fulfillment." In deploying the Peel Commission as attorney the committee communicated its opinion on the Arab case rather clearly.

The report rejected the Arab view that the principle of self-determination had been intended to apply to Palestine in 1922. Taking then the accepted view the committee wrote: "it was not applied to Palestine, obviously because the intention to make possible the creation of the Jewish National Home and the *sui generis* Mandate for Palestine run counter to this principle."[69] It concluded that "there would seem to be no grounds for questioning the validity of the mandate for the reason advanced by the Arab States."[70] It should be pointed out that while self-determination was a political principle much in currency it did not acquire any degree of legal significance until several years after the United Nations had been established.

In making this assessment of the competing legal claims the inference might be drawn that UNSCOP was inclining towards the Jewish view. However, it should be born in mind that the Jewish argument was easier to make as it accorded with the dominant view of international law. The Arab case attempted to articulate a proposition that the committee should accept that there were fundamental legal principles which governed all international institutions and their instruments. However, the Arab states were never able to explain what those alleged principles were and at what point they had become part of international law. The committee would thus reject the invitation to challenge the legitimacy of the international legal order.

The report then assessed the proposals for the future of Palestine that had been put forward by Jews and Arabs. It considered that three options had been placed before it: (1) partition into two states, (2) a unitary state or (3) a single state with a federal, cantonal or bi-national structure.

As several Jewish organizations had made representations to the committee the report noted a variety of opinions. While most submissions favored a Jewish state some did not. Two organizations in Palestine, *Ihud* and *Hashomer Hatzair*, supported the creation of a bi-national state with complete equality between the two nations. A third, the Communist Party, opted for a bi-national or federal state. One submission from the American Council for

Judaism opposed a Jewish state as "a threat to peace and security of Palestine."[71]

The Jewish Agency for Palestine was described as representing "the opinion of the majority of organized Jewry in the country" which advocated the Zionist Organization's program,[72] which proposed:

(a) That Palestine be established as a Jewish Commonwealth integrated into the structure of the democratic world;

(b) That the gates of Palestine be open to Jewish immigration;

(c) That the Jewish Agency be vested with the control of immigration into Palestine and the necessary authority for the upbuilding of the country;

(d) As regards partition, the Political Survey 1946–1947, submitted to the Committee by the Jewish Agency states on page 71:

> "… A solution on partition lines, if it is to be acceptable, can hardly be regarded as other than a *pis aller* [last resort]… Any solution of the Palestine problem which may be proposed will be judged by the Jewish people by reference to whether it ensures large-scale immigration and settlement and leads without delay to the establishment of a Jewish State."[73]

The report was thus able both to include a variety of Jewish voices and to note the flexible tone of the main representative organization. By not insisting that all of Palestine should be a Jewish state it suggested that compromise was possible. The core of the Jewish proposals were thus for a sovereign state on a territory that could sustain unrestricted Jewish immigration. Partition was the logic of the Jewish Agency's proposals.

In the absence of a submission by the Arab Higher Committee, UNSCOP considered constitutional proposals on the future of Palestine put by the Arab League to the London Palestine conference in 1946. Through this device the committee was able to construct submissions from both Palestinian communities. The Arab League proposals were that Palestine should be a "unitary state, with a democratic constitution and an elected assembly."[74] The constitution would guarantee freedom of religion and "full civil rights for all Palestinian citizens." However, under a proposed naturalization clause many Jews would be ineligible for citizenship unless they had been continuously resident in Palestine for ten years. The impact of such a proposal would have disqualified from citizenship about 100,000 Jews either in Palestine or in British detention camps, many of them Holocaust survivors. There would be safeguards of the "religious and cultural rights of the Jewish community."[75] The constitution was also to contain articles that would limit Jewish representation in the "democratic assembly" to one-third irrespective of the size of the Jewish population. In addition all of Jewish immigration was to be prohibited and Jews would not be able to buy Arab-owned land.[76]

This 1940s Arab vision of a Palestinian state is all too little commented upon. Too often it is assumed that Palestinians and the Arab world sought a democratic Palestine based on the principle of self-determination, and that this was frustrated by Zionism. As UNSCOP makes clear, such a prospect was not put on the table. The actual proposal would have created a legally entrenched ethnic ascendancy, not unlike Northern Ireland at the time. In the subsequent debates Arab delegates were to suggest that this was a reasonable proposal which contained a major concession in that all Jews who arrived in Palestine by 1937 would be allowed to remain. Most subsequent accounts of the partition debates omit reference to the Arab position. In 1967, for example, the Institute of Palestine Studies said that Arab proposals were that Palestine would have "a democratic constitution with an elected legislature."[77] It would represent "all important sections of the citizenship in proportion to its numerical strength."[78] There was no mention of the fixed limitation to one third for Jewish representation in the Assembly and complete silence on the clauses on land ownership and immigration. On naturalization a sanitized formula was used. "The law of naturalization and citizenship," it stated, would "provide among other conditions, that the applicant should be a legal resident of Palestine for a continuous period to be determined by the constituent assembly."[79] One can only assume that in retrospect the original proposals appeared less palatable for public consumption in the 1960s. Yet the reality is that the 1947 proposals would have created a Palestine where Arabs would be legally privileged over Jews. This is ironic as much of the Palestinian and Arab case against Zionism has been built around the argument that Jews would dominate Arabs. In reality this fear of domination appeared to have its roots in a project based on Arab ascendancy whose aim was to do precisely the opposite.

The view that Zionism is an ideology that essentially subjects non-Jews to Jewish domination is in common currency today. Many analyses of the Palestinian minority in Israel[80] rightly place emphasis on social and legal discrimination especially in the area of land ownership. Such practices, however, are not contained in Israeli basic laws and at times the Israeli courts have found such practices illegal. There is no restriction on the proportion of Palestinians represented in the Knesset. The only restriction on participation is on racist parties, a law introduced explicitly to ban the anti-Arab *Kach* party. Yet the Arab position that UNSCOP considered was for a state based on ethnic domination. The Jewish submission, on the other hand, advocated complete equality for Arabs within the Jewish state. The committee would surely have been hard put to agree with the proposal for a state based on constitutionally privileging one ethnic group over another – and to advocate such a state to the General Assembly of the United Nations.

At the end of this section the report comments that there was difficulty in balancing "two diametrically opposed claims, each of which is supported by strong arguments, in a small country of limited resources, in an atmosphere of great and increasing political and racial tensions and conflicting nationalisms."[81] In posing its task in this way UNSCOP had embraced the two-nations approach and rejected the Arab view that only one nation existed in Palestine. It also implied that the categorical and rigid Arab position that there was only one legitimate option had found no favor.

THE RECOMMENDATIONS

As a result of its deliberations the committee recorded that "it became apparent that there was little support for either of the solutions which would take an extreme position, namely, a single independent State of Palestine, under either Arab or Jewish domination."[82] The report continued that "there was no disposition of the Committee to support in full the official positions of the Arab States or the Jewish Agency."[83] Significantly the committee recognized that Arabs and Jews had "strong claims to rights and interests in Palestine, the Arabs by virtue of being for centuries the indigenous and preponderant people there, and the Jews by virtue of historical association…and international pledges made to them respecting their rights in it."[84] This careful balancing between the legitimate claims of both peoples meant that it was "indefensible to accept the full claims of one at the expense of the other."[85]

The committee then explained that having rejected the extreme solutions it had also found that various compromise proposals along bi-nationalism or cantonal lines were impractical. As a consequence there were only two options worth exploring: partition into two

states, or a federal state. Of the nine unanimous recommendations the principal one was that the mandate should be terminated
and that no new system of international supervision, such as
trusteeship under the United Nations, was suitable. As a result
independence should be granted as soon as practical as "the Arab
and Jewish peoples, after more than a century of tutelage under
the mandate both seek a means of effective expression for their
national aspirations."[86] Despite this objective there would need to
be a transitional phase under UN responsibility. This was necessary
as finding a solution fully acceptable to both sides was "utterly
impossible, the prospect of imposing a solution upon them would
be a basic condition of any recommended proposal."[87] This part of
the recommendation was subsequently forgotten after the partition
plan was adopted – and indeed one might suggest that international
amnesia has continued ever since.

Another unanimous recommendation included extremely elliptical
formulations on "Jewish displaced persons." Having visited some
displaced persons camps in Europe the committee no doubt felt
bound to make some reference to them. The situation of Jews in
these camps was coyly described as the "legacy of the Second World
War."[88] Again it is stunning that no actual reference was made
to the fact that these Jews were survivors of Nazi genocide. The
report mused that some sort of international initiative would be
appropriate to address this situation, although it contains no hint
of what this might be. Despite clear evidence to the committee that
most camp inmates wanted to go to Palestine that option appeared
to have been ruled out. Such a course would not allay "the fears of
the Arabs in the Near East that Palestine and ultimately the existing
Arab countries are to be marked as place for settlement for the Jews
of the world."[89] In order to send this message these "distressed
European Jews" should forgo their desires. However, other than
that negative position no other solution was suggested. This again
rather undercuts arguments that the United Nations saw a Jewish
state as a form of international reparation.

More evidence of the refusal to engage with the results of the
Holocaust is to be found in the first of the second category of
recommendations, those approved "by a substantial majority."
Recommendation XII deals with the "Jewish Problem in General"
which was adopted with two dissensions and one no vote. It stated
"in the appraisal of the Palestine question, it be accepted as incon-
trovertible that the solution to Palestine cannot be considered as a
solution to the Jewish problem in general."

In its commentary the committee explained this recommendation in various ways. First it said that Palestine was a small country and it was "most improbable that there could be settled in Palestine all the Jews who may wish to leave their present domiciles for reasons of immediate displacement or distress or actual or anticipated anti-Jewish attitudes in the countries that they now reside." Second, there was limited transportation available to convey Jews to Palestine. Third, the absorption capacity of the country was limited. A fourth position repeats the arguments on displaced persons: "serious account," it states, "must be taken of the certain resentment and vigorous opposition of Arabs throughout the Middle East to any attempt to solve, at their expense, the Jewish problem, which they consider to be an international responsibility." Immigration to Palestine was emphatically ruled out even though Jews faced "immediate displacement or distress or anticipated anti-Jewish attitudes." It was also significant that in a section dealing with the "Jewish problem" there was no explanation of what the Jewish problem was.

The committee's minority which recommended a federal solution held similar positions. Under its plan the federal authorities would determine immigration for the entire state, and we have seen that this would have resulted in an Arab veto on further Jewish migrants. However, not content with this formula the minority were quite explicit in their reasoning. "It cannot be contemplated," they wrote, "that Palestine is to be considered in any sense as a means of solving the problem of world Jewry."[90] It continued: "no claim to a right of unlimited immigration of Jews into Palestine, irrespective of time can be entertained."[91] Its recommendations on the question were that for a three-year transitional period a nine-member international commission comprising three representatives from both the Arab and Jewish states together with three representatives of the United Nations would determine the absorption capacity of the Jewish state. Significantly no such arrangement would be made to determine the rate of immigration of any other nationality.

The propositions about the Jewish problem in both majority and minority recommendations seem to be in contradiction with earlier parts of the report which dealt with the Jewish case. In these sections we should recall the committee recognized that the terms of the Mandate on the Jewish national home constituted obligations made to the Jewish peoples as whole, and not just to the Jews of Palestine. This position was also repeated in the introduction to its recommendations where the committee recognizes the strength of the Jewish claim due to "international pledges: made to their rights in Palestine. These pledges cannot be other than those which existed in the Mandate." Yet within a few pages the report seems to change tack and alter the narrative significantly. Without explanation the committee appeared to have reversed its interpretation and to regard the pledges only effectively valid for the Jewish community in Palestine. While this community was endowed with the attributes of nationhood and attachment to the country, the Jews outside, including Holocaust survivors, are portrayed as "displaced persons" or "distressed Jews" lacking the entitlements to nationhood and abode in the national home. It appeared that Jews who had reached Palestine were part of the nation and those who had not were to be excluded from it.

The report then turned to the principal majority recommendation which detailed the provision for the partition of the country. As the report explained:

> the basic premise underlying the partition proposal is that claims to Palestine of Arabs and Jews, both possessing validity, are irreconcilable, and that among all of the solutions advanced, partition will provide the most realistic and practicable settlement, and is the most likely to afford a workable basis for meeting in part the claims and aspirations of both parties.[92]

The committee recognized that both "peoples have their historic roots in Palestine"[93] and that the "basic conflict in Palestine is a clash of two intense nationalisms."[94] It advocated partition on the grounds that it was the only option that would allow both peoples to take their place in the international community, that it provided "finality" and that it was realistic.[95] The report returned to the question of Jewish immigration which it claimed can be removed "from the arena of conflict," as the plan "definitely fixes the extent of the territory to be allotted to the Jews with its implicit limitation on immigration."[96] This passage continues: "the fact that the solution carries the sanction of the United Nations involves a finality which should allay Arab fears of further expansion of the Jewish State."[97] It is unclear whether this comment implied that the committee accepted the view that a Jewish state would be essentially expansionist. Nonetheless its purpose appears to be to offer an international guarantee against such expansionism.

The report then outlines the other aspect of the plan, the economic union, which had the aim that the "economic unity of the country should be preserved."[98] This was to address concerns about the viability of each state. The key areas of the economic union were specified as: (a) a customs union, (b) a common currency and (c) cooperation in transport and communications. In addition it was envisaged that there would be joint economic activity in areas such as irrigation and land reclamation. All these activities were to be coordinated by a Joint Economic Board equally representing the two states and the United Nations Economic and Social Council.[99]

However, the idea of the economic union did not really derive from the reality of the Palestinian economy. As earlier parts of the report have recorded, there were in fact two parallel economies. Cooperation did exist in some areas although these were the exception. Mostly agriculture, industry, much of the financial sector and the labor market were divided along communal lines. Despite this both communities were reliant on the same transport system and used the same currency. Partition was not intended to disrupt areas that were in common. Maintaining the free movement of goods inside Palestine and between Palestine and the outside world was regarded as central for the well-being of each state. The plan would also force both states to cooperate with each other in these crucial areas. The idea that both communities would soon replace armed conflict with wrangles over transportation might seem utopian. However, in the context of the early steps towards European economic integration so soon after World War II, such ideas were not without merit.

The other main area of cooperation would be Jerusalem. The proposed international zone included not only the city of Jerusalem but also the Bethlehem area. It contained a great many of the holy places of Judaism, Christianity and Islam. By removing those from either the Arab or the Jewish state UNSCOP intended to illustrate its objective of balancing between the parties. The city was to be administered by a Governor under the United Nations Trusteeship Council.[100] The area was to be de-militarized although the Governor would have at his disposal a police force recruited from outside Palestine. Existing local councils would continue in operation. The residents would become citizens of the city unless they opted to become citizens of either the Arab or Jewish state. Jerusalem would be integrated into the economic union. The international regime would last for ten years when its status would be reviewed and its citizens would be able to express their views on its future status. The idea of treating Jerusalem differently from the rest of Palestine was to some extent modeled on the 1937 Peel Commission which had allocated Jerusalem to British control.

The partition itself was to be effected in a two-year transitional period following September 1, 1947. During this period steps would be taken to create the infrastructure of both states. In addition 150,000 Jewish immigrants were to be admitted to the area of the Jewish state. It was envisaged that the British would continue to administer Palestine although under the auspices of the United Nations. The British decision to quit the country should have alerted the committee that Britain's cooperation with the United Nations was not a foregone conclusion. This was particularly the case as Britain would have been forced to oversee a reversal of its policy on immigration which had already been so costly in lives and money – and indeed Britain's reputation.

Both states would be required to adopt constitutions which followed strict guidelines. This was the first time that the United Nations was to become involved in stipulating the requirements of a constitution and to insist that its content was to be a condition for independence. While an international legal innovation it should be remembered that the victorious powers occupying Germany and Japan were also insisting on putting in place constitutions that were thought to help guarantee international peace and security. In Palestine this process was formalized in an international context.

Formally the constitutions of each state were to be drafted by elected constituent assembly, although the main features of the constitution were compulsory. The legislatures of both states were to be "elected by universal suffrage and by secret ballot on the basis of proportional representation."[101] In addition the form of government was to be parliamentary with an executive responsible to the legislature. The inclusion of proportional representation was to guarantee both adequate communal and political representation. It was also for this reason, one assumes, that the parliamentary system was regarded as the most suitable form of government as the executive would have to interact with the Assembly.

Other provisions were to be major innovations within any constitution as they dealt with matters of international relations. The first reflecting article 3 of the United Nations Charter would commit the state to settling all disputes by "peaceful means in such a manner that international peace and security, and justice are not endangered." The second was to incorporate article 2(4) of the United Nations Charter so that each state would accept the obligation to refrain in their "international relations from the threat or use of force against the territorial integrity or political independence of any State, or any other manner inconsistent with the purposes of the United Nations."[102] The exact aim of these provisions, given that both states were intended to join the United Nations and would in any event be bound by the charter, was not exactly clear. The effect of them was probably intended to be more political than legal. Through the act of incorporation each state would emphasize its commitments to the peaceful resolution of disputes and the rejection of the use of force. This requirement also reflected the spirit of the times and the desire to popularize the principles of the new international organization.

Another innovation also reflected the language of the new United Nations Charter as all persons were to be guaranteed "equal and non-discriminatory rights in civil, political and religious matters and the enjoyment of human rights and fundamental freedoms, including freedom of religious worship, language, speech and publication, education, assembly and association."[103] This certainly reflected the post-World War II consciousness of human rights, a new and as yet rather undefined concept – the UN Universal Declaration of Human Rights was being drafted at the time. Nonetheless it was an important and early use of the idea that human rights could play a role in conflict resolution.

Each constitution was to guarantee the freedom of "transit and travel" for citizens of the other state and for the residents of Jerusalem. This was subject to the *proviso* of security considerations. However, this was revealing of the way in which the plan was conceived by the committee. While each state was to be fully sovereign it was not the intention of the plan to interrupt the existing communities in Palestine. Partition was thus not to imply that boundaries would be complete with walls, electrified fences and border guards. The boundaries were conceived of as the meeting points of two states. It indicated a high degree of imagination on the part of the committee and an intention not to recreate the scenes of horror that had accompanied the partition of India – events that were unfolding as the report was being written. The boundaries between the Palestinian states were thus meant to be fluid so that everyday life could continue after partition as before.

The plan could be summed up as "political division and economic unity." The report explains that this will confer on "Arab and Jew, in its own territory, the power to make its own laws, while preserving to both throughout Palestine, a single integrated economy, admittedly essential to the well-being of each, and the same territorial freedom of movement to individuals as is enjoyed today."[104] The commentary continues by explaining that each state will be able to control residency rights and immigration although "free passage" is provided for all. How this would work in practice is not explained, especially as free passage implies a temporary journey. However, the partition lines would divide families and people from their work places and so the phrase does not capture the many practical issues that would arise.

The view that ethnic characteristics will be the solution to all problems is strongly expressed. "In the larger view," we are told, "here are the sole remaining representatives of the Semitic race. They are in the land in which that race was cradled." Before there is any confusion this is a reference to both Jews and Arabs we are reassured "there are no fundamental incompatibilities between them. The scheme satisfies the deepest aspirations of both: independence."[105] Having referred rather patronizingly to the "genius of each people" and to their contributions to civilization the committee then explains how they believe that this racialized vision of Palestine would work.

The Jews will bring to the land the social dynamism and scientific method of the West; the Arabs confront them with individualism and intuitive understanding of life. Here, then in this close association, through the natural emulation of each other, can be evolved a synthesis of the two civilizations, preserving, at the same time, their fundamental characteristics. In each state the native genius will have a scope and opportunity to evolve into its highest cultural forms and to attain its greatest reaches of mind and spirit. In the case of the Jews, that is really the condition of survival. Palestine will remain one land in which Semitic ideals may pass into realization.[106]

This passage of Orientalist excess well represented the times. It was of concern that racial determinism was assumed to be a cure for a national conflict. One assumes that this picture of Semitic solidarity was meant to comfort the international community that despite all appearances to the contrary Jews and Arabs were genetically bound together. These common roots were to guarantee two identical constitutions, free movement across borders and cooperation over Jerusalem. Equally problematic was the contrast between the "social dynamism" of the Jews and the Arab "intuitive understanding of life." Such terminology was, however, familiar in a world still marked by colonialism.

The actual proposals for partitioning the land followed the principle of drawing the boundaries near the greatest concentration of the Arab and Jewish populations. Jews had their main concentrations along the coastal strip and in the north, whereas Palestinians were located in the central parts of Palestine. However, large Palestinian populations could also be found in the Jewish areas such as Jaffa adjacent to Tel Aviv and Haifa. The latter city in particular illustrated the problem of partition for mixed cities and towns. The committee, in applying its principle, was forced to create a patchwork of six areas which were largely discontinuous. The one exception to this principle was the Negev which was allocated to the Jewish state despite Jews only comprising about 2 percent of the population; although home to 90,000 Bedouin. The allocation of the Negev to the Jewish state was on the basis that it left "considerable room for further development and land settlement."[107] This was a reference to the Bersheva sub-district which was described as "very sparsely populated and capable of development." The Negev itself was regarded as "desert land of little agricultural value" and only added to the Jewish state as it is "naturally linked" to the northern part of Bersheva. It is difficult to know whether Jews or Arabs would be the more disconcerted by this approach to the territorial delimitation.

In deciding on the population centers the committee had to rely on estimates of the population as there had been no census since 1931. However, the committee did not always use the same estimates and it was noticeable that the report contains three figures for the Jewish population: 600,000, 608,000 and 650,000. The Arab population was regularly put at 1,200,000, however this figure omits the 90,000 Bedouin of the Negev. It was also the case that as the British held 18,000 Jewish illegal immigrants in Cyprus and elsewhere this figure should have been considered when assessing the likely population. It would seem that it would have been more accurate to conclude that there were 1,300,000 Arabs and between 620,000 and 670,000 Jews. These actual figures were to be significant given the controversy over whether or not the Jewish state as proposed would even have a Jewish majority. In the report the population of the Jewish state was projected as 498,000 Jews with an Arab population of 407,000 although this does not include the 90,000 Bedouin. Added together, Jews and Arabs would have almost equal numbers. This assumed the lower estimate of the Jewish population was accurate; if it was not there would be 42,000 missing Jews. However two additional factors have to be taken into account. Under the plan the citizens of the Jerusalem area could opt for citizenship of either state. It could be easily assumed that the 100,000 Jews of the city would become citizens of the Jewish state thus meaning that resident and non-resident Jewish citizens would be 598,000 as against 487,000 Arabs. During the transitional period it should be remembered that 150,000 immigrants were to be admitted to the area of the Jewish state. Taking these figures into account the intention of the committee appeared to be that the resident Jewish population would be 650,000 rising to 750,000 citizens with the Jews of Jerusalem. In the event the plan was later modified as Jaffa with its 70,000 Arab population was to become an enclave and allocated to the Arab state.

As far as the Arab state was concerned it would incorporate the main Arab centers of population with the exception of Haifa (and initially Jaffa) and of course Jerusalem. The Arab state would have access to the sea via Gaza which would have an area almost double that of the current Gaza Strip. Its total population would be smaller than the Jewish state at 735,000, of whom only 10,000 were Jewish. This would have meant that only about 52 percent of the Palestine Arab population would be residents of the Arab state. However, this figure would rise to 55 percent once the Jaffa enclave was added and with the 105,000 Arabs of Jerusalem likely to become citizens of it, the total proportion of Arab citizens would be 70 percent. However, the very large minority of 30 percent of the Arabs of Palestine would be within the Jewish state in contrast to the very small number of Jews inside the Arab state (1.5 percent). In terms of land area the Arab state would have comprised about 45 percent of Palestine. The committee was concerned about the revenue viability of both states but particularly the Arab one as it would have far fewer wage earners than would the Jewish state. Ironically given the subsequent history, the committee consoled itself with the thought that as the Palestinian problem would have been solved, the expenditure on police and security could be substantially reduced. The expected peace dividend was to prove elusive.

There are many objections that can be made about the proposals for the Arab state. On the face of it, it seems unfair that only 45 percent of the territory would be allocated to 66 percent of the population. Partition also meant that a large number of Palestinian Arabs would live in the Jewish state. From the perspective of Palestinian national identity this would fracture the nation and undermine the right of Palestinians to self-determination. In particular it would transform a section of the Palestinian population – who regarded itself as part of the majority – into a minority in another state. Their status as Arab Palestinians would thus be changed merely by virtue of residence. However, the report aimed to deal with at least some of these issues through the constitutional requirements of each state. It should also be stressed that the inclusion of Arabs within the Jewish state did nothing to affect land tenure or land ownership. The committee also hoped that with free movement of populations in the context of the economic union the status of individuals would remain unchanged. The committee accepted that this was a weakness of the plan but thought that overall it was a price worth paying to create the basis for a permanent resolution to the conflict.

The partition plan thus provided for two sovereign states and intended that there would be clear majorities for Arabs and Jews in each. The boundaries between them were complex but these were intended to be easily crossed. The plan did not provide for any form of movement of populations between states and Jews and Arabs were expected to remain in their homes and to maintain their communities, irrespective of where the boundary lay. Privately owned land and leasehold property was to be undisturbed. Through the internationally guaranteed constitutions the minorities in each state would be protected and would be able to actively participate in government. The internationalization of Jerusalem aimed to remove it as a point of tension between the two communities and to allow access to all. The negotiating stance of the Arab Higher Committee meant that it was unable to consider the possible benefits of the scheme or to propose changes. Having ruled out any form of partition in advance it was unable to suggest modifications – such as extending the boundaries of the Arab state.

This position stemmed from the rejection by the AHC and the Arab League that two nations existed in Palestine. This political position was articulated as if it were legal doctrine. The opposition to partition was deeply rooted in the belief that Jews did not constitute a distinct people or nation and as such they could not have a legal entitlement to any form of collective legal existence. Equally strongly there was the view that Palestinian Arabs were the natural nation of the country and that as such were legally guaranteed the right to self-determination. As a result the Arab community had the exclusive title to Palestine. Such assumptions were without foundation as self-determination had not yet evolved into a legal right – and, as we shall see, when it did the recognition of a people with that right was not dependent on inherent charac-teristics. It was indeed the partition resolution itself that endowed

Palestine's Arabs with the right to an independent state. It was ironic therefore that just at the moment the United Nations recognized the Arab people of Palestine's right to self-determination, their representatives were to reject it. The AHC's commitment to Palestinian self-determination was premised on the rejection of the same right for the Jewish people. It was to be an exclusive right or nothing.

4
Law for War

The UNSCOP majority recommendations were incorporated into General Assembly resolution 181 which was adopted in November 1947. However, months before the debate opened Arab states and some supporters had lit a legal fuse to justify war as a means to block partition. After the United Nations voted to establish UNSCOP in May, Syria, Iraq and Lebanon formally announced to the General Assembly that they formally repudiated the "possibility of any partition of Palestine," as that would mean "sundering Palestine from its Arab hinterland." As a result each government declared it "entirely reserves its position in case any disturbance of peace and security takes place in the Near East as a result of the work or conclusions of the special committee."[1] This formula that would continue to echo through the United Nations chamber over the next year gave notice that the committee's work would take place under the threat to use force. This chapter will focus on the way in which the discourse of war was woven into the legal arguments advanced during the debates.

The Arab League had already adopted a military policy toward Palestine in June 1946. A confidential resolution had called on members to finance, equip and train volunteers in readiness for service in the country.[2] Having begun such military preparations the Arab states began to initiate a diplomatic strategy that would advance legal justifications for the use of force. Few opportunities would be missed to make such a case. At meetings with UNSCOP in June and July 1947 the willingness and justification to use force was clearly expressed – as it was in the written submission.[3]

International law on the use of force had undergone some changes with the arrival of the United Nations Charter. Any state threatening force was prima facie in contravention of article 2(4) that stipulated that members "shall refrain from the threat or the use of force against the territorial integrity or political independence of any state, or in any other manner inconsistent with the purposes of the United Nations." It was due to the latter phrase that the Arab states were to become so insistent that the United Nations itself would be acting illegally if it opted for partition. Such a position became rather thin when resolution 181 was adopted, as it could now be cogently argued that partition was a purpose of the United Nations. However, the Arab states also argued that partition would constitute aggression against Palestine. As such, Arab states asserted that self-defense would be justified in response. Self-defense had been reaffirmed by article 51 of the charter which reads, "nothing in this present Charter shall impair the inherent right of self-defense in the event of armed attack." The Arab states did not argue that a United Nations General Assembly resolution itself would constitute an "armed attack" but rather it would sanction Zionist policies which were inevitably, in their view, aggressive toward Palestine. The discourse of "Zionist aggression" lay deep in the Arab political narrative. Now it was to take on a legal coloration. Two immediate obstacles to the success of this legal argument were that neither Palestine nor the Zionists constituted a state. Both the relevant articles of the United Nations Charter only refer to the actions of states: either as perpetrator or the victim. Only states could make threats or use force, and only states could defend themselves. One of the ways in which the Arab argument addressed this problem was to construct Palestine as an "Arab issue" and to make the case that Zionism was a military threat to existing Arab states. Zionism as a political ideology could not be defined as representing a state; however, as we shall see, the Arab states went to great lengths to argue that Zionism was an instrument for the policies of other states – in particular the Soviet Union.

Systematic preparations by Arab states to use force were well in place before UNSCOP had reported. These became more advanced during September and October 1947 when the Arab League took the decisive step to establish a military committee under the Syrian General Isma'il Safwat. Its brief was "to decide the Palestinian needs to increase its defense; to coordinate and organize support provided by the Arab states."[4] This statement reflected a subtle shift in the Arab discourse. Palestine itself was to be treated as if it were a state already with defense requirements. Although Palestine itself was not to assess its own needs; that was to be the responsibility of the Arab League. This legal view of Palestine as both a state in its own right and as a ward of the Arab League was to become common in the debate that followed. The source of the threat was variously identified as "Zionist designs" and "Zionist gangs." However, in this period before the adoption of the United Nations resolution inter-communal violence was evenly matched. Much of the Zionist military activity was aimed at the British. It had been the British headquarters of the mandate at the King David Hotel that had been destroyed and in the summer of 1947 it was the killing of the two British sergeants that was in the news. Nonetheless for the Arab states all these incidents were to be seen as Zionist aggression against Arab interests. Indeed even the continued discussions about partition fostered the violence. The highly rhetorical language which portrayed Jews as foreigners, aliens, illegal immigrants, and revolutionaries sought to cast all their action as disruptive to a natural Arab order. Within this imaginative discourse aggression would be transformed from its military meaning into a broad term that would be used to cover the arrival in Palestine of destitute immigrants or the construction of a new building in Tel Aviv. This imagery became seductive within the Arab world and would become so deeply secreted within political narratives that "Zionist aggression" would come to be seen as an established fact. It also entered the bloodstream of the Arab and Palestinian legal discourse.

During 1947 various Arab militias supplemented by foreign volunteers were deployed in Palestine. These were formed around Palestinian groups (such as Najada) who were able to recruit volunteers from Arab countries through political and religious networks such as the Muslim Brotherhood.[5] The formation of the military committee was to some extent an attempt by the League to exercise control over military events. It appears that the decision was also intended to take the initiative out of the hands of the Arab Higher Committee, although irregular forces associated with factions of the AHC were to remain active on the ground. The committee was something of a diplomatic coup for Syria which jealously guarded its interests in Palestine, rightly fearing that Jordanians and Egyptians entertained hopes of strategic gains in any conflict. In 1946 the Palestinian Arab leadership had explained that "geographically Palestine is part of Syria; its indigenous inhabitants belong to the Syrian branch of the Arab family of nations."[6] It was a position that the Syrian government wanted to maintain. The formation of the military committee was a key stage in the process of mobilizing the forces of war against partition.

The UNSCOP report and that of General Assembly resolution 181 are difficult to read as an aggressive plan to attack Palestine. The UNSCOP majority report was carefully constructed around four core principles: maintaining the unity of the country; providing for political sovereignty for Jews and Arabs; guaranteeing individual and minority rights; and protecting the holy places. The plan involved no forced movement of populations, no dispossession of property or land and provided for free movement between the three parts of Palestine. As far as the Jewish state was concerned it was conceived only in the context of Palestine and was not as a response to the Holocaust – or indeed as the fulfillment of Zionism. No radical transformation of Palestine was proposed. It sought to maintain the unity of the country through the economic union and the international status of Jerusalem.

The plan was based on the recognition that both populations in Palestine constituted national communities with historical attachments to the country. The partition formula was presented as a genuine compromise between the competing claims. Palestine would neither be a Jewish state nor an Arab state, it would become both. Partition was seen as preventing either community being dominated by the other. The committee had been quite open about the drawbacks, in particular the existence of a large Palestinian Arab minority in the Jewish state. However, it regarded the constitutional requirements as at least in part addressing this question. It had also recognized that the division of Palestine into a patchwork of land parcels created difficulties for the contiguity of the states. Yet this, it was thought, could be turned into an advantage as it would force both sides to cooperate. This view was given voice by Andrew Johnson of the United States in the General Assembly debate:

> Although both the Arab and the Jewish States have been given a separate political existence within clearly defined boundaries, it is our hope that these boundaries will be as freely crossed as the boundaries which separate the individual states within the United States, and will be as friendly as the boundary which runs for three thousand miles between Canada and the United States.[7]

In the light of what befell Palestine for the next six decades this was a rather rosy assessment of the prospects. Johnson's statement does represent the frequently expressed view at the time that partition offered the best hope for reconciliation. Whether the authors of the UNSCOP majority report really imagined that moving between Hebron and Tel Aviv would be on a par with traveling between Albany and Boston is another matter.

The partition plan thus talked of two sovereign states but in fact projected a novel arrangement for the interaction between the two peoples. While perhaps not really the US model it was certainly markedly different from Indian partition. In coming to their recommendations the committee attempted to plot a middle course between what it referred to as two extremes. As we have seen, it summed up the Arab case for a unitary independent state under a permanent Arab majority with strict restrictions on Jewish representation, land rights and immigration. However, the Jewish case was much more flexible. As the committee had noted, the demand for a Jewish state contained the readiness to accept partition. The proposed Jewish state was not ethnically exclusivist and was to be based on equal political and economic right for all citizens.

This meant that UNSCOP in fact had a much more difficult task than choosing between two extremes. It had to balance between rigidity on the part of the Arabs and pragmatism on the part of the Jews. This must have placed the committee in great difficulty as any compromise scheme could be seen by the Arabs as necessarily rejecting their position and as a concession to the Jews. There was another problem for the committee that while the Jews made direct representations to the committee the Palestinians did not. This, as we have seen, did not mean that the Palestinian case was not put to the committee. The meetings with representatives of the Arab states did allow for direct contact with the Arab view, if not with the Palestinians themselves. In addition the committee carefully took into account the formal statements of the Arab Higher Committee. Despite its best efforts contact with the Arab population in Palestine was thus extremely limited. The active participation of the Jewish community with the committee meant relations went beyond formalities. Members of the committee and its staff interacted with Jews facilitating the visits which created personal and informal relations. Visits to *kibbutzim* and to Jewish towns also created a sense of contact. Unlike the Palestinian national movement, the Zionist movement did not attempt to prevent Jews who were anti-Zionist or who supported a bi-national solution from meeting the committee. This created a quite different environment in which the formal positions of the Zionist movement could be understood. The informal contact reinforced the sense that there was a degree of reasonableness in the Jewish position.

The more the Arab states spoke for Palestine the more Palestine became subject to the politics of the Arab League. While the Arab Higher Committee was formally recognized at the United Nations the distinctive Palestinian voice was somewhat muted. The combined effect of this meant that any Palestinian debate about the future options was stifled. The Arab Higher Committee monopolized Palestinian public opinion and the Arab League spoke for the

Arab Higher Committee. As a result all nuances in the Palestinian community were silenced by an increasingly homogenized Arab argument driven by the Arab League. It followed that UNSCOP could engage better with the Jewish than the Arab position. In the debates on partition Arab representatives at the United Nations were to continue with this approach and presented the case as a single Arab view. Palestine had to that extent disappeared within Arab unity. The defense of Palestine had become the defense of the Arab world.

In the debates the Arab states and the Palestinians were keen to advance their legal position. While its premise rested on the alleged illegality of actions of the League of Nations this was now extended to contend that the United Nations did not have the legal capacity to partition Palestine. While every challenge to the legality of the Mandate had been rejected by the League,[8] essentially the same argument was to be recycled in relation to the United Nations. Whereas in the 1920s the Covenant of the League of Nations had been the subject of attention, in the 1940s it was the United Nations Charter. In both instances it was suggested that both international bodies were legally unable to change the status of Palestine.

The arguments about legal capacity of the United Nations were based on several propositions. The first was that partition would be contrary to the United Nations Charter on the question of self-determination. This was connected with a second that the UN could not impose a policy against the wishes of the Palestinian majority. The third raised a constitutional issue that as under the charter the General Assembly only had the power to make recommendations; it did not have the competence to partition a territory.

The question of the right of self-determination of peoples which is prominent in the United Nations Charter might appear at first glance a winning position. However, as Rosalyn Higgins has explained the charter did not elaborate this principle as a legal one.[9] Indeed chapters 11, 12 and 13 of the charter are concerned with the governance of non-self-governing peoples. International law's colonial origins had ensured that self-determination had been an exclusively political right which was the preserve of the "civilized nations." Indeed even outside this context self-determination was not regarded as a legal right.[10] Self-determination emerged as a legal right through several instruments of the United Nations General Assembly in the 1960s and 1970s. The critical resolutions[11] did not create any objective criteria that a people require in order to be recognized as possessing the right to self-determination. The term "people" in this context should not be equated to nation for example. The international legal doctrine has rather developed through prohibiting barriers to self-determination such as colonial regimes, enemy occupations and racist regimes. International law thus did not and does not recognize self-determination as a natural right that derives from the national or ethnic character of a people. In deciding that the Jews and Arabs of Palestine were two peoples each with the right to a state, the General Assembly could not be said to be acting contrary to the charter. It was rather the opposite; it was an early example of the UN attempting to grapple with the application of the principle.

The argument is that the General Assembly did not have the competence to pass the partition resolution as it could only adopt recommendations is particularly weak. The Assembly has very wide remit and can debate any matter it wishes. Critically the charter provides that each organ can determine its own competence without interference. Such considerations did not prevent the most vigorous opposition to the legitimacy of the partition resolution.

This view was well represented by the representative of Yemen in the General Assembly, Prince Seif El Islam Abdullah, who explained:

> We have made it clear that the partition plan is illegal, being contrary to the United Nations Charter and unjust, since it imposes an institution upon a country without its consent. The partition plan is unworkable. Because of this injustice and illegality the Arabs do not agree to it.[12]

For the Prince the legal issue was clear and thus its assertion was taken as sufficient proof of his authority on the matter. The tone was also interesting as it was offered with some exasperation as if the obvious illegality had been pointed out many times. It also announced a categorical position: the "Arabs do not agree to it." These tones are then reiterated: "the United Nations is an organization of international law and justice, and not one of appeasement or force."[13] The use of the language of appeasement was no doubt an attempt to create a linkage between the position of Palestine in 1947 and Britain and France in 1939. With that historical reference in mind he went on to warn of the danger of disregarding "the rights of the Arabs" which would be a "denial of their just claims… If they resort to self-defence, are they to blame?"[14] This argument was to become a theme of the General Assembly debate. Partition was constructed as an illegal and violent intervention into the Arab world. As a result the Arab world as a whole, and Arab states individually, have the right to self-defense. Indeed Prince Abdullah ended his speech with a plea that the United Nations should not be made "an instrument of dispute, strife and bloodshed."[15]

The Iranian representative (Adl) called the partition plan a proposal that "has no foundation in law."[16] He also reiterated the proposition that the General Assembly would exceed its powers if the resolution were to be adopted, as it would "repudiate and even usurp the right of each people to give itself the laws which it thinks are desirable for preserving its own national life."[17] He also suggested that the result would in any event produce "fire and slaughter."[18] The Egyptian Ambassador, Mahmoud Bey Fawzi also took the view that it was "clear" that the Assembly "was not competent to impose any solution."[19] Although having argued that the legal situation was clear he then proposed that the entire matter should be referred to the International Court of Justice for an advisory opinion. The latter was not a new proposal and one which the Arab world had been advocating for some time. Much has been made in subsequent debates that this option was rejected at the time. However, the fact that such an opinion was thought worthwhile is surely evidence that despite the protestations of legal clarity, the issue may not have been so straightforward.

Amir Faisal Al Saud of Saudi Arabia was undeterred by any legal doubt. He argued simply that the vote on partition would decide whether "justice or tyranny will prevail."[20] Al Saud fully utilized the view of Palestine as a state as he explained the Saudi understanding of the charter. "Remember," he said,

that in the preamble of the Charter you have pledged before God and history that you will stand firm against the aggressor and direct your effort to establish world peace and international security. Is not what is being attempted today in Palestine a case of flagrant aggression? Is it not tyrannical that an international organization is intervening to partition a country in order to present a part of it to the aggressor?[21]

If we were in any doubt as to the identity of the aggressor Al Saud soon enlightens us when he warns that the entire plan "is to please the Zionist gang and those accomplices lending their support."[22]

Amir Arslan, the Syrian delegate, strangely ignored the contributions that had gone before, and began his speech by claiming that "no one" had "really taken into account the legal side of the question."[23] However, much of his contribution ranged far wider as he was keen to set the law in context. It was he said important to understand that the debate was taking place against the background of "intrigues" and "manoeuvres" to present the plan as humanitarian. On the Jewish claim of a "historic right" to Palestine, he comments, "even supposing that this right existed, it could not be equal to the historic and acquired rights of the Arabs."[24] However, such a claim was non-existent as he claimed to have proved that "the Jews of Eastern Europe are not related in any way to Israel and that they are purely of Russian Khazar origin." He then supported this argument with a quotation from Benedict and Weltfish's work *The Races of Mankind*[25] where he says the authors wrote, "Jews are people who acknowledge the Jewish religion. They belong to all races. The European Jews are very varied in origin and biological type."[26] Both views were very revealing of the approach to national identity at the time in which nations were conceived as naturally occurring phenomena which are rooted in racial or biological characteristics. Thus the argument here was quite clear: if Jews are not a race, they could not be a nation, and thus they have no claim to a state. Arslan's reliance on Benedict and Weltfish is misplaced. The authors provided cogent arguments against basing any analysis of human activity on the basis of claims of race. Indeed their article went against the grain of the discourse of the European Enlightenment where for example in the works of Montesquieu and Hegel race was assumed to be a key determining factor in history. For Arslan and other opponents of Jewish statehood the idea that Jews did not qualify as a race seemed particularly alluring, endowing the argument with the aura of science. Such ideas have proved to be particularly persistent in the Palestinian–Israeli conflict, where the argument that the lack of racial homogeneity amongst Jews disqualifies them to any claim to be a people or nation is still made frequently. Arslan's emphasis on the proposition that Jews are a "people who acknowledge the Jewish religion" was also significant. The view that Jews have an exclusively religious identity is also still maintained by those who seek to argue that Jewish nationalism is counterfeit. Interestingly not all supporters of the Arab case in 1947 adopted this position; the Pakistani representative, Sir Muhammad Zafrullah Khan, had no problem in referring to the "Jewish race," nor did he reject the idea that Jews were a nation. This was a telling comment from a representative of a state that had been formed in 1947 on the basis that Muslim Indians constituted a distinctive nation.

Arslan then turned his attention to discuss the implications of his views on Jewish identity for Palestine. Were Jews just fleeing from persecution, then, he claims, they would be welcome in Palestine and indeed all Arab countries. However, "as everyone has realized, we are faced, in this case with no more than a political scheme of an imperialist nature in which all the ambitions coincide and two extremes meet."[27] The slippage from Jews as belonging to a religion to having political designs was not explained. These political designs having been first described as of an "imperialist nature" were then to be revealed as a communist plot. Having referred to the US anti-communist policies, Arslan continued:

> But if the Black sea ports could pour half a million communists into Palestine today, the delegation of the United States would be all the happier so long as Palestine was swarming with Jews. They are not satisfied with the one hundred and fifty thousand communists who are already in Palestine.[28]

The argument that Jewish immigration to Palestine was connected with the spread of communism was not new, and as we have noted, had been referred to since the 1920 May riots. In the 1940s with the new international position of the Soviet Union this argument was embellished with fear of Soviet influence. It was noticeable how Jews had been reconstructed from a religious group into an ideological one. In this guise Jews were now to be seen not as a threat merely to Palestine but to the political stability of the region. "The whole affair is only a conspiracy," Arslan commented, recycling an unfortunate image. The scope and impact of this conspiracy was enormous:

> The truth is that the Zionists and their friends have other aims in mind. That is proved by the fact that they have made the territory of the Jewish State extend to the Red Sea; that is a threat to the Suez Canal, the Islamic holy places in the Hedjaz, the interests of all Arab countries in the Red Sea region, and the interests of Ethiopia. In short the United States delegation and other delegations in favour of this plan consider it impossible and unjust to subject six hundred thousand Jews to a decision making Palestine one state; but these same delegations want the Arabs in Palestine and all independent Arab States, with a total population of thirty million people, to be subject to an illegal decision contrary to the Charter and their vital interests.[29]

The partition plan is thus posed as a threat not just to Palestine but to the whole of the Arab world and even to Ethiopia. Arslan conceives of the Jews as instruments of Soviet penetration into the region – although with the support of the United States. He is convinced that the United States went along with this project due to the fact that Zionists dominated US policy-making. He hoped that "the good people of this great and truly democratic country, the United States will wake up one day, open their eyes, see things clearly and demand that their country's policy shall be independent of that of the Zionists."[30] Jews were portrayed as communists, Soviet instruments, and controllers of US policy who were able to hoodwink the American public. In each role Jews were portrayed as powerful, disruptive and manipulative. The Syrian speech ends with a warning that partition would never be recognized and that Syria would "reserve the right to act accordingly."[31]

This speech contained all the main elements of the Arab argument. Jews had no natural national identity and so could have no national claim to Palestine. As a consequence any support for a Jewish state would be illegal. While Jews were a religious group that lacked any national characteristics, they did possess collective features that enabled them to act as an influential group in world politics as both conveyers of communism and manipulators of superpowers. What united Jews or gave them this élan to coordinate such a level of activity was not explained. However, what was central to the argument was that Jews possessed a shadowy power that once exposed could be undermined. Part of the purpose of the debate was to unmask what Arslan called a conspiracy. The concluding statement that Syria reserved the right to act against partition became a familiar theme of Arab representatives in the debate.

Arslan was succeeded at the podium by the Lebanese representative, Camille Chamoun, who developed the theme of manipulation. "I can well imagine," he explained, "to what pressure, to what manoeuvres your sense of justice, equity and democracy has been exposed during these last thirty-six hours."[32] He suggested that delegations have been pressured "in hotel rooms, in bed, in corridors and anterooms" and that there were threats of economic sanctions or offers of bribes to vote for partition. It was undoubtedly the case that there was a high degree of lobbying taking place on all sides but this was normal in the United Nations on all critical issues. The purpose of this intervention was to question the validity of any vote in favor of partition. "The United States is wearing the fatal shirt of Nessus," he declared, recalling the Greek myth of Nessus who cunningly persuaded Dejamina to pass his poisoned shirt to the hero Hercules which led to his death. In this modern story of deception the Zionists are manipulating the United States to poison the United Nations against Palestine.

With this colorful image of deception Chamoun turned to the doctrine of self-determination which he said was so clear that "there is no need for me to dwell at length on it." It was an obligation that is "imposed on us by the categorical terms of the Charter, to safeguard the right of the peoples to govern themselves and to decide their own destiny."[33] This principle had been breached he said because there had been no attempt to ascertain the wishes of "the majority of the inhabitants of Palestine." This was erroneous as it was the AHC that had boycotted the United Nations precisely at the moment that the organization had sought Palestinian views. Despite his apparent clarity on the question of self-determination Chamoun did introduce some interesting speculation on its possible application. He pondered the question of whether if the right of self-determination applied to the Jews as a minority in Palestine, would it equally apply to the Arabs who would become a minority in the Jewish state? If so he suggested there would have to be re-division of the Jewish state so that the Arab majority could gain their rights. Unfortunately this was posed only rhetorically. However, had this much more subtle and serious argument been pursued the Arab states and the Palestinians could well have influenced the course of the debate. To do so of course would have been to accept the legitimacy of Jewish claims of national rights.

When the turn of Iraq came to address the Assembly its representative Fadhil Jamali delivered a speech which re-iterated the now familiar legal arguments but which was perhaps the most explicit in putting the objections to the creation of a Jewish state. He began from the proposition that peaceful relations have become impossible "because of the growing political designs and ambitions of the newcomers." He regarded the partition plan as just the first step of a greater strategy:

The Zionists continued to cherish their designs and ambitions. They very effectively exploited the miseries of the victims of Hitler to their own political ends. Now they want a state in part of Palestine, later on in all of Palestine, and, eventually to penetrate the rest of the Arab world.[34]

The explicit reference to the Holocaust as being used manipulatively by Zionists was one of the first and most public articulations of a position that has now become common in some anti-Zionist circles. In Jamali's account Hitler's victims are not identified as Jews. They remain faceless although subject to exploitation by the Zionists. The victims were not to be given their own voice and the overwhelming desire of the Jews in the displaced peoples camps to be permitted to emigrate to Palestine was to be dismissed as the result of manipulation. This crude intervention appeared to address arguments that were not contained in the UNSCOP report which had been dismissive of the Holocaust and had rejected the creation of a Jewish state as a solution to the "Jewish problem." Jamali was convinced that "those who drafted the plan had only the Jewish Agency and its wishes to take into consideration."[35] Indeed the proposal was "Zionist-designed, and was adopted by a pro-Zionist committee, which gave all its care and attention to Zionist demands, leaving to the Arabs what Zionist benevolence permitted."[36] This underlined the problem that faced the committee in making its recommendations. As we have already noted, any proposal that was less than the Arab position could be seen as pro-Jewish. Despite the fact that many aspects of the plan were not received favorably by the Zionist movement, in particular the severing of the Jews of Jerusalem from the Jewish state and the character of the boundaries, the fact that a Jewish state was proposed at all could be used to portray the committee as pro-Zionist.

In outlining the dangers of a Jewish state Jamali linked Zionism with both communism and Nazism:

A Jewish State in Palestine would be a great danger to international peace in that part of the world. It would be a place where conflicting power politics would play a role. A recent trial of underground communists in Baghdad who were precipitating a subversive movement against the constitution of the country revealed that these communists were financed by Zionist sources in Palestine from the sale of all forms of merchandise, the returns of which were spent on subversive movements. This, by the way, is a method which was used by the Nazis before the last war. The immigrants coming into Palestine – the origins of many of whom are not known – carry the seeds of many a subversive movement into the Near East.[37]

This return to the communist theme underlined that while there were general comments about imperialism in some of the speeches, anti-communism was regarded as the strongest card. This was interesting in the light of the turn of events, especially after 1967, which saw the emergence of the Arab and Palestinian analysis of Israel as a colonial-settler state. In 1947 there had been no mention of a colonial project but a great deal about how the Jews and Zionists were in cahoots with communism. The use of the "communist menace" might have been thought an argument that could appeal to Western states. However, this argument was at odds with the position that the United States was already under the sway of the Zionists. The idea of the communist plot does have a resonance with the anti-Semitic image of Jews as a shadowy group conspiring for power. Jewish stereotypes were further reinforced by reference to a comment by the Anglican Bishop of Jerusalem who had expressed "distress at the growing industrialization and commercialization" of the holy places in Jerusalem and Bethlehem as well as in the Galilee. It would seem odd that the Jews would be responsible for the commercialization of Bethlehem whose religious sites must have been under the control of Christian authorities. Nonetheless the purpose of using the image of the Jew transforming holy places into commercial enterprises was evident. In case there was any doubt of the poisoned well from which he was drawing, Jamali stressed that, "trouble starts the minute Jews begin to cherish dreams of domination."[38]

His fellow Syrian delegate (El-Khouri), widened the theme of Jewish influence in the debate. "You see to what extent their influence has extended here," he stated.

> In the United States they are one to thirty whereas in Palestine they are one to three. Living in this democratic country they have extended their influence into all circles. They have even extended it to the centre of the United Nations and intimidate speakers by hissing at them. This is the proof that they are influencing and dominating people here even though they are one to thirty in this country. We should take account of that, and the United States, and the people of the United States should be careful for the future which awaits them.[39]

Thus the legal argument that the General Assembly did not have power to adopt the partition resolution was also accompanied by the argument that the Assembly was acting under duress. This was laying the ground to claim that if adopted the resolution would be void. The portrayal of Jews in the debate is very disturbing. As we have seen, Jews are depicted as deploying deception, manipulation, intimidation and duress as they are intent on domination, not just in Palestine or indeed the rest of the Middle East but also in the United States. The anti-Semitic discourse used by several delegates, it should be noted, was never challenged by other participants. It was allowed to stand as if it were just another legitimate opinion. It was extraordinary that the very ideology that led to the Holocaust was on display in the United Nations so soon after the war. It was particularly grotesque that this image of the powerful Jew was deployed so soon after the evident weakness of the Jews to prevent their own destruction in Europe.

While not addressing anti-Semitism delegations supporting partition were keen to take up the legal issues. The American representative, Andrew Johnson, made a reasoned argument on some of the key legal questions but he readily accepted that there was "no direct precedent in international law for the problem with which the General Assembly is now confronted."[40] Nonetheless he contended that the partition plan fell

> properly within the scope the Charter and within the powers and responsibilities of the organs of the United Nations… The problem is international, not domestic… The General Assembly may make any recommendations with respect to this question which it deems just and equitable, and in accordance with the principles and purposes of the Charter.[41]

He pointed out that part of the uniqueness of the situation was that Britain had unilaterally declared the end of the Mandate and expressed its refusal to carry out any policy that did not have the agreement of the two communities. This, he rightly pointed out, this placed a "heavy moral responsibility" on the United Nations. He also outlined his views on the legal status of Palestine that made this responsibility all the more acute:

> Palestine, as a territory under mandate, is not a state. It is not an international person but is in a sense a ward of the international community. In the circumstances now prevailing, the General Assembly of the United Nations is the effective voice of the international community in determining the new forms and structures of government which should prevail in Palestine when the Mandate is terminated.[42]

The USSR had a two-nation position that had originally led it to favor a Jewish–Arab federal state. As that had proved impractical the USSR was to become an enthusiastic supporter of partition. In addition the USSR was the only delegation at the time to make the additional argument that a Jewish state was justified by the inaction of the Western allies to prevent the Holocaust. In the May debate, Andrei Gromyko had argued:

> The fact that no western European state has been able to ensure the defense of the elementary rights of the Jewish people, and to safeguard it against the violence of the fascist executioners, explains the aspirations of the Jews to establish their own state. It would be unjust not to take this into consideration and to deny this right to the Jewish people to realize this aspiration. It would be unjustifiable to deny this right to the Jewish people, particularly in view of all it has undergone during the Second World War.[43]

This was the clearest expression of the argument that the creation of a Jewish state was a necessary step so that Jews could protect themselves. Such a view was never articulated by any of the Western participants in the debates. Poland which had a pro-Soviet government was the only other state to express similar sentiments. Western states at the time seemed extremely reluctant to comment at all on the implications of the Holocaust. It was easy to avoid mention as the UNSCOP report had de-coupled the two issues. It makes the subsequent commonly expressed sentiment that support for the Jewish state was the result of Western guilt all the more curious. In the debates the Western allies of World War II clearly did not regard themselves as bearing any guilt toward the Jews. They saw themselves as part of the alliance that had vanquished Nazism. They had clean hands.

In the debate on resolution 181 Gromyko addressed the question of whether the plan was directed "against the Arab population of Palestine and against the Arab states in general." He concluded that it was "not directed against either of the two national groups that inhabit Palestine. On the contrary…this decision corresponds to the fundamental national interests of both peoples."[44] In answer to the charge that partition is a "historic injustice," he replied:

> After all the Jewish people has been closely linked with Palestine for a considerable period in history. Apart from that we must

not overlook…the position in which the Jewish people found themselves as a result of the recent world war. I shall not repeat what the USSR delegation said on this point at the special session of the General Assembly. However, it may not be amiss to remind listeners again that, as a result of the war which was unleashed by Hitlerite Germany, the Jews, as a people, have suffered more than any other people. You know that there was not a single country in Western Europe which succeeded in adequately protecting the interest of the Jewish people against the arbitrary acts and violence of the Hitlerites.[45]

This conscious reiteration of the position illustrated that this was the considered position of the USSR and was not a mere rhetorical flourish. It was of course also a highly political remark that sought to distinguish the Soviet Union from the West. This was after all the early days of the Cold War. Gromyko was frank when he turned to the political position of the Arab states in the new world order. He explained that the Soviet Union had great sympathy for the Arab peoples in trying to "rid themselves of the last fetters of colonial dependence." He distinguished between the "nations of the Arab East" and their governments, "we do not identify with the vital national interests of the Arabs, the clumsy statements made by some of the representatives of the Arab States about the foreign policy of the USSR in connection with the question of the future of Palestine."[46] The anti-communism of many of the speeches was no doubt aimed at influencing the United States and its allies but little thought was given to the fact that the Soviet Union and its allies would be unlikely to countenance those who claimed that the creation of a Jewish state would be evidence of Soviet expansionism. Such views Gromyko said were made "under the stress of fleeting emotions," and cannot represent the "basic and permanent interests of the Arab people." The pro-Western governments of the Arab world were not to the liking of the Soviet Union and undoubtedly a key aspect of the support for Zionism was part of an effort to weaken those regimes.

Gromyko's comments, however, clearly went beyond the attempt to play politics with the region. He returned to the question of principle and legality: "The solution of the Palestine problem based on a partition of Palestine into two separate states will be of profound historical significance," he said, "because this decision will meet the legitimate demands of the Jewish people, hundreds of thousands of whom…are still without a country, without homes…"

This framing of Jewish demands as legitimate was undoubtedly an attempt to refute any doubts that the Jews had the right to self-determination. The USSR was, it should be noted, including Jews outside Palestine as having that right as well as Jews inside Palestine.

In the final part of the speech Gromyko addressed the legal issue of the competence of the United Nations to take the decision. He said that the submissions that challenged this competence had failed "to adduce any convincing arguments apart from various general and unfounded statements and declarations." In his opinion:

> The General Assembly, as well as the United Nations as a whole, not only has the right to consider this matter, but in view of the situation that has arisen in Palestine, it is bound to take the requisite decision. In the view of the USSR delegation, the plan for the solution of the Palestine problem which has been drawn up by the Ad Hoc Committee, and according to which the practical implementation of the measures necessary to give effect rests with the Security Council, is in full accord with the interest of maintaining and strengthening international peace and with the interest of increasing cooperation between states.[47]

After several days of debate the stage was set for the vote on resolution 181. An Iranian attempt to delay the vote for six weeks failed and the resolution was adopted 33 votes for 13 against and 10 abstentions. Three permanent members of the Security Council voted in favor (USSR, USA, France) and two abstained (UK, China). All Arab members and those with significant Muslim populations (except the Soviet Union and Yugoslavia) voted against. However, the yes column was not just composed of Western states; the five "socialist" states voted together with the USA, Canada and Australia; the Scandinavian countries voted alongside South Africa and the Benelux countries with ten Latin American states. This was the last vote of the General Assembly that was not to divide on ideological grounds for many decades. Although clearly adopted by the required two-thirds majority the voting pattern revealed a great deal of division amongst the Western powers. Two blocs were united, the socialist states and the Arab League, although pitted against each other. Subsequent suggestions that partition was a policy by Western imperialism to impose its will on the Middle East hardly squared with either the actual debates or the way the votes were cast on the resolution.

The reaction to the vote by those who opposed the resolution was immediately expressed in the Assembly. Representatives from Saudi Arabia, Pakistan, Iraq, Syria and Yemen recorded not only their opposition to the resolution but their intention to defy it. Amir Faisal Al Saud (Saudi Arabia) announced: "Saudi Arabia registers, on this historic occasion, the fact that it does not consider itself bound by the resolution... Furthermore, it reserves to itself the full right to act freely in whatever way it deems fit."[48] For Pakistan a delegate read a statement by Sir Muhammad Zafrullah Khan which had been written before the vote and had anticipated the result. He suggested that states that opposed partition had been forced to change their vote in favor, although how he would know this in advance was questionable. The resolution, the statement read,

> totally lacks legal validity. We entertain no sense of grievance against those of our friends and fellow representatives who have been compelled, under heavy pressure to change sides and to cast their votes in support of a proposal the justice and fairness of which does not commend themselves to them. Our feeling for them is one of sympathy that they have been placed in a position of such embarrassment between their conscience on one side, and the pressure to which they and their governments were being subjected to, on the other.[49]

This drew on sentiments expressed during the debate that pressure and compulsion on members had been rife. Such views also presented the vote as a foregone conclusion due to careful and influential Zionist planning. However, most Zionists at the time were in fact anxious that the resolution might have been defeated.[50] The Iraq representative Jamali echoed Khan's view: "we understand very well," he said, "that it was great pressure and great influence that worked itself through UNSCOP...through the General Assembly itself to direct the matter in a course which led to this conclusion."[51] He continued:

> In the name of my Government, I wish to state that it feels that this decision is antidemocratic, illegal, impractical and contrary to the Charter. Therefore, in the name of my Government I wish to put on record that Iraq does not recognize the validity of this decision, will reserve freedom of action towards its implementation, and holds those who were influential in passing it... responsible for the consequences.[52]

The Iraqi Prime Minister was reported to have said that if there had been a secret ballot he would have been surprised if four votes would have been cast in favor. This was wishful thinking as to a large extent the Arab states had become a victim to their own arguments believing that there was only one possible view of the justice of the issue.

The Syrian Amir Arslan suggested that "even before the Assembly took this decision...most of the delegations had suspected a dictatorial attitude." He then rather abruptly announced that "the Charter is dead. But it did not die a natural death; it was murdered, and you all know who is guilty. My country will never recognize such a decision. It will never be responsible for it. Let the consequences be on the head of others, not on ours."[53] Prince Seif El Islam Abdullah from Yemen then repeated the same formula:

the partition plan is contrary to justice and to the Charter of the United Nations. Therefore the government of Yemen does not consider itself bound by such a decision for it is contrary to the letter and the spirit of the Charter... Yemen will reserve its freedom of action towards the implementation of this decision.[54]

Each of these statements is highly significant and founds a vital part of the Arab legal narrative of the conflict. The partition resolution was not just illegal and invalid. It was a contravention of the charter and the General Assembly did not have the power to pass it. Moreover, had there been no pressure and intimidation the resolution would not have been passed. In this account these multiple illegalities meant that the states who voted against it could not be bound by it. Indeed as the formula of reserving freedom of action was repeated the United Nations was being given notice that war was being actively prepared to prevent partition.

Within two weeks of the passing of resolution 181, the heads of Arab governments met in Cairo and approved the formation of the Arab Liberation Army (ALA) which was to be the military arm of the Arab League in Palestine. In Palestine itself violence greeted the resolution. Inter-communal violence that had been so graphically described in the UNSCOP report was about to escalate beyond the control of the British authorities. The British refused to cooperate with the United Nations after the vote. As a result the United Nations Palestine Commission that was intended to pave the way for the implementation of the plan was unable to do its work. Thus while Britain was too weak to prevent the outbreak of civil war it was strong enough to frustrate the UN plan.

The Palestinian Jewish community had welcomed the UN vote and the Jewish Agency headed by Ben-Gurion had accepted it. However, in the absence of any political means to implement it a dangerous vacuum was created. While crowds in Jewish towns and cities celebrated, Ben-Gurion brooded over the means of realizing the Jewish state. If the United Nations could not implement its own plan, who would? Ben-Gurion knew that only force of arms would decide the issue. In response to Arab preparations such as the ALA, the putative Jewish state began to take measures to create a military force capable of withstanding military attempts to prevent the creation of the Jewish state. While Ben-Gurion and other *Yishuv* leaders sought to build the Haganah into such a force, the CIA had already made the military calculations.

The CIA report,[55] published the day before the vote, predicted that "armed hostilities between Jews and Arabs will break out if the UN General Assembly accepts the plan to partition Palestine into Jewish and Arab states."[56] It estimated that the Arab world could mobilize between 100,000 and 200,000 fighters while the Jews could count on 200,000. In their estimate the CIA thought that without outside assistance the Jews, while initially taking the advantage, would go down in defeat within two years. This assessment was made in the context of analysis of the impact of such a UN vote on US interests in the Middle East. The report concluded that the United States, "by supporting partition, has already lost much of its prestige in the Near East."[57] It predicted that if partition were adopted the regional situation of the United States would become dire both economically and politically. Americans and American interests would become the target of attacks and "poverty, unrest and hopelessness upon which communist propaganda thrives will increase throughout the Arab world, and Soviet Agents (some of which have already been smuggled into Palestine as Jewish DPs) will scatter into other Arab states."[58] As can be seen the report reflected Arab concerns about the USSR's policy toward Palestine fearing that the turmoil in the region would allow the Soviet Union to establish "a base in the heart of the Near East." It continued:

The USSR has been actively but secretly assisting the Jews. In addition to reports that the USSR is assisting Jewish underground agents in Europe, large ships filled with illegal immigrants have been leaving the Rumanian port of Constanza. The British have watched with suspicion Soviet "lumber ships" leaving the Black sea for Palestine, which the British claim, are carrying arms below decks for both the Jews and Arabs of Palestine. In the event of Arab–Jewish hostilities, the USSR will continue to support the Jews and will probably also attempt covertly to aid the Arabs.[59]

The CIA's assessment that the Soviet Union would support the Jews militarily was prescient. The report demonstrated that US government officials were by no means united in their attitude to Zionism or to partition. This stems from two reasons, the most dominant of which was strategic. The USA had to guard its economic interests, especially those connected to oil, whereas support for partition would undermine its position in the Middle East. This was associated with the danger that the Soviet Union would be able to use the situation to its advantage which would weaken the United States both militarily and economically. The second reason seemed to be quite pragmatic: if a Jewish state could only survive for two years there would be little point in taking risks for a project that would end in failure. In the event the United States did support partition but interestingly took no steps at all to give any military aid to the Jews before or after the establishment of the State of Israel.

Once the partition resolution had been adopted a feverish nationalist wave swept the Arab world as mass demonstrations took place to "save Palestine." Governments which had been so free with their rhetoric at the United Nations and in their public statements now faced the demands of their citizens for action. Having denounced partition as tantamount to aggression against Palestine and the Arab nation the governments of the Arab states were forced to plan their response.

The Arab Higher Committee made immediate preparations for a military response to the resolution and appointed Abd-al-Qadir Al Husseini (a cousin of the Mufti) as commander-in-chief and dispatched him to Jerusalem.[60] However, he had a very difficult task in establishing any authority. The problem was not military but political. Within Palestine there was little semblance of national leadership as many members of the AHC operated from outside the country. The Mufti was based in Cairo and other members had offices in Beirut and Damascus. One key leader, Hussein Khalidi, did remain in Jerusalem and managed to establish an Arab police force with British support to protect Arab neighborhoods. That success only indicated the local character of Palestinian national organization at this crucial time. In, for example, Haifa, the mayor, Yussuf Haikal, became increasingly unable to exercise authority due to factional rivalries. Abd-al-Qadir therefore was unable to develop a military strategy within a coherent political structure. This had military consequences as loyalties to competing political factions and clans tended to weigh more strongly than discipline to a political center. As the militias were tied to these factions developing a coherent military plan was problematic. Thus as volunteers arrived to join the Arab militias they faced a confusing situation. In January 1948 the Arab League began to deploy the Arab Liberation Army in the country which added another complicating factor. The Palestinian militias and the ALA were of course operating while Palestine was still under British control which posed special difficulties. As 1948 wore on the plethora of militias and the ALA units were to enjoy only episodic coordination. While these forces were often successful at a local level they lacked a national strategic command.

The violence that met the adoption of the partition resolution left 412 dead, 208 Arabs and 204 Jews.[61] These casualties were the result of an intense inter-communal conflict in which the targets became roads, work places and residential areas. Attacks in this phase were initiated by Arabs, which produced a strong response from the Haganah. For the Jewish leadership dealing with such attacks had to be placed within a longer term political and military strategy of establishing the Jewish state that the partition plan promised. While partition had been premised on the ability of the United Nations to enforce it, it was evident that the organization had no will or means to do so. Any action by the United Nations would have needed to be approved by the Security Council, and although the charter provided that the Council would have an armed force at its disposal none had been created – and nor has it been since. In the absence of a genuine United Nations force only member states could be authorized to send forces. However, such an authorization would have been unlikely as both the main powers, the USSR and the USA, would fear (as the CIA report indicated) that the other would use the situation to their advantage. For the Jewish leadership in December 1947, then, the expectation of any international enforcement of the plan was non-existent. The continued bellicose statements by the Arab League and the Arab states, together with the reality of Arab violence in Palestine, reinforced the sense that the Jewish state would have to be created by Jewish arms.

The December inter-communal violence taught the Jewish leadership that there was no clear-cut distinction between military threats from outside Palestine and violence inside the country. The combination of Arab militias, foreign volunteers and the deployment of the ALA had already blurred the lines of demarcation between international war and civil war. This posed three interrelated challenges to the *Yishuv*: defense of Jewish communities from violence; controlling the area allocated by the United Nations for the Jewish state; and preparing for a military invasion from Arab states. The most pressing need was to protect isolated Jewish communities and the roads that supplied them. This was intimately connected to the attempt to develop a continuous Jewish territory along the lines of the partition plan. These objectives would create the minimum conditions for preparing for an international war.[62] As with the Arab side any military activity had to take into account the continued British presence.

For the Palestinian Jewish community the UN resolution provided international legitimacy for the creation of a state. The refusal of the British to implement it and the inability of the international community to act on it could not undermine its legal significance. The actions of the Jewish community to remedy these deficiencies were merely seen as supplying the modalities to bring about the policy of the international community. Jewish military actions and preparations were to be seen as part of a justified resistance to threats to frustrate the will of the United Nations. Thus the *Yishuv* would be able to cast itself as the defender of the United Nations.

Military preparations thus became the major concern of Ben-Gurion and the *Yishuv* leadership. The Haganah had evolved as an underground army and training had been limited by these circumstances. While there were members who had seen action in World War II, they were very much the minority. While the Haganah could call on large numbers it had few weapons and materiel. These had to be acquired from abroad and smuggled into the country avoiding British detection. While some American supporters were able to finance quite large amounts of small arms the major problem was to purchase heavier weapons including tanks and aircraft. This was to be sourced by the Soviet Union and supplied by Czechoslovakia. The Jewish war of national liberation was to take the pattern of many anti-colonial wars that were to come; popular anti-imperialist movements supported by Soviet arms.

For the Arab states, however, the increased military activity of the *Yishuv* was taken as evidence that partition was fostering the break-down of law and order in Palestine. Efforts to use force inside Palestine before the end of the Mandate on May 14, 1948 had had some tactical success but were strategically limited. As we have noted, the lack of decisive Palestinian political leadership had been a major stumbling block. With some important local exceptions this leadership had been weak and fractious during the early months of 1948. However, by the end of March almost the entire membership of the AHC had left the country, leaving Palestinians leaderless. Nor was the Arab League able to overcome this deficit. The League itself was deeply divided over its political and military objectives. As a result the member states competed for supporters amongst the AHC. The competition between Syria, Jordan and Egypt for influence in Palestine essentially meant that there were three conflicting strategies. King Abdullah of Jordan while formally objecting to partition had advocated a federation of Palestine with Jordan and with some form of Jewish local autonomy. When he realized that this was not a likely outcome he determined that as much of Arab Palestine as possible should be united with Jordan. As a consequence the Arab Legion prepared a plan to seize the West Bank including Jerusalem. The Egyptians on the other hand, having at first wavered about military action then set out to achieve a rapid military victory believing that Egyptian troops would conquer Tel Aviv within hours of the opening of hostilities. Syria sought to bring Palestine within its influence as a South Syrian province. Thus as Jordanians calmly planned the extension of their kingdom, the Egyptians dreamed of becoming the triumphal saviors of the Palestinians, and the Syrians maintained the dream of Greater Syria. These conflicting national ambitions would have been problematic enough had it not also been that the Arab military was not well trained or equipped. Nor did the Arab armies have much combat experience; for the Syrian army this would be its first experience of war. The one exception to this was the Arab Legion which was at least partially to achieve its aims by conquering the West Bank and East Jerusalem.

Once the State of Israel had been declared these three strategic options were played out with tragic consequences for all concerned. On the night of May 14–15, 1948, Egypt first informed the Security Council that it had entered Palestine to "establish law and order." Next day the Arab League issued a long declaration on Palestine which recounted its version of the history and the legal situation. Its main import, however, was to justify the invasion of Palestine.

The Governments of the Arab States, as members of the Arab League, a regional organization within the meaning of the provisions of Chapter VIII of the Charter of the United Nations, are responsible for maintaining peace and security in their area. These governments view the events taking place in Palestine as a threat to peace and security in the area as a whole and in each of them taken separately.

Therefore, as security in Palestine is a sacred trust in the hands of the Arab States, and in order to put an end to this state of affairs and to prevent it from becoming aggravated or from turning into chaos, the extent of which no one can foretell; in order to stop the spreading of disturbances and disorder in Palestine to the neighbouring Arab countries; in order to fill the gap brought about in the governmental machinery in Palestine as a result of the termination of the mandate and the non-establishment of a lawful successor authority, the Governments of the Arab States have found themselves compelled to intervene in Palestine, solely in order to help its inhabitants restore peace and security and the rule of justice and law to their country, and in order to prevent bloodshed.[63]

In invoking the authority of Chapter VIII the Arab League was relying on the regional collective security provisions of the UN Charter. These encourage regional military groupings to play a role in the suppression of aggression. This was an interesting shift from the earlier position that Arab states would be able to rely on self-defense alone if a Jewish state were to be created. The new position attempted to mobilize UN authority for action to thwart "Zionist aggression." The statement thus described the declaration of statehood in such terms. "Events which have taken place in Palestine," it asserted, "have unmasked the aggressive intentions and imperialistic designs of the Zionists." It is interesting that both Jews and Arabs sought legitimacy for their actions from the authority of the UN. Thus while the Jewish legal narrative relied on the partition resolution the Arab narrative attempted to construct a legal argument that its military intervention was consistent with suppressing aggression the main aim of the UN. The Arab League was "compelled to intervene" to prevent aggression. This latter stance necessarily rests on the assumption that the Arab League had the capacity to interpret the charter as it willed. It was and remains a difficult position to sustain as it would suggest that force can be used in the name of the United Nations to frustrate a policy of the United Nations. Such a conclusion would make the work of the United Nations impossible. However, the belief in this legal basis for military action in 1948 retains considerable support today. It should be noted that the declaration reiterates that the goal of the action was the creation of an independent state on the basis of the London conference proposals – for a single permanent majority Arab state. The declaration attempts to grant that state immediate legal status as the "governments of the Arab States recognize the independence of Palestine, which has so far been suppressed by the British mandate," and "has become an accomplished fact for the lawful inhabitants of Palestine." The first Arab–Israeli war had begun; a war in which both sides believed they had the law on their side.

5
Partition by Force

In the absence of the international will or ability to implement the United Nations partition resolution its fate passed into the hands of forces on the ground. A war of position broke out immediately with Jews attempting to consolidate control over the area allocated to the Jewish state and Palestinians and the Arab states waging a campaign to prevent partition. This chapter will examine the way in which the war established a new partition with political and legal consequences which have remained central ever since.

International factors were to play a major role in shaping the ability of the parties in Palestine to pursue their strategies. For the Jews this meant developing a relationship with the Soviet Union, while not disturbing their close contacts in the United States. This was a complex operation in the context of the sharpening Cold War. The Jews held a diplomatic advantage in that both powers had a common interest in undermining British and French influence in the Middle East and neither had strong ties with the Arab states.

In the United States the Zionist movement had become dominant amongst American Jews and had a powerful lobbying arm which gave it access to most centers of power. While influential it would be an error to assume that this translated automatically into the US administration espousing pro-Zionist policies. Despite tenacious attempts in the first half of 1948 the Zionists had failed to win much support in the State Department. This was demonstrated when the State Department abandoned support for partition and proposed that a United Nations Trusteeship regime should replace the mandate in the spring of 1948. As we have seen the CIA was also unconvinced that American interests lay with the creation of a Jewish state. As a result the USA was an enthusiastic supporter of the Security Council arms embargo against Palestine. This meant that the US government never contemplated arms sales or any form of strategic support for Palestine's Jews. While the Zionist movement was able to raise money that could be used to buy arms, acquiring them was somewhat furtive. It was against this rather unpromising background that Chaim Weizmann's ability to win

President Harry Truman to the support of the Jewish state was remarkable. Truman it appears fought a protracted personal battle with the State Department over the issue which continued until Israel's declaration of independence.[1]

The Soviet Union's support for partition was much more consistent and did not waver. Critically the USSR did not support the UN arms embargo. Serious Zionist contacts with the Soviet Union began in December 1947 when the supply of arms was discussed. It was in the course of these negotiations that it was decided that Czechoslovakia would supply the *Yishuv*.[2] From April 1948 shipments were to arrive in Palestine which included machine guns, rifles, mortars and ammunition. By the end of May four Messerschmitt BF 109 planes had also arrived.[3] These were supplemented by ten tanks in June.[4] That such small amounts of arms could prove decisive highlights the unsophisticated character of the 1948 War – David Tal estimates that about 80 planes and 60 tanks were deployed in all.[5] Yet without this level of Soviet support it is unlikely that the Jewish state could have been secured.

While the Jews were obtaining strategic supplies from the Eastern bloc the Palestinian Arabs increasingly became subject to the politics of the Arab world. While Palestinian militias were formally under the control of the Arab Higher Committee in Jerusalem military decision-making was effectively in the hands of various Arab states. With the Mufti in Egypt AHC members were forced to travel frequently outside Palestine for consultations thus further frustrating attempts to consolidate a coherent leadership. As the Mufti was regarded with great suspicion by Arab governments any important decision of the AHC had to be ratified by them. Rather than directing events in Palestine, the Palestinian leadership was to be found shuttling from one Arab capital to another. Palestinian interests were to be increasingly marginal to governments in Damascus, Cairo, Baghdad and Amman whose main concern was to counter the influence of their rivals.

The British prepared the withdrawal from Palestine almost as soon as the UN vote had been taken. By the end of March 1948 increasing areas of Palestine ceased to be under Mandatory control. In the place of the British, Palestinians aided by the Arab Liberation Army and the Jews by the Haganah attempted to exercise authority. The British having refused to cooperate with the United Nations concentrated on an orderly withdrawal of their forces. Less orderly was the transfer of administration with the result that the civilian population was threatened with a complete collapse of government services. The Palestinian population was particularly exposed to this dislocation as there was no Arab equivalent to the Jewish Agency and it was thus reliant on the British administration. For the Jewish population the situation was quite different as the Jewish Agency already provided key services. Thus while the Jewish community found itself beleaguered its institutions and leadership were able to offer the rudiments of self-government. Palestinians on the other hand had lost the administrative structures of the mandate and lacked either institutions or effective leadership to take its place. Jewish society became more cohesive while Palestinian society was increasingly atomized.

DECLARATION OF THE JEWISH STATE

Before the British mandate ended the Jewish Agency had begun to convert itself into a provisional government. On April 12 the Jewish Agency Executive authorized the transformation of the existing organs into state-like institutions. A Peoples Council was to act as legislature, and a Peoples Administration was the executive. These were not merely changes of nomenclature but represented a determined step toward creating the Jewish state. When the mandate ended on May 14, 1948, it was in the name of the Peoples Council that the declaration of the State of Israel was made. The decision on statehood had been taken by the Peoples Administration two days before by a narrow 6–4 vote in favor. The hesitancy on the question as expressed in the vote was due to the precarious military situation. This was dramatized by events the following day when Kafr Etzion (near Jerusalem) fell to the Arab Legion with the massacre of those who surrendered, combatants and civilians alike. However, it was also international developments that made the decision on statehood pressing. At the United Nations concrete proposals for withdrawing partition and turning Palestine into a UN Trust were under discussion. Ben-Gurion realized that the end of the mandate would create a decisive moment. He was also concerned that delay would increase the hesitations on Jewish statehood in the US administration. A day before the declaration Ben-Gurion would have known that the USSR was positively disposed. Mier Vilner, leader of the Communist Party, needed Moscow's pre-approval for his signature of the declaration of independence which he received on May 13.[6] By making the declaration at the same moment as the British withdrew Ben-Gurion knew there would be no uneasy interregnum and the Great Powers would have less room for maneuver. The high command of the Haganah was not sanguine about the battle ahead.[7] Nonetheless on this occasion politics was to be the order of the day. As the British left, Jewish forces had been successful in bringing about 20 percent of Palestine under its control.[8]

On the night of May 14, 1948, David Ben-Gurion read the Declaration of the Establishment of the State of Israel at the Tel Aviv museum. The declaration carefully balanced the legitimacy for the state on the basis of historical claims and the way that these had been recognized by the international community. The declaration thus placed itself within the objective set by the founding Zionist conference in 1897 to establish the Jewish national home by "public law." There was no invocation of a divine right to the state. The declaration narrates the secular Zionist story of a people "being forcibly exiled from their land" and who "never ceased to pray and hope for their return to it and for the restoration in it of their political freedom."[9] As a consequence, "Jews strove in every generation to reestablish themselves in their ancient homeland." Thus the trope of exile and return were woven into the text. This was reinforced by the reference to Herzl who is described as the "spiritual father of the Jewish state" and to the first Zionist conference as proclaiming the "right of the Jewish people to national re-birth in its own country." The declaration continues:

This right was recognized in the Balfour Declaration...and reaffirmed in the Mandate of the League of Nations, which in particular, gave international sanction to the historic connection between the Jewish people and Eretz-Israel and to the right of the Jewish people to rebuild its national home.

The declaration then turns to the Holocaust which was not given as the justification for the creation of the state but as the acute modern example of why the Zionist movement's project of overcoming the homelessness of the Jewish people was necessary:

The catastrophe which recently befell the Jewish people – the massacre of millions of Jews in Europe – was another clear demonstration of the urgency of solving the problem of its homelessness by reestablishing in Eretz-Israel the Jewish state, which would open the gates of the homeland wide to every Jew and confer upon the Jewish people the status of a fully privileged member of the comity of nations.

Survivors of the Nazi holocaust in Europe, as well as Jews from other parts of the world, continued to migrate to Eretz-Israel, undaunted by difficulties, restrictions and dangers and never ceased to assert their right to a life of dignity, freedom and honest toil in their national homeland.

This passage was important as the Holocaust is carefully positioned in the text, as part of the narrative of the Jewish people. As time has elapsed there has been a widespread assumption that the Holocaust was the central reason for the creation of a Jewish state. However, within the declaration no such claim is made in the name of the Jewish people. Thus as we have seen, with the exception of the Soviet Union, none of the main actors at the time saw Israel's creation as recompense for the Holocaust.

The arguments for statehood were rooted in a series of references to the international community's legal recognition of the existence of the Jewish people and their national rights in Palestine:

On the 29th of November, 1947, the United Nations General Assembly passed a resolution calling for the establishment of a Jewish State in Eretz-Israel; the General Assembly required the inhabitants of Eretz-Israel to take such steps as were necessary on their part for the implementation of that resolution. This recognition by the United Nations of the right of the Jewish people to establish their state is irrevocable.

This was an interesting interpretation of the resolution which, while it did call on all parties to assist with its implementation, was characterized as a requirement in the declaration. In this account the creation of the state became an act of compliance with the United Nations. However, the text also referred to the creation of the state as emanating from a "natural right." This reinforced the earlier formulation that the international community's positive law grants recognition to already existing rights rather than establishing them. This is an important argument that was to become increasingly central to the Israeli legal narrative. It had aspects in common with the Palestinian view which also had claimed similar natural rights existed.

In the operative paragraph of the declaration this becomes clear:

Accordingly we, members of the People's Council, representatives of the Jewish community of Eretz-Israel and of the Zionist movement, are here assembled on this day of the termination of the British Mandate over Eretz-Israel and by virtue of our natural and historic right and on the strength of the resolution of the United Nations General Assembly, hereby declare the establishment of a Jewish state in Eretz-Israel, to be known as the State of Israel.

The declaration continued to outline guarantees to all citizens "irrespective of religion, race or sex," promised to safeguard the holy places and to be faithful to the United Nations. The reference to the partition plan, however, continued in a part of the declaration that has often been overlooked. The State of Israel "is prepared to cooperate with the agencies and representatives of the United Nations in implementing the resolution of the General Assembly of the 29th November 1947, and will take steps to bring about the economic union of the whole of *Eretz-Israel*." This could have been used by the Arab states and the Palestinians to good effect at the end of the war. However, having rejected partition in principle they were unable to do so.

The declaration thus placed the new state entirely within the legitimacy of the United Nations. It can be read as an instrument to implement the partition resolution, as the last quotation makes clear. This fealty to the United Nations was critical in making the case for recognition of the state and also for applying for UN membership itself. It also seized the legal ground from the Arab cause; the declaration of the new state was the implementation of the will of the international community. Arab opposition was to be seen not merely as an assault on the Jewish state but as an attack on the international community.

While the Palestinians and Arab states denounced the declaration as illegitimate no corresponding declaration of Palestine was forthcoming. There was indeed some confusion in the Arab League about the legal status of Palestine after the end of the mandate. While reference was made in the May 15 Arab League statement to Palestinian independence, no steps were taken to appeal for recognition or to form a Palestinian government. At the time, it should be pointed out, Palestinians and the Arab Legion controlled the lion's share of the country. The Mufti did suggest the creation of such a government but wrangling in the Arab League and the complete opposition of the Jordanians prevented it. Even after the first two phases of the 1948 war (May 15–June 11 and July 8–18) while the Arab side still retained control of most of Palestine no government was formed. The arguments within the Arab League continued about the creation of a Palestinian government, but without any agreement. Those parts of Palestine under Arab control were placed under the command of district governors but there was no attempt to coordinate these at a national level.

It was only at the beginning of September that the Arab League was to announce that AHC member Ahmed Hilmi would become the "head" of civil administration for Palestine. On September 20 Hilmi was named as the Prime Minister of an All-Palestine Government to be based in Gaza. While the Arab League had taken the decision, the Jordanians had vigorously opposed it and refused to let the government operate anywhere on the territory it controlled. When the AHC eventually issued a communiqué announcing the formation of the government it claimed that "the inhabitants of Palestine, by virtue of their natural right to self-determination and in accordance with the resolutions of the Arab League, have decided to declare Palestine in its entirety... as an independent state."[10] A Palestine National Council was then convened in Gaza presided over by the Mufti which issued a formal declaration of independence. However, on the same day (September 30) the Jordanian government convened the rival "First Palestine Congress" in Amman. It was attended by several thousand delegates (as opposed to the 75 who had gathered in Gaza) and adopted resolutions denouncing the Gaza government and defining Palestine and Jordan as a single territorial unit.[11] The All-Palestine Government issued passports and attempted to revive the militia, the Holy War Army, but did little else. Within two weeks of its formation all its ministers were transferred to Cairo due to the last phase of the war. Once in Cairo the government decomposed although it limped on as a "department" of the Arab League until it was finally dissolved by President Nasser in 1959.[12] The Jordanians disarmed any units of the Holy War Army in the West Bank and stamped out any sign of support for the Gaza government. The Second Palestine Congress (December 1, 1948), sealed the unity of Arab Palestine with Jordan with the "election" of Abdullah as King.[13] This resulted in the formal incorporation of the West Bank and East Jerusalem into Jordan, a process completed in 1950. The Palestinian leadership had become captive to the rivalries of the Arab League. It was due to the League's prevarications that no initiatives were taken to declare a state and form a government. The political ease with which the Hashemites were able to effect their plan of integrating as much of Palestine as possible into their kingdom underlined the collapse of an independent Palestinian perspective.

The Arab League having taken responsibility for Palestine was to prove incapable of protecting Palestinians or the legal integrity of the Palestinian territory their forces controlled. The erosion of Palestinian leadership and the failures of the Arab League left the Palestinian population exposed to the disaster of the war. This had been evident as the inter-communal war intensified when the British pulled back their forces in the early months of 1948. Lacking protection, administrative institutions or any clear political perspective thousands of Palestinians began to flee the country. At first it was the wealthier sections of the population but rapidly wider sections of the population joined them. The insecurity of the Palestinian population was evident as the battle lines moved between the countryside and the mixed towns. Increasingly, civilians became victims of the fighting. While many fled the constantly moving front line others were terrorized by the fear that incidents such as Deir Yassin (where at least 110 civilians were massacred by the Irgun in April) would become the pattern of the future. As a result of this combined process by May 14 some 300,000 or 23 percent of the Palestinian population had fled their homes. The Palestinian refugee problem had begun.

In the international war following Israel's creation the rate of flight was to increase. Within the first four weeks of fighting a further 100,000 fled. By the end of the war in December 1948 the total figure of displaced Palestinians was put at 726,000 by the United Nations. As with all statistics, so with the numbers for Palestinian refugees there has been a war of figures. Palestinian estimates have sometimes reached 1 million whereas the Israeli official position was that 530,000 Palestinians left the area that became Israel. In the most authoritative study of the issue Benny Morris thinks a more accurate estimate would be between 600,000 and 760,000.[14] Whatever the exact figure it was clear that after the war ended some 369 villages within Israel's territory had been abandoned[15] and hundreds of thousands of Palestinians had become refugees in neighboring countries or displaced within Palestine itself. Within the newly formed State of Israel the remaining Palestinian Arab population was somewhere between 140,000 and 170,000, compared to the 722,000 who according to mandate estimates were living in these areas at the end of 1946. This was a disaster for the individuals who lost their homes and land and were thrust into the limbo of the dispossessed. For Palestinians as a people the disaster went much deeper than personal tragedies to become the defining moment of Palestinian contemporary history.[16] This intertwining of personal dispossession and national displacement has become known as the Palestinian *nakba* (Arabic for "catastrophe").

Political and legal responsibility for the Palestinian refugees and the demise of Palestine in 1948 has been much debated and remains central to contemporary efforts to resolve the conflict. At the heart of any just solution is the resolution of the refugee issue. Both Israelis and Palestinians regard each other as bearing both moral and legal responsibility for the situation. Thus while Palestinian leaders hold that it was Israel's creation that led to the problem, Israeli governments argue that it was Arab aggression which created the conditions for mass flight. These arguments have been engaged with by a group of Middle East scholars who attempted to provide evidence that the refugee problem was the consequence of the Zionist project. The creation of a Jewish state, it has been argued, was premised on the removal of the Palestinian population. Indeed the 1948 refugees were in reality expelled. This issue goes to the heart of the possibilities for resolving the conflict as proponents of the view that refugees were expelled as part of a Zionist plan tend to view Israel itself as the obstacle to peace.

The discussion of the refugee question refracts some of the key issues raised in the debate over partition. The official Zionist narrative on the refugees holds that Palestinian flight was a result of the specific conditions of the war. As the war was initiated by the Arab states, Israel cannot be held morally or legally responsible for its consequences. Indeed in some versions of this history it was the Arab and Palestinian leadership which advised the population to flee. The Zionists had no intention of displacing Palestinians who had been offered full equality in the Jewish state.

Since 1948 a Palestinian counter-narrative has solidified which claims that the Zionists took advantage of the war to expel the Palestinian population in order to create space for a Jewish state. This was the result of a premeditated plan that was intrinsic to the expansionist nature of Zionism. Israel therefore must bear the full responsibility for the refugees.

In order to explore these arguments I am going to engage with three scholars who have worked on the topic: Nur Masalha, Ilan Pappé and Benny Morris. For Masalha[17] Zionism contained within it the logic of the forced transfer of Palestinians from its inception. Pappé characterizes the events of 1948 as "ethnic cleansing" which had been planned in advance.[18] Whereas Masalha and Pappé build the argument that any such expulsions would be morally and legally unacceptable, Morris takes a rather unique position in claiming that the expulsion of Palestinians would have been justified.

Masalha's core argument is that Zionism was based on the policy of Palestinian transfer out of the projected Jewish state. For him the mass flight in 1948 confirms this thesis:

> The general endorsement of the transfer solution and the attempt to promote it secretly by the mainstream labour leaders, some of whom played a decisive role in the 1948 war, highlight the ideological intent that made the 1948 refugee exodus possible.[19]

The term "ideological intent" is perplexing as ideologies are incapable of possessing intention, as intentions can only be possessed by an individual human being. However, one assumes the author was suggesting that Zionism rested on a determinist premise from which it could never escape. Yet at the same time Masalha asserted that Zionist leaders generally "endorsed" this premise but promoted it "secretly." Such formulations are widely in circulation and need to be assessed.

The idea of transfer or exchange of populations was indeed discussed in the Zionist movement. It was true that some leaders of the movement did advocate such a policy vigorously. Usefully, Benny Morris, in his role as supporter of transfer, attempted to produce evidence that this idea was deeply embedded in Zionism by reviewing statements on the subject by Zionist leaders from Herzl onwards.[20] He began with reference to Herzl's 1895 diary entry when he mused that for the Jews to secure their home they might need to "spirit the penniless population across the border." At the time Herzl was thinking of a Jewish state in Argentina. However, as Morris admitted, the idea did not reappear in his writing and was not part of his *Jewish State*. Indeed in Herzl's utopian novel *Altneuland*, published in 1902, his character Rashid Bey expresses surprise at a question asking him if the Jews had forced the Arabs to leave the country.[21] Morris next turned to Arthur Ruppin, head of the Zionist Organization's Palestine Office, who is quoted as recommending a "limited population transfer." This conditional remark was made on one occasion and Ruppin abandoned any such idea when he became a founder in 1925 of the *Brit Shalom* movement whose purpose was to work for full equality between Jews and Arabs.[22] Leon Motzkin and Israel Zangwill are produced in evidence and the latter in particular did make the case publicly for transfer or exchanging populations before and after World War I.[23] However, he stood out precisely because his views seemed to garner little support and were indeed regarded as extremely provocative.[24] No articles, speeches or official resolutions of the Zionist movement can be produced on the subject.[25] Morris ignored the discussion at the closed debate of the seventh Zionist Congress (1905) which exhaustively discussed Jewish–Arab relations without proposing transfer. It was at that conference that Yizhak Epstein had argued for an alliance between Jews and Arabs against Ottoman rule. This he said would ensure that Jewish immigrants would act not as conquerors but as participants in a struggle for liberation alongside the Arabs. While there were disagreements with his views on tactical grounds it was not because he assumed the Arab population would remain in place.[26] Morris is forced to admit that the revisionist Zionist leader Zeev Jabotinsky was totally opposed to transfer, explaining in 1931 "we don't want to evict even one Arab from the left or right banks of the Jordan."[27] As we can see Morris can produce only meager evidence for his view.

Interestingly the idea of transfer of populations was discussed by the British and the Jordanians. John Glubb wrote that he personally discussed Jordanian plans for partition and population exchanges with Lord Moyne, Britain's Middle East Minister in the early 1940s. "Any necessary exchanges of population could have been carried out without unnecessary hardship," he recorded.[28] It was, however, the Peel Commission's proposal for partition based on exchanges of population that provoked the widest discussion of the issue in the Zionist movement. Ben-Gurion seized on the idea of any Jewish state even if it only comprised 20 percent of Palestine. In arguing against those who rejected the idea he did emphasize the population exchange element of the plan. The proposal had come from the British and not the Zionist movement. It is difficult to cast Ben-Gurion as the author of transfer in such a context. This can be seen clearly when later he rejected outright the policy of the British Labour Party for a Jewish state based on the transfer of the Palestinians.

It is not only Morris who relies on marginal and contingent evidence for Zionist transfer policy. In attempting to make his case Masalha claims that Weizmann had a formulated plan for transfer as early as 1930.[29] The evidence for this plan is said to be recorded in conversations with British officials. However, on further investigation we find that these discussions were in response to the 1929 disturbances which had led to the deaths of 133 Jews.

PARTITION BY FORCE 141

The British it appeared had suggested to Weizmann that one of the reasons for the violence was landlessness caused by land sales to Jews. Weizmann apparently suggested that the British could help solve the problem by offering Palestinian land in Transjordan. He was hardly proposing the transfer of the entire Palestinian population and was no doubt attempting to embarrass the British into taking responsibility for what was in fact their own policy.

All those searching for evidence of a transfer strategy alight on the figure of Yosef Weitz who campaigned for the Zionist movement to adopt such a policy both before and after the creation of Israel. He was the head of the Jewish Agency lands commission and served as an advisor to David Ben-Gurion on many occasions. In May 1948 he proposed that the provisional government should establish transfer committees to implement his plan, but this was rejected by Ben-Gurion. His open espousal of the policy and its regular rejection by all official bodies in the Zionist movement and then the Israeli government hardly lend credence to the view that transfer was central to Zionism. Had it been so it would be curious that Weitz would have had to raise the issue repeatedly and to express regret that his views were equally regularly rejected.

As Yosef Gorny convincingly argues[30] the central concern of Zionist thought was to formulate the best form of state structure that could accommodate a Jewish national home. As he demonstrates, the Zionist movement in its pre-state existence advocated a variety of options all of which envisaged some form of power-sharing with the Arabs – most through some form of federalism. Jabotinsky supported parliamentary federalism, the labor movement favored autonomous federalism, Ben-Gurion advocated parity federalism and Hashomer Hatzair was committed to a bi-national state.[31] The merits of these different projects were continuously discussed from 1905 until 1946. None of these plans involved the transfer of populations much less the expulsion of the Palestinians. There were no proposals for a unitary state based on a homogeneous Jewish population. Ben-Gurion and other factions often placed great emphasis on creating a Jewish majority in Palestine, but that was to be achieved by immigration of Jews not the eviction of the Palestinians.

In the absence of any substantial documentary evidence the proponents of the view that transfer is essential to Zionism are often forced to suggest that the policy was so critical that it had to be kept secret. This would mean that we have to accept that the movement was able to keep this central tenet of its policies secret for half a century and that all proposals not containing this vital element were an elaborate smokescreen. In addition we would have to believe that no note or memo would survive and that every memoir of those involved would have been censored. Given the democratic nature of Zionism, its pluralism and frequent acrimonious factional struggles this would seem unlikely. It would also imply that a movement with few resources would have had the capacity to silence debates in the lively Hebrew press not just in Palestine but internationally. Nor of course would this explain why those who did advocate it, such as Weitz, were permitted to breach this silence.

There is another problem with the notion of secrecy. Zionism like any other political movement was sustained by education and motivated by belief. Transfer would need to be part of the program, explained and advocated in order to mobilize the membership. Thousands of people would have to be armed with the ideology and capacity to carry it out.

It is also the case that if secrecy had been at such a premium it would be odd that Ben-Gurion would so publicly endorse the Peel Commission's proposals. Yet Masalha, who believes that secrecy was critical, specifically refers to Ben-Gurion's remarks on the issue as evidence that it was a Zionist policy.[32] Masalha would have to explain how such a public position could have come about. Either transfer was a secret policy or it was not. It would also be odd that Zionist leaders would not refer to the policy in privately circulated documents. Yet when in the 1940s Ben-Gurion's plan for the ambitious Palestine-Jordanian confederation was written only for the few members of the Jewish Agency Executive, transfer was not mentioned.[33] Masalha's argument also means that we would have to believe that all the Jewish Agency's statements to the United Nations during the partition debates were dissimulation. In those debates it should be pointed out that the official position of the Jewish Agency was that not a single Arab in Palestine should be moved from their home and that the Jewish state would guarantee for all equality to its citizens without discrimination. As we have seen the latter commitments were contained in the declaration of independence. Such positions were in stark contrast to the Palestinian policy for a state that would constitutionally guarantee an Arab ascendancy and deny citizenship to tens of thousands of Jews.

In producing the first systematic study of Palestinian mass flight in 1987 Benny Morris worked a great deal on previously unpublished Israeli archives. He divided the exodus into four waves. The first takes place entirely in the context of the inter-communal war (December 1947–March 1948); the second from the end of the civil war into the first phase of the international war (April–June); the third from July to October; and the fourth in October and November. Each of these phases was mapped onto particular stages of the military conflict. In Morris' first phase the Arabs held the initiative in the fighting although Jewish forces began to assert themselves at the end of the period. During this first period according to British figures the hostilities had left 895 Jews and 991 Arabs dead,[34] indicating a higher proportional death rate for Jews than Arabs. However, as the conflict became international the advantage seized by the Jews was consolidated and over the second half of 1948 the area of Jewish control grew dramatically from 20 percent of Palestine at the beginning of the war to 78 percent at its end. Morris' study found that some 450,000 Palestinians were to flee or be exiled during this period. These are enormous figures and produced a human tragedy on a massive scale. Morris concluded his 1987 study with the assessment that:

> The Palestinian refugee problem was born of war, not by design, Jewish or Arab. It was largely a by-product of Arab and Jewish fears and of that protracted, bitter fighting that characterized the first Israeli–Arab war; in smaller part it was the deliberate creation of Jewish and Arab military commanders and politicians.[35]

By 2004 while not substantially changing his view that "war not design" caused the Palestinian exodus Morris develops a new position in his approach which regards displacement of the Arabs as "inherent in Zionist ideology."[36] However, he had a curious argument for this which is quite distinct from the positions of Masalha or Pappé. For Morris, what happened in 1948 was the logical outcome of the land purchase and settlement that had been taking place since the arrival of the Zionists in Palestine in the late nineteenth century. It is difficult to equate land purchased at the market rate with the mass flight of Palestinians in 1948. As we have pointed out, in any event land purchases had been relatively small during the Mandate and most Jews lived in the cities. Landlessness that was created in Palestine was not substantially different to landlessness created through the commodification of land elsewhere. While in Palestine land transactions had national implications for both communities, they were not of the same type that took place in European settlement colonies in the Americas, Australasia and parts of Africa. In those cases the indigenous population was forcibly removed and land was allocated to settlers at nominal prices. The Jewish acquisition of land followed a quite different pattern and was extremely modest. It seems rather overblown to conflate such prosaic land transfers with mass expulsions and massacres such as occurred at Lydda in 1948 where 250 people died.[37] Morris' new assessment was explained in his *Haaretz* interview where he reveals his conversion to the idea of transfer. It appears that he revised his book on the refugee issue not as a result of new historical evidence but due to his changed political position.[38]

Morris' views on transfer thus involve not new evidence but a new reading of the existing documents. In this he adopts a position similar to Pappé who takes a postmodern deconstructive hatchet to some key 1948 texts. His central focus is Plan D produced by the Haganah National Command in March 1948. Before turning to the details of the plan it is critical to reflect on the context in which this military strategy was written.

If the Arab states had been weak in military preparations they had been extremely strong on bellicose rhetoric. The regular threats to use force were accompanied by speeches of some invective against the Jews. Arab League Secretary Azzam's statement in an October 1947 speech, that "this war will be a war of extermination and a momentous massacre which will be spoken of like the Mongol massacres and the Crusades,"[39] was a telling example. If such remarks which were widely reported in the Arabic press were meant to raise the morale of the Arab cause, they certainly delivered a sobering message to the Jews. Two years after the Holocaust a new extermination was being threatened. Azzam's statement, it should be stressed, was made only a month after holding talks with Abba Eban and David Hurewitz representing the Jewish Agency in a bid to avoid war. The Secretary of the Arab League made ominously clear at the meeting that there was no need for any agreement as the Jewish presence in Palestine would only be temporary.[40] Azzam's sentiments were not unrepresentative at the time. The war aims of the Arab states appeared even more drastic than their political program. This would have to be taken into account in Jewish military planning.

It is against this background that Pappé claims that Plan D was a "blue print for ethnic cleansing."[41] His case relies on a particular interpretation of one part of Plan D. The clause appeared in a section of the plan entitled "Consolidation of Defense Systems and Fortifications" and reads:

Mounting operations against enemy population centres located inside or near our defensive system in order to prevent them from being used as bases by an active armed force. These operations can be divided into the following categories:

Destruction of villages (setting fire to, blowing up, and planting mines in the debris), especially of those population centres which are difficult to control continuously.

Mounting search and control operations according to the following guidelines: encirclement of the village and conducting a search inside it, in the event of resistance, the armed force must be destroyed and the population must be expelled outside the borders of the state.[42]

There is no doubt that this provided for the expulsion of civilians. However, was this part of a coordinated and systematic plan? To answer this question we need to look more carefully at the clause and to place it in the context of the overall plan. Its objective was "to gain control of the areas of the Hebrew state and defend its borders. It also aims at gaining control of areas of Jewish settlement and concentration which are located outside the borders against regular, semi-regular, and small forces operated from outside or inside the state."[43] The plan that followed was thus aimed at securing the area allocated for the Jewish state and to provide protection to Jewish communities outside those boundaries. The key area of Jewish settlement outside the UN borders was of course Jerusalem where some 100,000 Jews lived. The plan, however, envisaged that the Israeli forces would have to deal with a multi-faceted armed threat that would be operated from bases "outside and inside the state." The plan then outlined a series of assumptions about the enemy whose forces were specified as:

- The semi-regular forces of the Liberation Amy affiliated with the Arab League, which operate from already occupied bases or bases to be occupied in the future.
- The regular forces of neighboring countries, which will launch an invasion across the borders, or will operate from bases inside the country (the Arab Legion).
- Small local forces which operate, or will operate, from bases inside the country and within the borders of the Hebrew state.[44]

It was noticeable that the plan distinguished the territory of British Mandate Palestine in general (the "country") from the UN area for the Jewish state. This made clear that the expectation of the military planners was that international enemy bases would be established inside the Jewish state as well as in other parts of Palestine. As a result under the operational objectives the plan stated that the Israeli forces must restrict "the capability of the enemy by carrying out limited operations; occupation and control of certain of his bases in rural and urban areas within the borders of the state."[45]

Plan D was based on a reasonable assessment that threats to the Jewish state would not come from a classical invasion by neighboring armies crossing a clearly established border but that the strategy of the regular armies would be to link up with irregular and other armed groups already acting behind the lines. This would in part take the form of establishing bases from which to operate. Thus the clause that Pappé had placed so much emphasis on needs to be read carefully in its context. As the text reads, expulsion occurs in the event of "resistance" by an "armed force." This was certainly more conditional and limited a plan than Pappé suggests. If there was any doubt about the conditional character of expulsion the following clause made this clear:

> In the absence of resistance, garrison troops will enter the village and take up positions in it... The officer in command of the unit will confiscate all weapons, wireless devices, and motor vehicles in the village. In addition he will detain all politically suspect individuals. After consultation with the [Jewish] political authorities, bodies will be appointed from the village to administer the internal affairs of the village. In every region a [Jewish] person will be appointed to be responsible for arranging the political and administrative affairs of all [Arab] villages and population centers which are occupied within that region.[46]

From this we should understand that the villages referred to are viewed from the military and not the ethnic viewpoint. The overwhelming concern was whether or not the village concerned was being used as a military base. The type of war envisaged was one where there would be no clear front line and in which civilian areas would become drawn into the military conflict. The issue was not that all civilian areas would be problematic but rather those locations that commanded strategic advantage for the adversary. This was certainly the case given the character of UN borders for the Jewish and Arab states. As we have noted, many in UNSCOP thought that the borders themselves as they weaved through the country could breed intimacy between the two peoples. In war time such intimacy was to prove deadly. As a result civilian areas could be quickly transformed into military sites. It was rarely the case that the people themselves wanted to transform their homes into military encampments. However, through clan loyalty, intimidation and the course of the hostilities tens of thousands of civilians found themselves in such a situation.

The idea that Plan D's principal objective was to expel civilians hardly appears consistent with the May 11 statement of Israel Galili (head of the Haganah National Command), that "up to May 15 we must continue to implement the plan of military operations [i.e. Plan D]...which did not take into account the collapse and flight of the Arab settlements following the rout in Haifa." He added, however, that "this collapse facilitates our tasks."[47] This comment sheds a great deal of light on the events of this period. That the author of Plan D was surprised by the flight undermines the argument that this had been its aim. It was also evident from the context that the tasks Galili was referring to were military and not a reference to a political program.

There is no question, as the work of Morris and Yoav Gelber demonstrates, that through 1948 the IDF was involved in the expulsion of thousands of Palestinians from their homes. The course of the battle seemed to dictate the intensity of these operations. However, only a minority of displaced Palestinians were removed by such means. That should not obscure the fact that these actions could have been responsible for the flight of many times more civilians who feared the same fate and took matters into their own hands. It was also evident that the pattern of flight differed from theater to theater, and to some extent was dependent on those in command. This can be seen in the pattern of Arab residence after the fighting was over. Few remained in the corridor between Tel Aviv and Jerusalem although the Galilee retained a large Arab population. This would undermine the argument that there was a systematic plan and that Plan D was it.

At the time there was little Palestinian or Arab comment on the legal implications of the flight itself. The concept of ethnic cleansing was not to be developed until the 1990s when the term emerged in the Balkan wars. That was part of a political design by some sections of the Serbian leadership to lay the basis for a Greater Serbia without Muslim or Croat inhabitants. In that case the purpose of the war was to remove the undesired population. In 1948 the situation was rather different. The *Yishuv* and then Israel fought a defensive war against those who wanted to destroy the Jewish state. The war was not initiated by Israel but by the Arab states who had been threatening to use force since 1946. During 1947 in the public debates of the United Nations they had laid their legal basis for launching the war. In those debates and the contemporary statements from the Arab League the aim of preventing or defeating the Jewish state often merged into threats to remove the Jews from Palestine by one means or another. While much research has been done on the Zionists and 1948 there has not been as serious attention paid to the Arab military strategy and political aims.

However, it is evident that in the areas of Palestine that the Arab forces did succeed in holding – the West Bank, Gaza and East Jerusalem – all Jews were expelled. As the course of the war favored the Israelis there were less opportunities to assess Arab treatment of Jewish civilians. However, in the inter-communal war and in the areas with Jewish civilians that fell to Arab control there seems little doubt that Jewish civilians were seen as targets for attack and expulsion.

At that time the legal rights of civilians in time of war were regulated by The Hague Conventions and Regulations of 1899 and 1907. These groundbreaking treaties had elaborated the principles for the conduct of war on the basis of the distinction between civilians and the military. What the 1948 war proved was the difficulty in making this distinction in an armed conflict where civilian centers became military theaters. World War II had demonstrated this problem on a grand scale as the battlefield often became the city. In Palestine, as we have seen, the consequence of this was that towns and villages became enemy bases. As a result military commanders began to view the civilians themselves as a factor in the fighting. Thus in the terms of Plan D Palestinian civilians living in enemy controlled areas became a justified target. According to this view by removing those civilians a military threat could be eliminated. The return of civilian Palestinians was also seen in this light. In June 1948 the head of IDF's Military Intelligence Department made this clear when he wrote:

> There is a substantial return movement of the villagers who had fled to neighboring countries during this cease-fire. There is a serious danger that these returnees will refortify their villages

which lie deep behind our front lines, and with the renewal of military activities they will become a fifth column, if not effective nests of resistance.[48]

As the war wore on Israeli casualties mounted (1 percent of all Palestinian Jews were to die), and as the conditions in Jewish areas worsened the IDF became more determined to eliminate all sources of threats against the new state.[49] Civilians were increasingly seen as at the very least collaborators with the enemy. Those attempting return were seen as effective reinforcements for the Arab war effort.

Civilians were seen as a threat to peace not only in Palestine in the 1940s. In the wake of World War II not only were the borders of Europe changed in favor of the victors but the German population of Eastern and Central Europe including the Eastern territories of Germany itself were forcibly removed. In all between 10 and 12 million Germans were moved from their homes. Normally given little notice and only allowed to take one small bag they were evicted at gunpoint. In the mass movement west virtually no assistance was given to the victims. Most were forced to walk long distances without medical attention; 1 million died. This great forced removal of civilians was done when there was no military threat; it was largely an act of collective punishment. By cleansing the Eastern territories of Germans the Soviet Union could expand west, in the process transforming Koenigsberg into Kaliningrad. It was justified as an act to safeguard the people of Europe. Anyone who spoke up for the German refugees was to be denounced as a warmonger. Israel's actions appeared to be less calculated than this policy that was broadly supported in the West as well as in the USSR. The brutality suffered by civilians in both cases has not been equally remembered by the international community. There is virtually no popular and very little academic interest in Europe's dispossessed of the 1940s unlike those of Palestine. However, both Israel and the European states will not entertain the return of the expellees or their descendants. Rightly there is concern about the fate of the Palestinian refugees, although by contrast little is even remembered of the German experience of mass expulsion in the period 1945–49.[50]

Israel, as it was fighting over its borders, appealed for international recognition and for membership of the United Nations. President Truman on behalf of the United States recognized the state *de facto* within hours. This action was against the advice of the State Department and almost caused the resignation of the entire

US mission at the United Nations – which was still pursuing its trusteeship line. Jan Smuts, the South African Prime Minister, and the long-standing Zionists soon followed suit. It was the Soviet Union which on May 18, 1948, accorded Israel its first *de jure* recognition by a major power. The recognition of the Jewish state by the two main world powers within days of its creation was another major achievement for Zionist diplomacy.

The parties to the conflict partitioned Palestine according to the course of the war. The Jewish state emerged with more territory than allocated to it by the United Nations. The Jordanians had expanded to their west and Egyptians had won control of Gaza. It was to be a partition of Palestine without Palestine itself. Palestinian society had been shattered and hundreds of thousands of Palestinians were displaced.

The Palestinian disaster was not merely the result of Israel's military success. Nor was it brought about by a big power conspiracy in which the United States or the USSR had acted to eliminate a people. The Palestinian leadership under the Mufti had been inept internationally and poorly organized in Palestine itself. As a result, the Arab League in attempting to step into the vacuum had merely imposed the rivalries of the Arab states on the Palestinians as each jockeyed for advantage. The Jordanians undoubtedly came out on top, at least for the next two decades. The Arab states' belief that ultimately force could prevent partition had been proved wrong. However, the idea that force of arms would ultimately win justice for the Palestinians had not died and was to intensify. The legal arguments against partition were now turned against Israel which was denounced as an illegitimate state, one that could hardly be mentioned by name in Arab League circles. It became the "Zionist entity."

The term attempted to convey the counterfeit nature of Israel and to imply that it was transient in nature. The assumption that the Zionist moment in the Middle East would be fleeting became a common view in the Arab world. The prediction of the Arab representatives in the General Assembly debates appeared to be coming true. Jewish expansionism had been proved by Israel's new size and the large number of refugees. However, as Walter Laqueur commented, Zionism was not "bound to result in the evacuation or expulsion of many Palestinian Arabs from Palestine." He continued:

Had the Arabs accepted the Peel Plan in 1937, the Jewish State would have been restricted to the coast plain between Tel Aviv and Haifa. Had they not rejected the UN partition plan, most of Palestine would have remained in their hands. The Arab thesis of inevitable Zionist expansion is a case of self-fulfilling prophecy; the Arabs did everything to make their prophecy come true by choosing the road of armed resistance – and losing. The Zionist movement and the Yishuv matured in the struggle against the Arab national movement. Eventually it reached the conclusion that it was pointless to seek Arab agreement and that it could achieve its aims only against the Arabs.[51]

This assessment might seem harsh in many ways but the commitment to armed resistance has dogged the Palestinian–Israeli conflict. It might be more accurate to say that both sides have seen force as their ultimate means of national survival. It was thus in the period 1946–49 that the lethal concoction of law and force was brewed. It was not that force was seen as a last resort but rather both sides began to believe that it was their legal right to achieve their aims through it. As we shall see in the next chapters, when negotiations began decades later such sanctified violence was rarely absent from the agenda.

6
From Mutual Denial to Mutual Recognition

The events of 1948 were to imprint themselves in the narratives of Palestinians and Israelis. For Palestinians the *nakba* became central to the forging of a discourse of dispossession; for Israelis 1948 was the moment of national liberation. The tropes of homelessness and return were to be reversed; exiled Jews had returned home, Palestinians had been exiled. For Jews the return was against the background of the destruction of the Holocaust in which the 1948 war was seen as a triumph of survival. Exile had been proved as a murderous trap. Winning the 1948 war was and could be seen as an essential prerequisite to continued existence. With the attributes of statehood Jews had the equipment to defend themselves. For Palestinians homelessness was both individual and collective. Individual losses coalesced with the loss of national entitlement. Dispossession could only be reversed by the return to the ancestral homeland. These discourses thus developed mutually exclusionary elements: Jewish survival became linked to Palestinian defeat while the restoration of Palestine required the removal of the Jews. Both peoples thus sought survival in the destruction of the other. This chapter surveys the way in which these discourses were to circulate even as outright mutual denial edged towards recognition and negotiations.

The 1948 war had partitioned Palestine into three territorial units, but not those envisaged by the United Nations. Israel had established itself within the Green Line of the 1949 Armistice agreements,[1] Jordan annexed the West Bank and Egypt became the occupier of the Gaza Strip. The Palestinian population found itself even more divided and dispersed not just living in the newly divided Palestine but also in large numbers as refugees in neighboring countries. The Jewish population of Palestine was entirely concentrated behind the Green Line. Jerusalem far from being internationalized had become a divided city with the east in Jordan and the west in Israel. One of the immediate results of the creation of Israel was the arrival of waves of Jewish immigrants. Over 100,000 arrived during the war year of 1948 alone. In the following three years Jewish immigration reached 560,000 meaning that the Jewish population had doubled in four years. Thus as Palestinians were experiencing the pains of dispersal Jewish Israel was consolidating itself. This process was not just demographic but also political and legal. Palestinians who remained in the non-Israeli controlled parts of Palestine became acculturated to the fundamentally different political and legal environments of Jordan and Egypt. Israel was meanwhile recognized by an increasing number of states and became a member of the United Nations in 1949. Palestine's partition by war seemed to have brought Palestine to an end.

This was certainly the reaction of the Israeli government. The results of the war seemed to remove the Palestine issue from the agenda. The Jordanian annexation of the West Bank only left the final disposal of Gaza to be decided. The new Israeli government did not consider the Palestinian refugees as their responsibility. Indeed as far as the Israeli government was concerned the Palestinian refugees had in fact been replaced by Jewish refugees fleeing from Arab countries. It was true that following the establishment of Israel the situation for the large Jewish communities in the Middle East and North Africa had become dire with political campaigns, legal restrictions and mob violence. As a result several hundred thousand Jews from the area migrated to Israel. Most had lost their property and arrived destitute. This population exchange was seen by Israel as an equitable result.

While the Zionist movement had historically related to the Arab presence in Palestine the newly formed Israeli state set out to deny the legitimacy of Arab Palestine at all levels. Israel viewed the rejection of the partition plan as the rejection of the Arab Palestinian state as well. By supporting what was regarded as an illegal war, the Palestinians had thus sealed their own fate. As a consequence Palestinians had lost their entitlement to national existence. All the results of the war, the refugees and the loss of territory were the responsibility of the party that had fought the war. The Arab states and not Israel were not just responsible for the refugees but also for the destruction of the right to self-determination. Having dissolved Palestine, the argument went, it was for the Arab states to resolve all the results, including absorbing the Palestinian refugees. The weight of this sentiment was to be felt once the Oslo peace process began as the Israeli side was to regard any steps towards Palestinian statehood, however limited, as a major concession which should be gratefully accepted by the Palestinians.

Variants of this Israeli account of 1948 endure to the current period and strongly influence the approach to current negotiations. While there is some merit in the view that the use of force in an effort to prevent partition was illegal it was problematic to then argue that the Palestinians had lost all legal entitlement or that all results of the Israeli use of self-defense were legitimate. Nor was it correct to argue that because the Israeli use of self-defense was justifiable that all military operations were conducted legally. While the forced movement of civilians was rooted in military considerations this did not mean that those military considerations were in conformity with the laws of war and The Hague Conventions. One of the problems with the highly rhetorical use of terms like "ethnic cleansing" and "transfer" in the work of scholars such as Pappé and Masalha, is that the actual breaches of international law during the 1948 war are often overlooked. War crimes committed by individuals are obscured by an ideological fog. Indeed it would be easy for Israel to dismiss these general charges of ethnic cleansing because the evidence, as we have seen, was so flimsy. The more ideological the prism through which 1948 is viewed, the less useful it becomes. This not merely affects general relations between Israelis and Palestinians but it would also become unhelpful in developing peace and reconciliation mechanisms that will be required in due course.

In dismissing Palestine in the 1950s Israel was not alone. The international community through the United Nations to a great extent focused on the humanitarian concerns of the refugees. In the resolutions of the United Nations General Assembly and Security Council there was silence about the issue of the Arab state in Palestine or the national rights of the Palestinians. This was to remain the case for two decades.

Even international concern for the refugees was muted. The United Nations General Assembly had adopted resolution 194 (III) in 1949 in which the topic was mentioned although in the context of a general resolution on the conflict. Refugees were dealt with in paragraph 11 – after access to the holy places, the internationalization of Jerusalem and the opening of transportation links to Jerusalem. This low priority is striking. It was also the case that the article did not unconditionally assert the right of the refugees to return to their homes. Rather, the General Assembly resolved that "refugees wishing to return to their homes and live at peace with their neighbors should be permitted to do so at the earliest practicable date, and that compensation should be paid for the property of those choosing not to return."[2] The way that the resolution was phrased seemed to assume that many refugees would not seek to return but would need compensation for their losses. This is significant given that the resolution was adopted so close to the flight of the Palestinians. Return was also conditional on the willingness to "live at peace with their neighbors." This phrase implied that Palestinians returning to their homes in Israel would at the very least have to accept the creation of the state and not to aid those wishing to destroy it. Given the general character of the resolution it is particularly significant that there is no mention of the need to create or establish an Arab Palestinian state. The refugees were placed under a special regime under the United Nations Relief and Works Agency for Palestine Refugees (UNRWA) established in 1949.[3] The definition of a Palestine refugee was "a person whose normal residence was Palestine for a minimum period of two years preceding the outbreak of the conflict in 1948 and who, as a result of this conflict, has lost both his home and his means of livelihood."[4] This definition was effectively to preclude Palestinians from relying on the later 1951 United Nations Convention on Refugees which was based on a different definition of a refugee.[5]

The incorporation of the West Bank into Jordan, although not internationally recognized, was nonetheless accepted as a *fait accompli*. The fact that most of Arab Palestine remaining after the establishment of Israel had been consumed by its neighbor was met with polite silence by the international community. Within the Arab world too, while the Jordanian action was not formally recognized a dignified ambivalence reigned. Jordan's own position on Palestine was opaque. It formally sought the recovery of all of Palestine from the Zionists but in the meantime Amman portrayed its incorporation of the West Bank as a protective measure. In reality Jordan had supported partition, although not the UN plan. As John Glubb writes:

> we in Jordan had produced our own solution…such parts of Palestine as were allotted to the Arabs would have to be incorporated into the neighboring Arab States. Galilee would have joined Lebanon, Samaria and Judea would have been united with trans-Jordan and Gaza-Beersheba district to Egypt.[6]

This was a revealing comment indicating that despite the Jordanian rhetoric about the defense of Palestine at the time of the unification in 1950 the real policy had been to dismember Arab Palestine all along. After 1950 Jordan would remain ambivalent about Palestine.

All Palestinians in Jordan were given citizenship and were integrated into Jordanian institutions. Nonetheless there were tensions between the two banks of the Jordan. The Jordanian government was to be wary of any signs of Palestinian nationalism. For the Palestinians attachment to Jordan also involved a degree of ambivalence on the issue of national identity. It was, however, to prove to be a critical experience that would continue to shape the political and legal culture of the West Bank even after 1967.

While Jordan began on the delicate path of unification with parts of Arab Palestine the rest of the Arab world was about to be swept by a new nationalist wave in which Palestine was to figure strongly. Palestine was to be subject to the new Arab politics much as it had been subject to the older version. The Egyptian Revolution (1952) and Nasserism were to play a major role in shaping Palestinian politics, leading most importantly to the creation of the Palestine Liberation Organization in 1964. As Palestine became increasingly central to the Arab nationalist cause, Palestinians themselves became more marginal.

Thus in some ways the politics of the Arab world was to reinforce the Israeli view that Palestine had ceased to exist as an independent issue. In Israel the first ten years of statehood was to see a ruthless campaign to remove all signs of Palestinian Arab existence. The destruction of abandoned villages was justified as a military measure but it also had far deeper implications as the place names were erased as well. It was not just the destruction of place, but also the attempted destruction of memory of place. The position of the Palestinian population that remained in Israel was highly compromised. Israeli law provided that Arabic was an official language along with Hebrew and that there was to be full equality for Arab citizens. However, for the first 18 years of Israel's existence the Palestinian population lived under military rule under the Military Emergency Regulations.[7] At one and the same time the Palestinians of Israel were to be equal citizens and a military threat.[8] Thus the Israeli government continued to see the civilian Palestinian population, much as it had during the war, as a security problem.[9] The remaining Palestinian population of Israel was not inconsiderable, numbering some 170,000.[10] While most remained in their homes, around 30,000 were internally displaced. In the early years of the Israeli state some 70 percent of Arab owned or tenanted land was expropriated.[11] Palestinians who did not end the war in their own property were rarely allowed to return. Many communities were moved wholesale. While security was often the justification the acquired land was to be consolidated into Jewish farms or became the basis for new Jewish communities.

Thus within Israel the Palestinian minority found itself highly subordinate to the requirements of Israeli state-building. The formal legal commitment to equality was constantly compromised by the view that Palestinians could not be loyal citizens of a Jewish state but rather constituted a fifth column to undermine it. Palestinians were also largely cut off from the rest of the Arab world which often viewed them with suspicion. Thus as the Israeli state consolidated itself, as many traces of Arab Palestine as possible were systematically removed. Palestinian Arabs were transformed into "Israeli Arabs" or the "Arab sector" in the official discourse. They were projected almost as a new people unrelated to their relatives in the West Bank, Gaza or the wider Diaspora.

In the United Nations and other international bodies Israeli representatives would reject all attempts to speak of Palestine or the Palestinian issue. This was an international reflection of domestic politics. The insistence on the denial of Palestinian existence became central to the articulation of Israel's case. It was as if mention of Palestine or of the refugees would in itself undermine Israel's legitimacy. Yet in not countenancing Palestine in such strong terms, strangely the country was constantly being referred to. The obsession with not referring to a place called Palestine or a people called Palestinian merely re-inscribed the centrality of both.

Israeli discourse from the state's inception began to draw extensively on Orientalism in constructing the Palestinian – although of course avoiding that name. In this the wars of 1948 were to play a major role in associating the Arab with violence. From the vantage point of 1948 the relationship between Arabs and Jews since 1920 could be seen as one in which Arabs used violence against Jews; 1920, 1929 and the Arab revolt (1936–39) all became preludes to 1948. Arabs and Muslims are linked to fanaticism and violence in Orientalist literature – Montesquieu famously contrasted the fanatic Muslim prince with the moderate Christian ruler in his *Spirit of Laws*.[12] Arab recourse to violence in the concrete circumstances of Palestine was to be seen as compliant with this perspective. As Palestinian guerilla groups began attacks on Israel this characteristic was confirmed. Thus the stereotype of the violent Arab became a central motif of Israeli discourse. It appeared in politicians' speeches, the popular media, films and books – and it shaped policy.

Palestine and Palestinian identity were thus crushed between Israeli state-building and Arab politics. The international community seemed to lose interest in Palestine but was willing to fund UNRWA. Palestinians had to grapple with acute situations on the ground and international disinterest. Palestinian attachment to the lost homeland manifested itself mainly through guerilla attacks on Israel. This necessarily put the focus on the Jewish state but also put pressure on the Arab states from which the actions were launched, in particular Egypt and Jordan. The development of an independent political movement was a highly sensitive issue as Palestinian efforts were often seen by Arab states as a threat to their own stability. For this reason Arab states were more supportive of anti-Israeli and anti-Zionist politics than the building of positive Palestinian nationalism. Thus in the 1950s and 1960s Palestinian nationalism which had been forged on anti-Zionism from the 1920s was nourished on opposition to Israel's right to exist.

Within the Palestinian and Arab narrative, Israel had been created as the result of aggression. As we have seen, the concept of Zionist aggression had been central to the objections to partition in 1948, but it lay deeper in Palestinian nationalism. The political origins of the term were to increasingly mingle with a legal use. At a broader historical level "Zionist aggression" in this view took the form of Zionist intrusion into Palestine. Israel was to be seen as a conqueror's regime to be placed alongside other occupations including those by the Greeks, Romans and Crusaders. Like these occupiers the belief was that the Zionists would be driven out. As Hadawi wrote in *Bitter Harvest*, three decades after Israel was created: "the Zionist intruders will return from whence they came and we shall have peace again in the Holy Land."[13] Sami Hadawi was a significant intellectual force in the Palestinian national movement and was the Director of the Institute of Palestine Studies from 1965. He saw Zionism purely as an ideological movement that used Jews as "pawns" to develop a Jewish population in Palestine.[14] Zionism was to be seen as either an ally of imperialism or an expression of it that led inevitably to oppression, racism and war. Many Palestinian intellectuals such as Hadawi were keen to stress the differences between Judaism and Zionism and to pose Zionism as a threat to Judaism. The portrayal of Zionism was to become increasingly sinister. It was linked with apartheid South Africa and even Nazism, especially after the 1967 war when the Soviet Union's anti-Zionist campaign began. There appears to have been little reflection on previous Palestinian and Arab arguments that had in fact associated Zionism with communism. Nonetheless the image of Zionists as imperialist, racist, expansionist, exploitative and wreaking violence on the Middle East was to be circulated within the Arab discourse about Palestine. Central to this image was the notion of Zionists as outsiders, who as Hadawi suggested could return to their homes as had the Greeks, Romans and the Crusaders.

Along with many other Palestinian intellectuals and activists Hadawi did begin to re-think the position that the Zionists would return home. In an edition of his book published a decade later he argued that

> the extremists on both sides are increasing in number; the Zionists who will not be satisfied with less than the total expulsion of the Palestinian inhabitants from the territory of the whole of Palestine, and those in the Palestinian camp who believe that the only solution is the total destruction of the state of Israel. If either side had its way the end result would be catastrophic for the people of the Middle East and would affect the rest of the world.[15]

This new position it needs to be noted stood side-by-side with the old analysis of Zionism, the character of the Jews and illegitimacy of the Mandate and the partition resolution. In the same period that Hadawi published the new edition of *Bitter Harvest* he also produced a rather lurid publication characterizing Israel as a terrorist state.[16] This demonstrated the uneasy relationship between the pragmatic acceptance of the two-state solution while maintaining the illegitimacy of Israel. This combination of ideological purity and pragmatic politics has become a marked element of Palestinian discourse since the late 1980s. It has done much to undermine relations once both sides resumed public contact.

As we have seen, the narrative that Jews did not constitute a people or nation and thus could not possess the right to self-determination had been entwined with the view that both the Mandate and partition were illegal. Israel's creation did not diminish such views. In some ways they became more entrenched. Israel's existence was seen as a temporary aberration that could not survive as it was based on such a false premise. Not only was the state not entitled to exist, it did not have the material capacity to exist for long, as Jews were not genuinely one people therefore it would inevitably disintegrate.

Much of the Arab and Palestinian discourse attempted to deepen the argument that Jews were in reality just a religious group. This was assumed to be a winning argument in a modern world that would be opposed to the creation of a state based on religion.

However, against the background of the creation of Pakistan, a state based on a Muslim identity – and a supporter of the Arab case – this seems a curious viewpoint. In many ways the Palestinian designation of Jewish identity as being solely religious paralleled the Israeli designation of Palestinians as "only" Arabs. In each case the assignment to each category seemed to allow the removal of any national issue. This reassignment of identity implied the Jews could return to live with any other Jews and Palestinians would be equally happily accommodating themselves to any Arab society. This mutual approach denied the right of autonomy to the other.

Palestinian intellectuals were to give a great deal of attention to history, anthropology, archeology and theology so as to construct Jews as anything other than a national group – although often with contradictory results. Palestinian arguments about the essential religious identity of the Jews were based on an assumption that Zionism had invented Jewish nationalism. Little attention was paid to the fact that the Zionist movement was founded by people who were often hostile or indifferent to religion. If Jews were only a religious group surely Jewish identity would have ceased once religion was abandoned? Historically Zionism had been a secular movement in which socialism was more central than religion. Despite the increasing Marxist tinge to Palestinian politics little consideration was given to the possibility that Zionism was the result of Jewish experience and had arisen in material circumstances. In the insistence that Jews were only a religious community the fact that discrimination and oppression against Jews in Eastern Europe did not focus on religious practices was ignored. Jews had been free to practice their religion. The discrimination that they had suffered had been social, political, legal and economic. Jews experienced discrimination in work, suffered education quotas, exclusion from the political process and even restrictions on where they could live. The pogroms in Russia did not stop at the doors of non-religious Jews. Nor had Nazism distinguished between religious Jews or non-religious Jews, or indeed between Jews who had converted to other religions. Attachments to ideological anti-Zionism therefore obscured any accurate analysis of how Zionism had developed and as a consequence blunted the ability to engage with it.

The view that Israel would disappear and that the Zionists would return home like other occupiers was based on the belief that Israel and Israelis had no authentic attachment to the region. This position was to some extent based on a biological conception of nation and nationalism. The Palestinian narrative, so insistent to deny any Jewish validity to national existence, ignored the way in which national identity really worked. If nationalism depended on a homogeneous biological group few nations would exist. The United States and Australia would surely have collapsed by now. Nor did Palestinian nationalism take into account sociological developments in Palestine and later Israel. The creation of a Hebrew culture and political institutions was well established by 1947 and as the decades progressed became more so. Whether Jews were creating or recreating a national culture can be debated but its existence would be hard to question. The reason that Jews fought so intensely to establish the state and then to defend it under great difficulties was testimony to a deep attachment to the land and to the society. This needed to be taken into account.

The argument that there was a major distinction between Jews and Zionism and that anti-Zionism was not anti-Semitism was and is frequently made. Yet many Palestinian intellectuals and politicians often fell back on Judaism as an explanation for Zionism; indeed openly expressed anti-Semitism was not unknown – as in the partition debate. While religion clearly plays a part in the construction of Jewish identity, this must be tempered with an analysis of the complex relationship between Judaism and the Jews. Judaism as it appears in the Torah seeks to explain the origins of humanity in general (Genesis), how the Jews came to be in Israel (Exodus) and the laws by which they should live (Leviticus). It is part theology, part national history, part morality – not unlike for example the sacred texts of Hinduism.

This interplay between religion and nation was not missed in some Palestinian analyses of Zionism. The phrase "chosen people" was frequently cited to indicate a Jewish belief in superiority that Zionism was alleged to incorporate. One writer who set out to outline the roots of Zionism in the Torah was Hassan Haddad, who wrote:

> This collection of myths, legends, historical narratives, poems, and prophetic and apocalyptic pronouncements is primarily responsible for the beliefs, conditions, and attitudes that produced Zionism and eventually led to the occupation and transformation of Palestine. We can summarize the beliefs as follows. (1) The Jews are separate and exclusive people chosen by their God to fulfil a destiny; the Jews of Europe in the twentieth century have inherited the covenant of divine election and historical destiny from the Hebrew tribes that existed more than three thousand

years ago. (2) This covenant includes definite ownership of the Land of Canaan (Palestine) as a patrimony of the ancient Israelites to be passed on to the descendents for ever: no other people can lay a rightful claim to that land. (3) The occupation and settlement of this land is the fulfilment of the duty placed collectively on the Jews, to establish a state for the Jews; the purity of the Jewishness of the land is derived from a divine command and is thus a sacred mission.[17]

As a result he concluded that "the Torah sets the divine basis for the exclusivist choice of Israel and is its title deed to Palestine."[18] He also emphasized that Jewish nationalism was present in the Torah. Even "non-Zionist Jews," he says, "who have spiritualized Judaism and the Bible beyond the level of ethnic nationalism cannot counteract this profusion of biblical texts concerned explicitly with Jewish nationalism and exclusivism."[19] Just to make sure his readers will understand the point he adds, "genocidal policy is to be found in the Torah as direct commands of Yahweh given through Moses."[20] Nor was Haddad alone in suggesting that Judaism was rooted in genocide; Sayed Yassin asserted that "the Torah contains many examples of mass exterminations."[21] Thus the attempt to distinguish between the Jewish religion and Zionism which often seemed central to Palestinian discourse was frequently blurred. In part this was perhaps due to the fact that once engaged with, the Jewish religious texts did indeed include the national story that Zionism drew on. Instead of engaging with this national narrative, all too frequently dubious conclusions were drawn about the characteristics of Jews who were essentially portrayed as occupiers, colonizers and racially-exclusive. Such views not only disarmed Palestinians in dealing with Zionism and Israel but also undermined the ethical case for Palestine.

Drawing connections between the characteristics of ancient and modern Jews was problematic for this argument. As it stood it would appear to accept the Zionist perspective. As a result it became essential that the Palestinian narrative would be able to distinguish between the ancient Hebrews and the modern Jews. As in the partition debate modern Jews were not to be seen as descendants of the Jews of the Torah. Hadawi attempted to give this a scientific aura by relying on a Mexican anthropologist who wrote:

The anthropological fact is that Jews are racially heterogeneous and there is no foundation for the claim that there is a Jewish race. Their constant migrations through their history and their relations – voluntary and otherwise – with the widest variety of nations and peoples have brought about such a degree of cross-breeding that so-called people of Israel can produce examples of traits typical of every people.[22]

As can be seen from the quotation above there is much to be desired in such statements which appeared to assume that there were genuine races which had a purity which clearly the Jews did not possess. Quite apart from the questionable provenance of such racial arguments once again it associated the Palestinian cause with highly problematic politics.

Hadawi, however, seemed to think that this biological argument was important evidence as it would break the historical connection and undermine any national claims by modern Jews. He constructed modern Jews as mainly the result of what he called "cross-breeds" and converts. He was sympathetic to the view that European Jews are descendants of the Khazars. As we have noted this assertion had been frequently advanced, including in the partition debates, however no evidence could be brought forward to support this thesis. Mostly such advocates of the view merely expressed surprise at the large number of Jews who lived in Eastern Europe, as if their ignorance of the ethnic make-up of a continent were a scientific fact.[23] The idea that people in Europe would have converted to Judaism in any numbers would seem at variance with the resultant discrimination – and worse – that would have followed. In any event if all of the arguments about the Jews not being Jews, or being descendants of Khazars, or half-breeds, were to be proven that would in no way affect the sense of national identity that Jews might feel and act upon. Chaim Weizmann replied to such comments with the simple observation that "I feel like a Jew and I have suffered like a Jew."[24]

Palestinian and Israeli narratives thus both attempt to construct the other in such a way as to question its legitimacy in Palestine. Each narrative assumed the other had so little attachment to the country that if life were to become uncomfortable it would leave. Both sides regarded the other's nationalism as fake and thus it would fade. The strength of national sentiment of each was constantly ignored as central political factor. These narratives were to form a backdrop to the political and military turmoil that were to mark Israeli–Arab relations through the Suez war in 1956, the Six Day war in 1967 and the Yom Kippur/October war in 1973. Despite the ingrained belief both sides had that the other would disappear, neither did.

RESUMING RELATIONS

It was not until the Oslo peace process began in 1993 that the Jews and Arabs of Palestine were to resume official public relations. The signing of the Declaration of Principles in September 1993 was preceded by the exchange of letters through which the leaders of Israel and the Palestine Liberation Organization recognized each other's existence. In the declaration itself both Israel and the Palestinians agreed to "recognize their mutual legitimate and political rights and strive to live in peaceful coexistence."[25] This somewhat tortured phrase nonetheless represented an important public acceptance that both peoples had a place in Palestine. The question remained what precisely that place was. Before turning to discuss Oslo in detail we need to discuss the historical context which produced the agreement.

The Oslo agreements dealt with the consequences of the 1967 Six Day war when Israel's lightning victory saw the conquest of the West Bank and the Gaza Strip as well as the Egyptian Sinai peninsula and Syria's Golan Heights. The war produced two important political building blocks of Israeli–Arab relations: the Khartoum Arab League meeting in September 1967 and UN Security Council resolution 242 in November 1967. The former, while reiterating the Arab world's rejection of Israel's legitimacy and its commitment to liberating all of Palestine, did adopt a staged approach to the policy. The first stage was to recover Arab land occupied by Israel in the war and the second to liberate all of Palestine. While there was to be no direct contact with Israel a political process involving third parties was regarded as being consistent with the policy. Resolution 242 envisaged such negotiations based on two key principles: Israeli withdrawal and the right of all states to live with secure boundaries in the region. The Arab League's politics of dividing the consequences of 1967 from 1948 combined with the legal framework of the UN resolution were to offer the possibility of negotiations.

THE OCCUPATION AND ISRAELI COLONIALISM

In the occupied West Bank itself reaction to Israel's victory produced several initiatives. In October 1967 a National Charter for the Arabs of the West Bank called for the return of the territory to Jordan – a policy consistent with the Khartoum conference. However, another group including the Mayor of Hebron Sheikh Mohammad Ali al-Ja'bari and the Ramallah lawyer Aziz Shehadeh, called for the creation of a separate Palestinian entity in the occupied territories.[26] The latter initiative was ignored by the Israelis[27] although it represented a significant move in the direction of a two-state solution and a return to the principles of the UN partition plan. It was, however, a marginal view at the time and most Palestinians would have rejected a proposal that meant accepting Israel and the loss of 78 percent of their homeland.

After 1967 the PLO under Fatah's leadership established itself in Amman. This was a strategic decision to transform Jordan into a state led by the PLO which would lead the final struggle against Israel. This challenge to the Hashemite dynasty was to be brought to a bloody end in September 1970 when King Hussein defeated the Palestinian National Army and drove it and the PLO leadership from Jordan.[28] Arafat then moved to Lebanon, home of the second largest Palestinian refugee community after Jordan. Here Arafat adopted a new strategy and built a PLO mini-state within the refugee camps. This was to destabilize the delicate political balance of Lebanon and was a factor that would lead to the Lebanese civil war. It was PLO attacks on Israel that led to the Israeli invasion of Lebanon in 1982. This was a disaster for Lebanon and a debacle for the PLO who were forced to withdraw to Tunis. Thus within 15 years of the 1967 war the PLO had been forced to move its political and military command from two countries and become geographically and strategically increasingly remote from Palestine.

Despite the PLO's emphasis on armed struggle and the use of terrorism during the late 1960s and early 1970s the main success of the PLO had been diplomatic. A series of United Nations General Assembly resolutions from 1969 had recognized the Palestinian right to self-determination and resulted in the seating of the PLO as an observer in the General Assembly as the "sole legitimate representative of the Palestinian people."[29] Its diplomatic accomplishments also included the adoption of UN General Assembly resolution 3379 (XXX) in 1975 defining Zionism as a form of racism. This involvement with the United Nations was to have an impact on the political trajectory of the movement. Its diplomatic gains stood in stark contrast to its military position.

From 1967 onwards a series of public political initiatives were launched to give shape to the principles contained in Security

Council resolution 242. The United States Secretary of State William Rogers was first off the mark in 1969. After an initial rejection he finessed his plan in 1970 which called for direct negotiations between Israel, Egypt and Jordan that would lead to Israeli withdrawal from most of the occupied territory in exchange for recognition of Israel's statehood. Although the plan collapsed through lack of support it popularized a formula that has since become embedded into Israeli–Arab peace-making. At the same time secret contacts between Israelis and Arab politicians began. The most developed appeared to be the relations between Yitzhak Rabin and King Hussein of Jordan.

The PLO had not welcomed the results of the Khartoum conference nor had they accepted resolution 242. After the Arab defeat the PLO, which had been created in 1964 by the Arab League and had been in Egypt's sphere of influence, began to emerge as an independent force. This was underlined by the adoption of a new covenant in 1968 and the election of Yasser Arafat as Chairman in 1969. The covenant now placed emphasis on Palestinian as opposed to Arab nationalism and Arafat's election represented the victory of Fatah and the strategy of armed resistance.[30] The PLO's covenant encoded the Palestinian legal narratives designating as illegal the Mandate and the United Nations partition plan (articles 19 and 20) and characterizing Zionism as "racist, fanatical, aggressive expansionist, colonialist, fascist and Nazi" (article 22). Jews did not possess a "nationality with independent existence" (article 20). The liberation of Palestine would "liquidate the Zionist and imperialist presence [in the Middle East]" (article 22). These sentiments meant that contact between Israel and the PLO would prove problematic.

The PLO thus saw the results of both 1948 and 1967 as proof that Zionism was inherently expansionist.[31] As a result negotiations with Israel would have been a sign of weakness that would have only strengthened this trend. With the signing of the Egypt–Israel Camp David peace treaty in 1978, however, that view became less tenable as Egypt was to recover all the territory that Israel had occupied. The treaty had also provided for Israeli–Palestinian negotiations on self-rule and a final settlement of the Palestine issue. The PLO along with the rest of the Arab world rejected Camp David as capitulation to Israel. Nonetheless for the first time an Arab country had ceased to treat Israel as an ideological construct and began, tentatively, to treat it as a state.

The PLO had other more immediate reasons to see Zionism as expansionist; the establishment of Israeli settlements in the occupied territories.[32] Almost as soon as the 1967 war was over Israel began to act as a colonial power. In East Jerusalem the Magrebi quarter adjacent to the Western Wall was destroyed and some 600 families were made homeless to make way for an open square in front of the wall. Almost immediately there was a clamor among some religious-Zionists led by Moshe Levenger for the settlement of the occupied land. He argued that the West Bank was after all the heartland of the Jewish people. Despite what Ben Ami described as the drunken atmosphere following the 1967 war[33] the Israeli government appeared to have no real plans for any of the territory captured except seeing it as a strategic asset which could be used as a bargaining chip with Arab neighbors. This was not true of some Israeli political circles. Such forces immediately made plans to move Israelis into the West Bank. Palestinians thus began to witness the beginning of a small but determined new Jewish population in the West Bank. Rather than the imagined colonialism of Zionism Palestinians had to confront the real colonialism of the Israeli state.[34]

Palestinian claims that Israel had a military plan to conquer all of Palestine after the 1948 war was of course correct. The IDF produced a series of contingency plans for conquering the area in the event of hostilities – indeed Gaza had been occupied in 1956 in just such circumstances. However, it would be wrong to suggest that these plans were part of a general strategy by Israel to seize the territory in order to annex it. Nor is it correct to view Israel as luring Arab states into war in 1967 to carry out such a plan. According to Mutawi:

> the war broke out as the result of inter-Arab rivalries and divisions. The issue of Israel was one of the principal axes on which the struggle for leadership of the Arab world revolved. Each Arab nation sought to outdo the others in its support for the Palestinians and thus brought the possibility of war ever closer.[35]

This view was also consistent with most accounts of the intentions of Israel's 1967 political or military leadership towards the West Bank or even East Jerusalem.[36] There was no evidence to suggest that their conquest was part of their thinking. In fact there appeared to be great indecision on whether even to enter East Jerusalem. Nonetheless the Palestinian and Arab view at the time was wedded to the belief that Israel's conquest was not merely part of a plan but the logical outcome of the expansionist policy inherent in Zionism. While an analysis of the causes of the 1967 war is beyond the scope of this discussion,[37] it would seem erroneous to regard the territorial results of 1967 as deriving from an expansionist impulse. It was in many ways an unhelpful analysis that disarmed the Palestinians for dealing with the situation. More often that not, 1967 was to be seen as a continuation of 1948, in which the same shadowy force, Zionism, was responsible. As a result policies were framed which were based on general ideological positions rather than on a concrete analysis that the Israeli state was sponsoring colonial designs on the occupied territories.

THE OSLO AGREEMENTS

The signing of the Oslo agreements on September 13, 1993, opened a new phase in the Palestinian–Israeli conflict. The opening of public and legally regulated negotiations was to become a new and permanent feature of Palestinian–Israeli relations. Despite the much talked about collapse of the Oslo agreements I will argue that their underlying purpose has proved to be rather resilient. The foundation of the agreement was the mutual recognition of each party to the conflict. For the first time through the medium of an exchange of letters the Palestine Liberation Organization recognized the State of Israel and Israel recognized the Palestine Liberation Organization as the representative of the Palestinian people.[38] Four days later Yitzhak Rabin and Yasser Arafat signed the Declaration of Principles in Washington. The declaration was the first of a series of documents to be negotiated. Despite the serious flaws in the agreements the underlying principles of mutual recognition, negotiation and Palestinian self-rule have survived the assassination and the death of its two principal architects, compliance failures on each side, international disinterest and violent breakdown.

As is now well recorded the Oslo process was the result of secret negotiations between the Rabin government and the PLO in 1992 and 1993.[39] The 1992 Israeli elections had produced a Labor-led government that had committed itself to peace with the Palestinians. Rabin as Labor Leader and then as Prime Minister had seemed to rule out any negotiation with the Palestine Liberation Organization and was firmly set against the creation of a Palestinian state. Nonetheless his period as Defense Minister during the first *intifada* (1987–92) had convinced him that military means could not resolve the conflict. The question that confronted the new government was what type of political initiative could be taken and who were the partners to take it with? The government included Shimon Peres as Foreign Minister, Yossi Beilin as Deputy Foreign Minister as well as members of the then new Meretz party. Peres was steeped in the most pragmatic wing of the Zionist movement whereas Beilin represented a new generation of leaders who had an ethical commitment to peace. They and the Meretz ministers (Yossi Sarid, Shulamit Aloni, Amnon Rubenstein and Yair Yzaban) formed a wing of the government that was open to negotiations with the PLO.

In the year before the formation of the new government the Madrid peace conference in November 1991, held in the wake of the Gulf war, had brought into being a series of multi-lateral and bi-lateral relations between Israel and its neighbors. Committees were formed which ranged over diplomatic, strategic and economic and social questions. A critical contribution to this process was made by a joint Jordanian–Palestinian team. As a result Israelis and Arab diplomats and specialists had become accustomed to meeting and exchanging ideas. However, it was unclear whether or not these meetings were going to progress and Rabin was not convinced that they were.[40] As a result his government decided to explore other avenues.

The opening of very tentative discussions between the Israeli academic Yair Hirschfeld and PLO official Ahmed Querie in London were to be the first of what was to become the Oslo process. The pair were brought together by one of the chief spokespersons for the Palestinians in the Madrid process, Hanan Ashrawi, but the talks were facilitated by the Norwegian academic Terje Rod Larsen. The aim of the meetings was to see if the two sides could frame a series of principles that could form the basis of formal negotiations. These contacts matured and a network of contacts involving the Norwegian Foreign Ministry, the PLO and the Israeli government consolidated the process. The channel of communication was upgraded as Ahmed Querie now representing the PLO and Uri Savir of the Israeli Foreign Ministry became the principal interlocutors. The talks were conducted in utmost secrecy. As a result, although at several removes the Israeli Prime Minister and the Chairman of the PLO were negotiating.

The Declaration of Principles provided a framework for negotiations and so was not in itself a document of substance. It rather set out the basis for talks, created an agenda for them, some interim goals and a timescale. The text provided for two periods of negotiations: the first for an interim agreement to create the institutions of Palestinian self-rule and then a second phase which would conclude a permanent settlement between the parties.

In setting the overall objectives of the exercise the preamble of the declaration states that the two sides

> agree that it is time to put an end to decades of confrontation and conflict, recognize their mutual legitimate and political rights, and strive to live in peaceful coexistence and mutual dignity and security and achieve a just, lasting and comprehensive peace settlement and historic reconciliation through the agreed political process.[41]

This objective had been carefully drafted and, as can be seen, the destination of the process remained ambiguously hidden behind the phrase "mutual legitimate and political rights." There was no mention of what these rights might be. The terms "self-determination" and "state" were also not used. One can assume that this wording would have appealed to Joel Singer, the international lawyer on the Israeli side who wanted to keep all options open. Many from the Palestinian legal community have been highly critical of the lack of legal input into the Palestinian negotiating team.[42] Whether this would have made any difference to the outcome is another matter. The ambiguity of the declaration was to become a marked character of all the texts produced through the seven years of the Oslo negotiations.

The specific aim of the declaration was to establish a

> Palestinian Interim Self Government Authority, the elected Council, for the Palestinian people in the West Bank and the Gaza Strip for a transitional period not exceeding five years, leading to a permanent settlement based on Security Council Resolutions 242 and 338.

> It is understood that the interim arrangements are an integral part of the whole peace process and that the negotiations on the permanent status will lead to the implementation of Security Council Resolutions 242 and 338.[43]

RESOLUTION 242

This rather crowded article set up the main dynamics of the process; the creation in the interim phase of an elected Palestinian authority and an agreement on the permanent status of the West Bank and Gaza within five years in accordance with the two Security Council resolutions. These resolutions were adopted in the wake of the 1967 and 1973 wars, with 338 (1973) merely reaffirming 242 (1967). The operative parts of resolution 242 outline a series of principles that must be applied:

(i) withdrawal of Israeli armed forces from territories occupied in the recent conflict;
(ii) termination of all claims or states of belligerency and respect for and acknowledgement of the sovereignty, territorial integrity and political independence of every state in the area and their right to live in peace within secure and recognized boundaries free from threats or acts of force.[44]

As can be seen the ambiguity in the declaration rests on ambiguities in the Security Council resolutions which were to be the basis for a settlement. It needs to be remembered that the negotiations over resolution 242 were conducted in the context of the Arab non-recognition of Israel, the Israeli non-recognition of the PLO and Israel's demand for "secure boundaries." In order to achieve the necessary measure of agreement for the resolution the drafters had to attempt to straddle several contradictory policies. This required carefully imprecise formulations that would allow all sides the ability to interpret the text as addressing their requirements. As a result no states are mentioned by name but all states in the region were to have the right to exist. However, it was doubtful the resolution envisaged that one of those states would be Palestine as the United Nations had not at the time adopted any resolution in favor of Palestinian self-determination.

The critical clause of resolution 242, with particular relevance to the Oslo agreements, refers to withdrawal. The text refers to "withdrawal from territory occupied" rather than "withdrawal from *the* territory occupied." The omission of the definite article introduced doubt as to the scope of the required Israeli withdrawal. In the drafting negotiations there was much debate about which language most accurately rendered the meaning of the resolution. In the French and Spanish translations it was grammatically impossible to omit the definite article (although this was not a problem in Chinese and Russian, the other official languages). It appeared that Gunnar Jarring, who mediated the process, insisted on using the English version only. It has been subsequently accepted that this is the authoritative text as the English rendition allows for the greatest impression.[45] This has allowed Israel to argue that there was no obligation to withdrawal from "all" occupied land, whereas the Arab states and the Palestinians interpret the resolution as requiring Israel to do just that. As Palestinians increasingly regained recognition through the United Nations General Assembly for their right to self-determination the latter interpretation gained widespread endorsement. In 2004 the International Court of Justice adopted the same position. However, in 1993 that authoritative legal determination was yet to come. Thus the reference to resolution 242 did not clarify the destination of the negotiation, but emphasized the different expectations of the parties.

The differences of interpretation were to haunt the negotiations. The Palestinians began from the premise that Israel was legally bound to withdraw from all the occupied territory. The Israelis on the other hand thought the extent of any withdrawal was negotiable, particularly as the resolution referred to the right of all states to live within "secure and recognized boundaries."[46] Palestinians thought that the creation of a state in the occupied territories would be a major concession as Israel retained 78 percent of British Mandate Palestine. Israel took the position that any withdrawal was a concession and that the Palestinians should demonstrate willingness to compromise by being flexible on the scope of Israel's pull-back.

Israel's attitude was also informed by a legal argument on the status of the West Bank. In June 1967 the West Bank formed part of Jordan. As we have seen, the Jordanian claim to sovereignty was based on an internationally unrecognized unilateral annexation in 1950. As this claim was therefore of dubious legality the question arose as to the character of the territory that Israel had occupied. Was Israel in occupation of part of Jordan? If the answer was no then the issue became to determine the legal character of the territory. Much was made of these questions by some Israeli politicians and lawyers.[47] They sought to suggest that if the Jordanians did not have good title this could create grounds for Israel's legitimate rights to them. From 1948 the international community, basing itself on the partition plan, had treated the legal status of the West Bank and East Jerusalem as parts of Palestine allocated to the Arab state or to the international regime respectively. Jordan's annexation had mostly been ignored at the formal legal level. As a result the official Israeli position was that the West Bank possessed no settled sovereignty and therefore it was disputed territory. In 1988 Jordan formally repudiated the annexation in deference to the PLO. However this did not change the Israeli attitude and so in 1993 it still regarded the legal status of the West Bank as "disputed." This legal designation encouraged the view that any Israeli withdrawal would be a major concession as it was legally unnecessary as no side had a settled title to the land. Thus by taking resolution 242 as the basis for resolving the conflict the ambiguity contained in the resolution allowed both parties to begin negotiations while holding radically different legal starting points on the status of the territory under discussion. The agreements thus encoded competing legal narratives while appearing to offer a clear basis for the negotiations.

The institutional aspects of Oslo were more precise. The agreement provided for democratic elections to a Council that would be at the center of the Palestinian Authority. The electorate was to include not just the residents of the West Bank and Gaza but also the Palestinian citizens of Jerusalem. The latter point was of great significance as Israel had purported to annex East Jerusalem. Also of great significance was the agreement that both sides would "view the West Bank and the Gaza Strip as a single territorial unit, whose integrity will be preserved during the interim period."[48] This later point and the inclusion of East Jerusalem residents in the electorate for the Council were gains for the Palestinian side.

The five-year time-frame was to begin as soon as Israel withdrew from the Gaza Strip and the Jericho area. As there were no maps attached to the agreements these areas remained imprecise and a further round of negotiations would be required. The exact extent of the area concerned would be important as the use of the term "withdrawal" has the legal significance, implying an end of the occupation. Israel's agreement to the use of the term is its first formal acknowledgment that it was an occupier. This marked an important breach in Israel's insistence since 1967 that all the territories were "disputed" not "occupied." Some of the territories were now acknowledged as having a different status.

In order to get to the stage of the withdrawal which in turn would allow for the creation of the Palestinian Authority a new phase of negotiations was required. This was needed in order to agree the maps, the modalities of the withdrawal and the details of Palestinian powers. It was not obvious from the declaration that such an extra stage had been intended as it appeared to provide for an easy transition to self-rule and then to the final agreement. This last stage, the permanent status talks, was to begin not more than three years into the operation of the process and would deal with the difficult questions: "Jerusalem, refugees, settlements, security arrangements, borders, relations and cooperation with other neighbors, and other issues of common interest."[49] Leaving these issues on one side it was thought would give time for confidence-building to create a conducive atmosphere for success. The end result was never specified although inclusion of discussions about borders could be read as a code indicating that the final result could be a Palestinian state. As we have noted, however, the studious avoidance of the term "state" or of the recognition of the Palestinian right to self-determination did not mean that this would not be the result.

The legal and political architecture of Oslo thus permitted quite different views of the past and visions of the future. In part this stemmed from the different Palestinian and Israeli legal narratives.[50] While these had undergone changes and shifts during the conflict the basic positions remained. Oslo's main advantage was that these positions could now be argued between the parties themselves. Oslo represented a new phase for both sides but decades of legal trench-warfare were to take their toll. Israelis and Palestinians found themselves trapped by this history.

Palestinians remained convinced that legal justice was on their side and that the creation of the State of Israel was a historic injustice. Nonetheless the new Oslo spirit represented an attempt to come to terms with the situation pragmatically. If Israel was not going to be removed then the question was how to rescue something for the Palestinian people in the form of an independent state – and achieve elementary justice for the refugees. These conclusions had in fact been drawn much earlier and had been concretized in the Algiers Declaration in 1988 which proclaimed Palestine a state.[51] Although this proclamation had been symbolic the content of the declaration included a provision that a state could be established on any part of occupied Palestine. This implication of a possible two-state solution represented an important public acknowledgment of a long debate in the PLO – and much international diplomacy.

The 1988 declaration had been made at a time of drastic change for the PLO's relations with the people of the occupied territories. For nearly a year a popular uprising against Israeli rule had been underway. The *intifada* was not the result of a policy of the PLO and continued for some time outside its control. A new layer of young leaders was to emerge which was not integrated into the PLO structures and who had no habit of obeying orders from a headquarters abroad. The *intifada* was a challenge not just to the

Israelis but also to the PLO. It also represented the first time that a PLO rival, Hamas, could compete for political allegiance amongst the Palestinian public. While this was to have long-term implications the creation of a large layer of independent activist youth meant that the PLO had to take careful steps to intercept and co-opt it for the movement. The *intifada* highlighted the overwhelmingly exiled character of the PLO which had had strong links with the refugees and the Palestinian Diaspora but which was less rooted in Palestine. The *intifada* had a profound effect in reinforcing the national consciousness of the people in the West Bank and Gaza and the resistance created a new sense of identity – and one that could not be easily shared by the Palestinians beyond the occupied territories. The *intifada* also underscored in practice the anti-Israeli rather than anti-Zionist politics. The struggle to end the occupation called for the removal of Israel, its military, its civil administration and its settlers from Arab Palestine. As a result it created a popular dynamic for a two-state solution. The emphasis was thus on the illegality of Israel as the occupying power, not on the illegitimacy of Israel itself.

Aspects of this new politics had been prefigured by the Algiers Declaration. This text marked a formal shift in the Palestinian legal narrative. Israel's occupation was to be seen as the most immediate obstacle to self-determination. The roots of this position stretched back to the 1967 Khartoum conference of the Arab League and its decision to divide resistance to Israel into two phases: first reclaiming the territory occupied in the war and second dealing with Israel itself. This essentially meant dividing the consequences of 1967 from those of 1948. The idea of a staged approach to the liberation of Palestine was not new in Arab political discourse. Egypt, for example, had held elections to a Palestinian National Union in 1961 to provide some level of distinctive Palestinian representation; though this had been limited to Gaza. This was followed by the promulgation of a Palestinian constitution which would be temporary until the complete recovery of the country. This policy had been designed to counter the Jordanian claims to the West Bank which Egypt rejected as illegal.[52] The Iraqi nationalist leader, Qassim, also envisaged a two-stage process. He projected the creation of an "immortal Palestinian republic" that would have political institutions and an army (trained by Iraq) that would eventually liberate the country.[53] These plans it should be noted preceded the 1967 war. Their existence engendered Israeli suspicions that all two-stage plans were based on the eventual elimination of Israel. This position is very much in evidence in Israel in the contemporary period. Many assessments suggested that a Palestinian state in the occupied territories would be a forward position from which to launch the conquest of Israel. However after 1967, while Palestine remained ideologically important, Egypt, Jordan and Syria prioritized actions that could recover their own territory. Palestine became an increasingly long-term question.

The staged approach to Israel at Khartoum was in the context of the three nos – no to peace with Israel, no to negotiations with Israel and no to recognition of Israel. As we have noted, negotiations with third parties were not ruled out. Under the influence of Nasser the Khartoum meeting placed great emphasis on a political process as well as a military one. Nasser was particularly keen that King Hussein of Jordan should pursue all political avenues to recover the West Bank.[54] Indeed following the adoption of resolution 242 several initiatives were undertaken through the United Nations and the United States. Therefore it would be a mistake to assume that the Khartoum meeting represented a consolidation of the Arab rejectionist position. In many ways it marked the beginning of a new political direction that would lead to the acceptance of a two-state solution. It was of course extremely early in this development and the staged approached was engaged with in different ways. The PLO had arrived at Khartoum without a formal invitation and were to remain extremely skeptical about the results of the conference.

LAW AND OCCUPATION

Nonetheless this approach did influence the way in which the Palestinians began to see the legal question of Israel's obligations as an occupying power. This was particularly focused on Israel's duties under the Fourth Geneva Convention of 1949. This convention outlines a regime of protection for civilians during armed conflicts including during occupations. For example, the convention requires that the occupier not only act humanely toward civilians but also permit them to use their own legal system. In addition there is strict prohibition on the transferring of the occupier's citizens into, or forcibly removing existing civilians out of the territory concerned. Nor are occupiers able to alter the status of the territory. As a result much of the Palestinian legal argument was focused on defeating Israel's various equivocations on the status of the West Bank, Gaza and East Jerusalem. This was in an effort to focus on the use of the Geneva Convention to prevent Israel from annexing territory or building settlements. The Palestinian argument was a powerful one against Israel's use of the terms "disputed territories," "administered territories" and "the territories" which had virtually no legal meaning. However, in demanding that Israel live up to its international legal responsibilities, the Palestinian argument necessarily meant recognizing Israel as a sovereign state. Under the Geneva Convention – and the law of occupation more generally – only states can have such obligations. Thus once the Palestinians rightly demanded that Israel live up to its international legal obligation this implied the recognition of Israel as a state. In addition, once the West Bank, East Jerusalem and Gaza were to be treated as occupied, did that imply that the 1949 Green Line constituted the legitimate borders of Israel?

Thus the more the argument was made about Israel's obligations as an occupier the more contradictory the Palestinian legal narrative became. It was difficult to maintain at one and the same time that Israel had international legal obligations as an occupier and that Israel did not have legitimacy as a state. The legal arguments about the character of the occupation were reinforced by the politics of the *intifada* which focused on the removal of Israel from occupied land. This was a classic anti-colonial rebellion premised on the demand that as Israel was the colonial power then it must return home. The question for the Palestinians was could they accept the 1949 Green Line as the boundary for that home?

The changing world political situation in the late 1980s was to have profound implications for the conflict. For the Palestinians the international landscape was not promising when the Algiers Declaration had been adopted. The PLO since its inception had ideologically defined itself as anti-imperialist and had become part of the non-aligned movement and had assiduously developed diplomatic ties with the Soviet bloc. This had been critical to the many successes that the PLO had scored in the United Nations. In addition the Soviet bloc countries had assisted the PLO and Palestinians practically, ranging from student scholarships to military training. Within a year of the Algiers Declaration much of this support was to be swept away by the popular overthrow of the communist regimes of Eastern Europe. That meant the withdrawal not only of practical assistance but also of diplomatic support. The new democratic governments rapidly renewed diplomatic relations with Israel and downgraded relations with the PLO. In the same period the Soviet Union also renewed its relations with Israel and lifted the ban on Jewish emigration. The PLO seemed unprepared for such a radical change in its diplomatic fortunes, which in part explains its decision to support Saddam Hussein's invasion of Kuwait in August 1990. Within days of the invasion the President of Iraq was to announce his "linkage policy." He was willing to withdraw from Kuwait, he said, if Israel withdrew from all occupied Arab land. The idea that to liberate one country you conquer another was an innovation in international politics. The PLO, almost alone in the Arab world, unwisely decided to support Iraq. When Iraq was defeated by the United Nations supported coalition the PLO found itself isolated. Eastern Europe had disappeared and the Arab world was hostile. Worse, most hostile of all were Saudi Arabia and Kuwait, both of which had been generous financial supporters of the organization. The funding virtually stopped which caused a major crisis in a movement that had been accustomed to a regular – and large – income. In addition for the Palestinian community in Kuwait the PLO's decision was to be disastrous and after liberation most were expelled and many bank accounts and other assets were frozen.

The PLO thus faced a crisis of direction in the 1990s and it was this which explained its willingness to become engaged in the Oslo process. It offered an opportunity to reinforce its centrality and to renew its diplomatic credentials. However, it was rebuilding itself from a weak position. Palestinian weakness was undoubtedly seized on by some on the Israeli side who sought to exploit it to their advantage. In some respects the 1993 declaration was less generous to the Palestinians than the agreement on Palestine that Israel and Egypt had come to in the Camp David treaty in 1978. Those proposals had also envisaged a five-year process of negotiations during which there would be a transfer of powers to an elected Palestinian Council. During this period there would be negotiations on all issues, "at the end of which the Palestinian people would be able to determine their own future." This seemed a more forthright formulation that approximated to self-determination – an outcome studiously avoided 15 years later.

Oslo was thus a paler version of Camp David. The PLO had objected to Egypt negotiating with Israel over their future and yet by the time they became the principal interlocutor they were to obtain a more problematic deal in worse circumstances. Israel's colonial occupation policy was much more advanced. Instead of a few thousand settlers in 1978 there were now over 120,000 in the West Bank alone. Beyond the support that the settlers received from Israeli government departments and the IDF, a broad political current to support settlements had become a powerful force in Israeli politics. Thus the Palestinians began the 1993 Oslo process from a position of considerable weakness. More of Arab Palestine was under Israeli control than ever before and the Palestinian leadership had become more estranged from the Arab world. Unlike in 1948 when decisions about Palestine had been mainly taken by the Arab League, in 1993 the Palestinians were now on their own. In 1948, as we have seen, the Palestinians were unable to escape the vortex of inter-Arab rivalries and as a result Palestine disappeared. In 1993 operating outside the framework of Arab unity the Palestinians were forced to attempt a deal with Israel on a basis not dissimilar to that which had been thwarted some 45 years before.

For the Israelis there were also important domestic and international factors that pushed them towards recognition of the PLO. The *intifada* had imposed a great strain on Israeli society and had to a great extent transformed the Israeli public's view of the occupied territories. Conscripts had had to face the first mass civilian uprising since the occupation and as such had been forced to confront large numbers of young activists only armed with determination and stones as weapons. As the uprising spread the West Bank became a no-go area for Israelis many of whom had regularly visited the region after 1967. Israelis living inside the Green Line rarely ventured into Palestinian areas except as soldiers. Israeli settlers in the West Bank and Gaza became increasingly reliant on the military to continue living there. Many began to travel in convoys and school buses had military protection. While the settlers in the main demanded drastic military action to defeat the *intifada*, for Israelis inside Israel a political solution seemed imperative. Israeli society had in any event by the early 1990s developed something of a siege mentality in response to wars and terrorism. This had produced a general exhaustion but the *intifada* made this all the more acute. It was this fact that propelled Rabin to power in 1992. Israeli leaders thus came under great pressure to develop policies that could end the violence. The letter from Arafat to Rabin included the commitment that the "PLO renounces the use of terrorism and other acts of violence and will assume responsibility over all PLO elements and personnel in order to assure their compliance, prevent violations and discipline violators."[55] The Israeli public might have been skeptical but these were the words that they wanted to hear and the sentiments that the Rabin government wanted to deliver as a trophy of Oslo.

Israel also saw the changed international situation as fortuitous for an agreement with the Palestinians. Israel had emerged from the Gulf war in a strong position. Israel's diplomatic position was strengthened not only with more ties with Eastern European states but also with many in Africa and Asia, most critically China. As a result of first Soviet policy and then the collapse of the USSR, Israel's population was rapidly growing with the largest wave of immigration for a generation – nearly a million Russian Jews had arrived within five years. In the Gulf war, despite being a target for Saddam Hussein's Scud missiles, Israel had shown great restraint at the request of the United States and had not entered the war. In the aftermath the United States set about attempting to deal with Middle East tensions by addressing the Palestinian–Israeli conflict. Part of Israel's price for attending the Madrid peace conference was the rescinding of the 1975 United Nations anti-Zionist resolution.[56] This was done easily and must have represented to Israel an important symbolic transformation of its international relations. Thus Israel found itself more secure on the diplomatic front than for some time and thus could approach the weakened Palestinian camp with expectations that it would be able to gain important concessions. It was with this sense of strategic superiority that Israel approached negotiations with the Palestinians.

According to the Declaration of Principles, Israel was to transfer powers to a Palestinian authority at the time it withdrew from the Gaza Strip and Jericho area. The areas of competence that the Palestinians were to gain were: education and culture, health, social welfare, direct taxation, and tourism.[57] This rather modest list of powers led Edward Said to comment that the Oslo agreements would lead to setting up a municipality rather than a state: "clearly the PLO has transformed itself from a national liberation movement into a kind of small town government."[58] He also argued that the accords appeared to be transferring the day-to-day responsibility for the Israeli occupation from Israel to the Palestinians.[59]

Despite the modesty of the transfer of powers it was many months more before Israel and the PLO were able to agree on how the handover of powers would take place. It was not until May 1994 when the Cairo Agreement was signed that these modalities could be put in place.[60] The central text was quite short but the annexes and maps reveal the incredible detail that the negotiations entailed. Its critical clauses provided for the withdrawal of Israel from the relevant areas, the transfer of powers and the creation of the Palestinian Authority and its jurisdiction. The maps that accompanied the text were an ominous warning of what Israel's negotiation strategy on withdrawal would be. This was not an expansive withdrawal (as had been indicated in Camp David) so much as a modality for an argument over every square kilometer. While the Declaration of Principles had referred to Israel's withdrawal from the Gaza Strip, the Cairo Agreement revealed that the withdrawal would not include the Israeli settlements or Israeli military installations. As a result some one-third of the Gaza Strip would be retained by the Israelis after this withdrawal. In addition the pattern of the settlements and bases meant that Israel would control the main roads and so Palestinians would not be able to exercise control over a contiguous territory. The Jericho area, although larger than the Israelis had originally proposed, was only about 1 percent of the West Bank. Its borders were also dictated by the pattern of Israeli settlements in the area. As a result it can be seen that the term "withdrawal" was rather conditional – and conditional on preserving Israel's interests including its colonial settlements.

There was a general colonial feel to the text of the Cairo Agreement. The Palestinian Authority's 24 members were subject to Israeli approval as the "PLO shall inform the Government of Israel of the names of members of the Palestinian Authority and any change of members. Changes in membership…will take effect upon the exchange of letters between the PLO and the Government of Israel."[61] Israel assumed the right to vet Palestinians who were to be responsible for "self-rule." Israel also wanted to ensure that the Authority would have no jurisdiction over any Israeli citizen. Not only would it not have competence over Israeli settlers or military bases, it would not have jurisdiction over any individual Israeli passing through its areas. The latter point was repeated to underline its significance.[62] A special clause also made it clear that individual Israelis in Gaza and the Jericho area were to remain under the authority of Israel.[63] The development of this form of personal jurisdiction was highly problematic for the functioning of a normal legal system as the authorities could only act on the basis of an individual's nationality not on the basis of their behavior. The main intent of the provision was clearly to protect the status of Israeli settlers and to assure them that they would not be at risk of falling under the control of Palestinians in any circumstances.

The colonial theme was also evident in the sections that dealt with the powers and responsibilities of the Authority. It was banned from engaging in international relations. However, as a concession the PLO was able to act on behalf of the Palestinian Authority and to "conduct negotiations and sign agreements with states or international organizations" on economic questions with donors supporting the PA's functions, on certain regional development initiatives and in the areas of culture, science and education.[64] This is interesting in that the PLO had received a great deal of international recognition at this point and not only represented Palestine as observers at the United Nations but had also signed international treaties. The PLO was keen to ensure that the agreement would not undermine this position. It appears that the Palestinian negotiators were successful in maintaining a division of labor between the PA and the PLO, so that the latter maintained its freedom to act in the international arena while offering its services to the Authority in economic and cultural areas. Needless to say this was somewhat of a legal fiction as the key personnel were the same, symbolized by Arafat who was to be both Chairman of the PLO and President of the PA.

The Cairo Agreement took many months to negotiate but once it was signed on May 4, 1994, the five-year timescale was set in motion. Critically this meant that a permanent settlement of the conflict was due by May 4, 1999. While the agreement can be criticized from many angles it did represent a major step forward in creating Palestinian institutions on Palestinian soil. As a result Yasser Arafat returned to Gaza from Tunis to head the Authority and with him went many thousands of officials, activists and members of the Palestine Liberation Army. The latter were to form the basis of the "strong police force" that was to be created.[65] In the summer of 1994 many in the Tunis leadership joined Arafat and the Palestinian Authority rapidly established itself in Gaza and Jericho. Although small in scale these newly freed areas did provide a glimpse of freedom from Israeli rule. However, the border posts between these areas and Israel and the rest of the occupied territories hinted at a new form of confinement that was about to begin.

7
Negotiating Palestine

The age of negotiations had begun. For the next decade and a half, Israelis and Palestinians were to encounter each other in various parts of the world to discuss in intimate detail arrangements for Palestinian self-rule, economic cooperation and ideas for comprehensive peace. The Oslo plan confidence-building approach to peace-making assumed that small concrete steps would help the parties trust each other and so create a positive atmosphere to resolve all aspects of the conflict. However, the way in which Oslo was to work produced the opposite effect. Far from promoting confidence-building it was to breed suspicion and allegations of bad faith. After signing Oslo the Palestinians were to witness an increased level of settlement activity which appeared to consolidate Israeli control over the occupied territories. Israeli civilians were to experience a wave of terrorist attacks. Israeli and Palestinian leaders instead of offering their respective peoples a clear vision of the future spoke ambiguously which encouraged anti-peace forces to mobilize for their maximalist policies. Israelis prevaricated over the creation of a Palestinian state; Palestinians were equivocal about their terms of recognizing Israel. Neither side would unveil a map of the future. The lack of an agreed destination hung over the talks at each stage. This concluding chapter will discuss the way in which the legal narratives of Palestinians and Israelis were reinforced rather than challenged by the Oslo process and so sustained rather than resolved the conflict.

Once the Palestinian Authority had been established in May 1994, Israeli and Palestinian negotiators set about working on the interim agreement that would create the democratically elected council to represent all Palestinians in the occupied territories. The negotiations were to last for over a year and as with the Cairo Agreement each team devoted attention to the minutest detail. Central to the agreement was the extent of the Israeli redeployment from the West Bank and the structure and powers of the Palestinian Authority. The interim agreement was eventually signed by Rabin and Arafat in Washington in September 1995.

The agreement and its annexes are several hundred pages long as with the Cairo Agreement, accurately recording the immense detail of the negotiations. Perhaps most critical of the annexes was the map of the West Bank. The map did not merely detail the area of Israeli redeployment but sub-divided the West Bank into three areas: A, B and C. These areas were not contiguous blocks of land but disconnected plots dictated, as with the 1994 Gaza map, by the pattern of Israeli settlements and military bases. Israel was committed to granting the PA full control only over area A. Area B was to be under the civil control of the PA although Israel was to have "over-riding responsibility for security." In area C Israel would remain in full control although it would allow the PA some jurisdiction over Palestinians but not over the territory.

Area A which comprised a mere 3 percent of the West Bank contained the main urban areas: Jenin, Nablus, Tulkarem, Qalqilyah, Ramallah and Bethlehem. Hebron was omitted as no agreement could be reached on Israeli redeployment from a city where a handful of settlers lived under army protection in the city center. Some 65 percent of the Palestinian population lived in area A. Area B which was 22 percent of the West Bank was comprised of 450 towns and villages. Israel would redeploy its troops and dismantle bases but would retain the right of freedom of movement in the zone. Area C contained the bulk of the West Bank giving the Israelis full control over the settlements and the strategic Jordan Valley. There was provision for three further redeployments from "West Bank territory" during the life of the agreement. However, the details of those redeployments were not specified. The term "redeployment" does not convey the same sense of permanence as "withdrawal." While Israel had withdrawn from the Gaza Strip and the Jericho area it would only redeploy from areas of the West Bank. Redeployment seemed to contain the possibility that Israel could easily return to the areas that the troops had left. This did turn out to be the case after 2000.

What had not been appreciated at the time were the full consequences for Palestinian society of dividing the West Bank into the three zones. After implementation of the agreement there was a rapid installation of Israeli checkpoints which followed the new demarcation lines. Oslo increasingly became the medium through which the daily lives of Palestinians would become more regulated by Israel than previously.[1] Israeli checkpoints appeared on the roads accessing the towns and cities in area A. Initially Palestinians mimicked these checkpoints and established ones of their own. As a result civilians seeking to move quite small distances were constantly waiting in queues to show their documents on land designated by both the agreements as one territorial unit.

While the amount of land handed over to Palestinian administration was tiny Palestinian negotiators had more success in creating self-rule institutions. Initially the Israelis had conceived of the elected Council as a joint executive and legislative body with about 30 members. This type of body was more familiar in local government structures and was rejected by the Palestinians. As an alternative the Palestinians argued for separately elected executive and legislative organs. At the time Israel, while retaining the parliamentary system, had a directly elected Prime Minister and the Palestinian side argued for a similar structure. The Palestinians wanted the elected organs to have the status of national institutions which could prefigure the creation of a state. Another aim was to ensure that the legislature would be large enough to provide for broad representation of the political spectrum. As a result the agreement provided for a directly elected head of the executive known by the Arabic term *Ra'es* and an 88-seat Palestinian Legislative Council. *Ra'es* means the head of an organization and could equally mean President or Chairperson. For the Palestinians the term would convey President, and indicate a step towards statehood. Israel could think of *Ra'es* as a Chairperson thus leaving open the final designation of the Palestinian territories.[2]

When the agreement was adopted by the Israeli cabinet it was not with the support of the then new Interior Minister and future Prime Minister Ehud Barak. In the Knesset the right-wing parties led by Likud denounced it as a capitulation to Palestinian terror. Religious-nationalist parties went further and claimed that to leave any part of *Eretz-Israel* was a breach of the Jewish people's divine covenant. Mass demonstrations and rallies against Oslo II took place addressed by opposition leaders Benjamin Netanyahu and Ariel Sharon who frequently used terms such as "betrayal" and "capitulation" to describe it. The backbone of these demonstrations was the settlers and their supporters. It was as a result of the mobilization of the right that left-wing Israelis and the Peace Now Movement organized the rally at which Prime Minister Yitzhak Rabin was assassinated. Israel was to go through a traumatic period in the immediate aftermath which was marked by great introspection which did not help the peace process.

Rabin's funeral illustrated the possibilities of the period for Arab–Israeli relations. Both King Hussein of Jordan and President Hosni Mubarak of Egypt not only attended the funeral but also eulogized the murdered Prime Minister of the Jewish state. Many other Arab countries, despite having no diplomatic relations sent representatives. Arafat while not attending the funeral paid a condolence visit to Rabin's widow. This was a tantalizing moment indicating the possibility of a radically transformed Middle East.

Shimon Peres, who had been closely associated with the secret Oslo phase, became Prime Minister and by the end of December implemented the redeployment from area A. Israel removed its military personnel and dismantled its bases. As the redeployments took place Palestinians celebrated the liberation of their cities with mass demonstrations. There was a great sense of momentum as the peace process expressed itself in a popular form for the first time. The redeployments also opened the way for the first Palestinian elections which were held on January 22, 1996.

The elections were not held under ideal conditions. Most Palestinian territory was still directly occupied. Only in the newly liberated enclaves were there any real zones of freedom in the West Bank. The electoral campaign had to face the hurdles of Israeli checkpoints and other obstacles outside area A. Palestinians in still-occupied Hebron and in East Jerusalem faced many more serious problems and it was difficult to argue that the conditions existed for a free campaign. Nevertheless the Palestinian elections were the freest and fairest held in the Arab world. Despite the restrictions of occupation and the harassment of some candidates and voters by the Israeli authorities (especially in Jerusalem) the international observers endorsed the elections as free and fair. Yasser Arafat was elected *Ra'es* or President and his Fatah party held a good majority in the Legislative Council. For the first time national democratic institutions had been established in Arab Palestine.[3]

While most Palestinians in the West Bank and Gaza had welcomed the Oslo agreements as offering the possibility of change, Hamas and many Palestinians in the Diaspora had rejected them. For Hamas this rejection had extended to the institutions created by the agreements and so they had boycotted the elections. Despite the boycott participation in the elections was relatively high with a 77 percent turnout (73.5 percent in the West Bank and 86.8 percent in Gaza). In East Jerusalem only 40 percent of voters cast their votes at the Post Office.[4] Nonetheless overall the elections marked a high level of endorsement for the peace process.

The combination of the redeployments and elections were real signals that the national movement was making gains through negotiations. This did consolidate a sense of national consciousness and pride. However, the experience added yet another factor to the distinctive political culture of the West Bank and Gaza which exacerbated differences between the Palestinians in the occupied territories and the Diaspora. Whereas the *intifada* had been an anti-colonial revolt the elections appeared to point Palestine towards independence. For the Palestinians in Palestine ending the occupation was the central objective; for the Palestinian refugees the issue of return was central. This led to serious fissures in Palestinian politics. The pragmatic wing of Fatah focused on creating as many national facts in Palestine as possible. Its success in creating national institutions and in establishing the principle of Israeli withdrawal gave it a degree of power in the early months of 1996. However, this was to ebb dramatically as the momentum slowed.

In the spring of 1996 Hamas began its suicide attacks against Israeli civilians with the aim of destroying the peace process. The bus bombings became emblematic for Israelis that despite Oslo Palestinian terrorism was not over. In signing the Oslo agreements the PLO had not only renounced violence but was also committed to preventing violence. The problem for the PLO was that the 1996 wave of violence came from its opponents who rejected its authority. Hamas was based on the Muslim Brotherhood which organized at several levels a secretive military wing and a public network of religious, education and welfare organizations.[5] As with other Islamist organizations in the region, its social activities often filled the chasm in education and health services. Hamas played this role both during the occupation and after the mid 1990s under the Palestinian Authority. Its armed wing was thus able to operate within a supportive social space. When it had established itself in the 1980s Hamas had opposed the use of violence on the grounds that it would only lead to Israeli reprisals – and denounced the PLO for their violent provocations.[6] After Oslo the positions were reversed.

The aim of the Hamas suicide bombing campaign to de-rail the peace process met with some success. Shimon Peres would cancel Oslo-related negotiations after each incident on the grounds that it was impermissible to "give in to terrorism." As a result Hamas learnt that its attacks could halt the peace process. The immediate impact of the interruption of the discussions was the delay in agreeing on a timetable for further redeployments. These were critical as the Palestinian public needed to be confident that Israel was serious in handing over territory to the Palestinian Authority. Even the appearance of delay would undermine confidence that the peace process could deliver results. The agreements provided for three phases of redeployment (over an 18-month period) which would take place once the Legislative Council had been installed.[7] The object was to expand the control of the PA to "cover West Bank and Gaza Strip territory."[8] Peres had scheduled Israeli elections for May 1996 in an effort to secure his own mandate and his response to the suicide bombings was intended to burnish his security credentials. However, by appearing tough by calling off negotiations with the Palestinians committed to the peace process he allowed Palestinians who were opposed to it to set the agenda. As the legislative council had taken office in February the negotiations for the first redeployment should have been well advanced in the spring of 1996 so that the August deadline could have been met. The cessation of talks meant that no preparation had been made and the momentum that had been evident in December and January was broken. Undoubtedly Peres believed that he would be more likely to win the elections if he had a tough posture on terrorism. It was his Likud rival Netanyahu, however, who was able to use the suicide attacks as evidence of the failure of Oslo. He appeared before the cameras at every bus bombing to blame Oslo for the increased insecurity for Israelis. As a result terrorism not the peace process became the central electoral issue.

Peres may well have thought the time lost in the talks could be made up after he had won the election and that he would have had more authority to negotiate. However, in order to win the elections he needed to demonstrate the link between the peace process and long-term Israeli security. The focus on Hamas was to boost the organization's reputation for resistance while it weakened Fatah's reputation for gaining results by negotiations. Peres was also coy on what the objective of Oslo was. During this period Yossi Beilin[9] and Abu Mazen[10] were rumored to have worked out the details of a final settlement outside of the formal negotiations. The rumors were true but neither side had the courage to publish the plan. It provided for the creation of a Palestinian state in 1999 based on most of the West Bank and Gaza with its capital in East Jerusalem. Israeli settlements would remain and the settlers would be offered Palestinian citizenship if they wished. Palestinian refugees would have the right to return to the Palestinian state and to compensation for moral and economic losses.[11] This plan offered a vision that both Israelis and Palestinians needed to debate. Its compromises on sensitive issues were such that political forces on each side did not want to deal with it in public. Arafat constantly feared that revealing his hand too early would weaken his negotiating stance.

He also wanted to avoid provoking the wrath of his critics in Fatah and beyond, particularly in the refugee community. Peres operated on the basis that Israeli voters would balk at talk of a Palestinian state and that the settlers would mobilize against being "handed over" to the Palestinians. Both Arafat and Peres had constituencies who had little interest in any compromise. Neither leader was prepared to confront them.

Instead of outlining any concrete destination for the peace process, Peres chose to fight the election on a manifesto which merely stated that Labor was not opposed to the creation of a Palestinian state. Likud denounced the leaked Beilin–Abu Mazen plan as a recipe for national capitulation. The party though did not run on a program of opposing Oslo. Its manifesto merely said that a government it formed would maintain Israel's international commitments – a code for formally, at least, maintaining Oslo.

When Netanyahu narrowly beat Peres, Likud was now able to dictate the pace and character of Israel's implementation of Oslo. Oslo was about to be transformed from a process that offered the Palestinians the prospect of freedom into a mechanism to prolong the occupation. Ariel Sharon was prominent in the government serving as infrastructure minister with a special brief for the settlements. Shortly before he took office, in an interesting opinion piece in the *Jerusalem Post* in late 1995 he had decried the West Bank redeployments which he saw as a step towards a Palestinian state in area A. That he said was bad news. However, the good news was that the Palestinian state was very small.[12] The question was how to keep it as small and weak as possible. This stance was to influence Netanyahu's view of Oslo as he set out to change the character of the negotiations. His aim he said was to lower Palestinian expectations. He resumed negotiations but concentrated first on Hebron. In January 1997, after six months of painfully slow talks, an agreement was reached that would allow Israel to retain control of the center of a city with over 100,000 Palestinians so that it could protect 400 Israeli settlers.

It took a further ten months for Netanyahu to agree to the first redeployment as stipulated in the agreement. By the time the Wye River Memorandum to give effect to this was signed in October 1998 all the redeployments should have been completed. As a result Netanyahu proposed to merge the first two phases of redeployments. The style of negotiating over every square kilometer was much in evidence. Under the Wye agreement Palestinians would obtain full control over only 17 percent of the West Bank and partial control over a further 22 percent. This result meant that five years after the signing of Oslo and less than a year to its supposed climax, Israel still controlled 61 percent of the West Bank.[13] This was what Netanyahu had meant by lowering expectations and it appeared to be a calibrated implementation of Sharon's small state policy.

Palestinian expectations had been that the three redeployments would have meant that within 18 months of February 1996 70–80 percent of the West Bank would have fallen under the Palestinian Authority. With that in mind Palestinian negotiators had worked on the basis that each redeployment should affect about 25 percent of the West Bank. The interim agreement was especially vague on the matter and worryingly referred to "West Bank and Gaza Strip territory" rather than *the* West Bank and Gaza Strip territory. This echo of the wording of resolution 242 could leave doubt as to the real extent of any Israeli redeployment. The way the document was drafted left Israel as the only partner with any initiative. Thus the phrase "further redeployments of Israeli military forces to specified military locations will be gradually implemented in accordance with the DOP [Declaration of Principles]," was quickly taken advantage of by Netanyahu to mean that Israel alone could determine the scope of the redeployment. The Palestinians had expected that the permanent status negotiations would begin when they controlled the bulk of occupied Palestine. The key questions then would be the fate of the Israeli settlements, the status of Jerusalem and the future of the refugees, but these would be negotiated against the background of full self-government in the West Bank and Gaza. This was the result that Netanyahu wanted to prevent.

Netanyahu came to the issue of the occupied territories with a clear vision of their future. In his book published in 1993[14] he had outlined his autonomy solution. "There is no reason," he had written, "why every lonely cluster of Arab houses should claim to need autonomy over the entire mountain on which it is perched. Thus autonomy is primarily applicable to urban centers in which an Arab population can make decisions on day to day life."[15] For Netanyahu the Palestinian population could make do with little land. Nonetheless he regarded even these areas as problematic as they could be used as a base from which to attack Israel. The Palestinians would need to be kept under the watchful Israeli eye: "to combat terrorism, Israeli military and security forces must have access to every part of the territory, including the urban centers from which terrorists may strike and to which they may return for safe haven."[16] However, under his plan the Palestinians of the

West Bank would be able to exercise limited autonomy. "It would be appropriate," he continued,

> ...to develop a system of four self-managing Arab counties: Jenin, Nablus, Ramallah and Hebron. Each of these counties comprises a city and the small towns and villages adjacent to it. Together these counties encompass the great majority of the West Bank's Arab population, and they take up no more than one fifth of the land.[17]

Having become Prime Minister it seemed that it was this vision that was to inform his negotiating position with the Palestinians. He was quite explicit about what "lowering expectations" meant, explaining on television that he "was not prepared to accept Palestinian sovereignty... A Palestinian or Arab state here, in the heart of our country, means an Arab army, alliances with Arab countries and dangers."[18] He explained that he was "prepared to give them many powers, but not in any areas that can threaten the existence of my country." During this period of "lowering expectations" many officials in the government began to publicly comment on solutions to the occupied territories that would result in less than statehood. In a press briefing in December 1996 David Bar-Ilan, the press aid to Israel's UN Ambassador, talked about a future Palestinian entity having the status of Puerto Rico or Andorra. Bar Ilan had overlooked that the latter had statehood and was a member of the United Nations. Nonetheless the message was clear: call it what you might the Palestinian entity that the Likud government had in mind was to be something less than a sovereign state; it would be an entity with limited powers and little territory. Netanyahu spelt out in some detail what this would look like. Speaking to a Jewish American audience in November 1997, he explained:

> I have not drawn any precise maps to define what we have in mind for an agreement with the Palestinians. But I do know that I represent a very broad national consensus when I declare that the Jordan Valley must be Israel's strategic border, that Israel will not give up control of airspace and water resources, that it must keep strategic zones that it considers vital; that it will not allow a Palestinian army equipped with heavy weapons or non-conventional arms to form West of the Jordan, and, above all Jerusalem will stay the undivided capital of Israel for ever.[19]

Drawing the map to those specifications would not have been difficult. Indeed earlier in the same year he had referred to his plan as "Allon-plus map." In the 1970s General Yigal Allon had produced a plan for withdrawal of central areas of the West Bank with Israel retaining the rest.[20] Like Netanyahu's proposals 20 years later Palestinians would have been entirely encircled by Israel and living on less than 50 percent of the West Bank. Netanyahu had in fact ordered officials to prepare a detailed map which was leaked to the press in 1998. It was strikingly similar to the Allon plan. There were to be three Palestinian areas although geographically separated from each other. The bulk of the West Bank would be retained by Israel. Netanyahu was able to justify his proposals as entirely consistent with the Oslo agreements as the permanent status phase was subjected to negotiations with no specified outcome. He was merely outlining Israel's proposals for a settlement.

Netanyahu, the politician who had gained so much from opposition to Oslo, was to cast himself in the role of its most enthusiastic defender. Oslo began to be presented as the document that contained the fundamental legal principles that regulated relations between Israel and the Palestinians. The ambiguities of the text and its silence on its ultimate goal were used to good effect. Netanyahu seized on the fact that the PLO had agreed to negotiate on such key questions as settlements and refugees as proof that the Palestinians had accepted that the legal issues at stake were no longer settled. The Geneva Conventions, United Nations General Assembly and Security Council resolutions on these topics were to be seen from the vantage point of Oslo. Indeed the willingness of the Palestinians to negotiate the permanent status issues at all was taken to mean that even the right to self-determination was not absolute. For Netanyahu and his government Oslo was the prism through which all legal obligations should be viewed. By entering Oslo the PLO had signaled its readiness to give up other legal entitlements.

Netanyahu attempted to use Oslo to place the Palestinians in a legal vice. At the same time he mounted a diplomatic offensive to convince the international community that Israel was adhering strictly to the principles of international law according to the Oslo agreements. Israel could determine the pace and scope of the redeployments which were subject to its security requirements. As a result talks with the Palestinians became increasingly protracted as every forest, hill and wasteland was mulled over. This resulted in minute increases in the amount of territory controlled by the PA which was to amount to 42 percent under full or partial control.

This was presented to the international community as progress and indeed as a sign of Israel's generosity.

The main objective was to use Oslo to teach the Palestinians that they were the subordinate party. It was meant to lower their expectations not only of the amount of land they would obtain, but also of what type of legal and political entity they might expect to build. Israel meanwhile continued to expand the settlements and construct the vast road network which allowed Israelis to travel between Israel and the settlements without passing through Palestinian areas. The infrastructure of the colonial occupation was made to appear permanent. The pace of settlement building did slow in the West Bank during these years – but not in East Jerusalem. Nonetheless the number of settlers continued to grow. In 1993 when the peace process began there were 120,000 settlers in the West Bank; by 2000 that number had doubled.

One of the myths of Oslo was that the Israelis had committed themselves to a settlement freeze. However, both parties had agreed in the Declaration of Principles that the "outcome of the permanent status negotiations should not be prejudiced or pre-empted by agreement reached for the interim period."[21] A similar clause was to appear in the Cairo Agreement[22] and in the interim agreement.[23] The latter also provided that "neither side shall initiate or take any step that will change the status of the West Bank or the Gaza Strip pending the outcome of the permanent status negotiations."[24] Thus if the parties continued to treat the West Bank and Gaza as they had at the outset of the process they would not be in breach of the agreement. This offered maximum maneuver to the most powerful party, Israel, to continue with its existing policies. Moreover the combined effect of these clauses was to allow Israel to maintain that it continued to have legal rights and claims in the West Bank and Gaza.

It is important to bear in mind that at the time the Israeli position on the West Bank and Gaza was either that they were disputed territories or indeed that Israel had a degree of legal title to them. This was certainly the case with Jerusalem and the West Bank. Yehuda Blum, the permanent representative of Israel to the United Nations (1978–84) and a legal scholar, made the case that as Jordan had used force illegally in 1948 it was not entitled to annex the West Bank and East Jerusalem. As Israel's use of force in 1967 was self-defense and therefore legal, Israel's claim to the area was greater than Jordan's or any other state's. To support this view he quotes Stephen Schwebel's[25] argument that "where the prior holder of territory had seized that territory unlawfully, the State which subsequently takes that territory in the lawful exercise of self-defense, has against the prior holder, better title."[26] In addition Blum made the case that the historical connection between the Jewish people and the West Bank was "an integral part of world history" that added, he thought, legal weight to the argument about 1967. This led him to argue that Jewish settlements, which he called "Israeli villages," were legal and built for the most part on what was Jewish-owned land. It was true that some settlements were built on land that had been owned by Jews before 1948. However, the settlements had acquired far more land from the category of *miri*[27] or public land which the British Mandate had made relatively easy for the state to acquire through expropriation. The Israeli authorities had ruthlessly used this "legal" device. Technically Israeli governments attempted to hide behind the fiction that such land was not "Arab-owned" in the sense that it was tenanted and the actual holder of the land was the state. It was for this reason that legal arguments claiming Israeli title to the West Bank, despite their absurdity, were clung to as it would mean that such land ultimately belonged to Israel and not to the Palestinians who lived and worked on it. It is also the case that at least 30 percent of the land the settlements are built on has been expropriated from Palestinian private owners. Netanyahu acted on the basis that this questionable legal account was the starting point for talks with the Palestinians over the West Bank. Offering the Palestinians half of the West Bank was seen by him as reasonable given that he considered all of the West Bank as legally Israel's to dispose of as it wished. The rejection of such discredited positions by the international community was dismissed on the grounds that Oslo should be seen as the exclusive basis for any settlement.

Israel under Netanyahu thus presented legal issues of the occupied territories as especially complex. Israel had good title and Israelis had long-standing interests in land. Palestinians should be prepared to negotiate in this context and should reject not only their sweeping claims to all of Palestine but also the international community's legal consensus that Palestinians were fully entitled to self-determination. Netanyahu was to stick doggedly to his view that it was Israel, and not the Palestinians who had title to the West Bank – and although on different grounds, to Gaza as well.[28]

This negotiating stance would thus cast any Israeli withdrawal from any amount of territory as a major concession. It would represent "giving up land." As a result it would be reasonable for

Israel to continue to argue over every square kilometer of land. Mahmoud Abbas (Abu Mazen) had been fully aware that Israel would take this position even during the Rabin and Peres period. Before Netanyahu's election he wrote, "Israel seeks to annex parts of the West Bank and of the Gaza Strip, and will try to control the water resources and will strive to annex Jerusalem."[29] Abbas' comment demonstrated that the Palestinian side knew well the basis on which any Israeli government would approach the question of territory. Netanyahu's views revealed a methodology that went well beyond the confines of the Israeli right. This became quite clear when Labor regained office under Ehud Barak.

The Netanyahu period saw the same pattern of incredibly detailed talks that had characterized the first phase of Oslo which was used to slow the process. So detailed and drawn out were they that when the time-frame came to an end in May 1999 no permanent status agreement was in sight. As May 4 approached many in the Palestinian camp debated the virtue of unilaterally declaring an independent Palestinian state. At first this was seen as a challenge to the Israeli government's refusal to bring Oslo to a conclusion. A declaration would be seen as taking the initiative and providing the basis for winning diplomatic recognition and possibly United Nations membership. The Clinton administration was against the idea fearing that it would destabilize any attempt to rescue Oslo. Clinton no doubt hoped that the Israeli Labor Party would win the upcoming elections and the spirit of 1993 would be revived. The Labor Party was also opposed to any unilateral action by the Palestinians.

While Netanyahu was also formally against the declaration the broader right in Israeli politics – including parts of his government – viewed the idea with some favor. As the Palestinians still controlled less than half the West Bank in areas A and B, amounting to only 10 percent of mandate Palestine, such a declaration was seen as fortuitous. This conveniently tiny and fragmented territory would also lack borders with other states. Such a Palestinian state would conform to the small weak state that Ariel Sharon had thought might be acceptable. On the West Bank it would be comprised of scattered areas surrounded by Israeli control. Once declared, Israel might opt for further negotiations but that would be from a position of considerable strength as it had been the Palestinians who had unilaterally declared their state within such borders. As these considerations surfaced Palestinian support for a Declaration of Statehood faded and Arafat let the date pass by. This incident perhaps demonstrated the power that Oslo still exercised over the parties and its international supporters. Despite the passing of the time-frame the core principles of withdrawal from land, the creation of Palestinian institutions and negotiations remained intact.

The June 1999 elections saw a crushing defeat for Netanyahu and the election of Ehud Barak as Prime Minister. Barak who had been Israeli Chief of Staff before entering politics was seen as something of a protégé of Yitzhak Rabin. However, he had not been an enthusiastic supporter of Oslo and as we noted had abstained in the cabinet vote on the interim agreement in 1995. There was great enthusiasm in Israel on his election and a feeling that there would be a serious return to the peace process. Barak, however, turned his attention to negotiations with Syria rather than moving quickly to deal with the Palestinians. The Syrian talks ended in failure and months had gone by in which the situation in the Palestinian areas had worsened politically and economically.

By 1999 the Palestinian Authority was well established and it had been able to create a series of political, legal and economic institutions. These positive developments had been hamstrung by the continuing conditions of Israeli occupation. Checkpoints began to turn Palestinian cities, towns and villages into prisons. A system of passes was introduced for Palestinians visiting East Jerusalem or to pass through any part of Israel including for journeys to Ben-Gurion international airport. Even for Palestinians traveling within the West Bank many journeys necessitated passing through several checkpoints. Some 700 such checkpoints hampered a population of under 2 million people going about their daily business, on their way to work, schools, hospitals or to visit relatives. At many checkpoints at busy times large queues formed; sometimes they were closed and crossing them at night was impossible. Simple journeys became lengthy and humiliating. Increasingly the checkpoints also became the scenes of human rights abuses. The disruption to civilian life was thus drastic. Checkpoints also had a disastrous impact on the fledgling institutions and the economy. Officials found it difficult to carry out their functions. School inspectors, for example, were often unable to reach a school and return to their offices before the checkpoints closed. Similarly businesses were subject to the same difficulties in the movement of goods and labor. As the conditions in occupied Palestine deteriorated, unemployment and frustration grew.

The fragility of the Palestinian Authority was underlined by the manner in which it was financed. Most of its revenue came from the return of VAT receipts on goods sold and from international donors. As a result the Authority was reliant on Israel for the return of the VAT and the good will of the international community. Thus the Authority grew highly dependent on both. This became all the more problematic as the payroll of the PA grew to some 130,000, the largest employer in Palestine. More widely Palestine became a donor-dependent society as universities, community groups and other parts of civil society competed for the attention and grants of governments and charitable foundations. Funding became a way of molding Palestinian society and setting its agendas. While donors were often motivated by good will the effect was to deepen Palestinian dependency and often undermine any sense of empowerment. Small pockets of individual initiative and economic enterprise did exist but they had to battle against these difficult conditions.

Palestinians had every reason to be wary of the direction that Arafat's leadership was taking their society. While heroic efforts were made to base the Authority on the rule of law and the highest standards of professionalism, these were often marginalized. From the creation of the Palestinian Authority in 1994 an important project to create a Basic Law to ensure that it was regulated by law and not political expediency was established. Academics, community activists, lawyers and politicians worked assiduously to produce a text of the law and the legal culture that would be required to sustain it. Many drafts of the Basic Law were produced but the President seemed reluctant to promulgate it. At the same time many of the key members of the Authority had been more used to running an exiled liberation organization than addressing the more mundane activities associated with day-to-day administration. Particular practices and values that might have been appropriate in exile became problematic in government. Very rapidly loyalty to individual leaders could turn into cronyism and corruption.[30] Debates in the Palestinian Legislative Council in the late 1990s often focused on these issues, and at times even called for the removal of particular ministers and officials.

CAMP DAVID 2000

It was against this unfavorable background in Palestine that Barak began to return to serious negotiations. He had a rather clear idea of what should be the result. Instead of beginning with the delayed third redeployment Barak wanted to go immediately to the permanent status stage and to obtain an end of conflict agreement.

However, serious redeployment – perhaps doubling the areas under Palestinian control – could have been a useful confidence-building move which could have changed the atmosphere. Instead he held out for once-and-for-all talks to conclude the process. US President Bill Clinton convened the Camp David conference for this purpose. However, months were wasted while the arrangements were being put in place which weakened both Arafat and Barak. Arafat needed to be able to show movement on the ground but as the economic situation worsened and the checkpoints tightened he was unable to offer a credible political horizon. Had Barak carried out a significant redeployment that had consolidated Palestinian control over a contiguous area of perhaps 70 percent of the West Bank and released several thousand Palestinian prisoners, Arafat might have been able to pose as a leader whose strategy had achieved real gains. Barak, however, acting like every Israeli leader since 1967, saw control over land and the prisoners as bargaining chips that he wanted to keep in his hand for the final deal.

July 2000 was an inauspicious moment for the talks that were advertised as ending the Palestinian–Israeli conflict. Clinton, Barak and Arafat all arrived at Camp David with ebbing political capital. Clinton was in the last six months of his presidency; Barak's coalition had collapsed and he was facing elections in six months; and Arafat, as we have seen, led a dependent Palestinian entity with very little to show for opting for the peace process. The discussions thus took place amongst leaders who were either too weak to make an agreement or in the case of Clinton were losing the political muscle to push them toward one. When inevitably the conference failed, each side attempted to blame the other. According to the Israelis this was the conference where the Palestinians rejected a generous Israeli offer that would have given them 95 percent of their demands. By rejecting the offer the Palestinian leadership was said to have demonstrated bad faith. Worse, it was claimed, Arafat had calculated that he would gain more by a return to violence than by maintaining negotiations.

The story of a generous Israeli offer began to circulate in the world's press. Arafat and the Palestinian leadership were portrayed as irrational in rejecting it. As the participants to the conference reported their experiences, however, a more complex reality emerged. In media accounts the Israeli offer to the Palestinians consisted of offering a Palestinian state on 95 percent of the West Bank and Gaza with its capital in the Palestinian neighborhoods of Jerusalem. However, no such offer was made by Barak at Camp

David. While accounts of the conference differ in details all agree that the main failure was the refusal of Barak and Arafat and their teams to meet directly and to consider concrete proposals together. Both sides remained in their respective cabins and Clinton's chief Middle East expert Dennis Ross engaged in a form of cabin-to-cabin diplomacy. Ross and other officials would discuss possible positions with each team and then President Clinton would meet, first with Barak and then with Arafat to assess their reaction to them. In this way the famous Clinton parameters emerged. Thus while a deal of sorts was in the air at Camp David, it was not an Israeli one and it really contained a series of US principles that would need to be developed.

The Clinton parameters[31] began with the allocation of territory for the Palestinian state. The position articulated was that "the solution will need to provide sovereignty over somewhere between 90 and 100 percent of West Bank territory."[32] The emphasis was on the word "between" as the intention was to allow Israel to annex the most populous settlements, although "there will need to be swaps and other territorial arrangements" to compensate the Palestinians.[33] This would mean that between 4 and 6 percent of the West Bank would be annexed by Israel, although the Palestinians would only receive between 1 and 3 percent of Israeli territory in exchange. However it also appeared that arrangements would be made for Israel to lease areas of the West Bank in addition. On Jerusalem, Israeli neighborhoods would be Israel's and Palestinian neighborhoods would become Palestine's with a complex sovereignty sharing agreement over the Haram al-Sharif/Temple Mount area. When Israel had annexed Jerusalem significant parts of the West Bank had been brought within the city boundaries. By 2000, some 180,000 Israelis lived in East Jerusalem and the allocation of those areas to Israel meant that Israel would gain far more than 5 percent of the West Bank. In addition 2 percent of land would be gained by Israel in exchange for a narrow strip of Israeli territory being attached to Gaza. Israel would also lease another 2 percent of the West Bank. The Clinton parameters would have seen Israel take at least 10 percent of the West Bank. Ehud Barak also revealed that there would have been a thin Israeli corridor that would run from Jerusalem through to the Jordan Valley thus cutting the West Bank in two.[34]

The proposed Palestinian state would be "non-militarized," although there would be a "strong Palestinian security force." Its borders would be eventually protected by an international force.

Israel would be allowed to retain three early warning military bases on the West Bank. In addition if Israel declared a "state of national emergency" Israel could deploy armed forces in Palestine along agreed routes. Palestine was to have control over its airspace although both sides should work out "special arrangements for Israeli training and operational needs." In the first three years the international borders of Palestine would be patrolled by Israeli forces after which they would hand over to the international force. As can be seen Palestinian control over its own territory would have been rather tenuous and would have been subject to Israeli security requirements. In addition the Palestinians would have had to trust that Israel would keep to the three-year time-line on handing border control to the international force.

On the critical question of refugees Clinton proposed one of two possible formulations: either "both sides recognize the right of Palestinian refugees to return to historic Palestine" or "both sides recognize the right of the Palestinian refugees to a homeland." These principles could be achieved in a number of ways. Palestinian refugees could: (1) return to the Palestinian state, (2) return to areas in Israel being transferred to the Palestinian state, (3) be rehabilitated in a host country, (4) be resettled in a third country, or (5) be admitted to Israel with the proviso that such admission was to be consistent with Israel's sovereign decision.[35] Thus under this scheme refugees' rights were treated collectively as far as any return was concerned.

The Clinton parameters thus did provide for Israel's withdrawal from about 90 percent of occupied land and the creation of a Palestinian state – although the latter was highly subject to Israeli-defined security needs. On the refugees the option was similar to many other attempts to find a compromise on the issue of return. Clinton himself summed up the proposals thus:

> It gives the Palestinian people the ability to determine their future on their own land, a sovereign viable state recognized by the international community, al Quds as its capital, sovereignty over the Haram, and new lives for the refugees.

> It gives the people of Israel a genuine end to the conflict, real security, the preservation of sacred religious ties, the incorporation of 80% of the settlers into Israel and the largest Jerusalem in history, recognized as your capital.[36]

The comments offer a positive spin on a series of principles that would have had to be drafted into a real agreement. It should be pointed out that they were offered to parties with no accompanying maps. As a result the exact shape of the Palestinian state was still to be decided. Given that Camp David took place well over a year after the Oslo process was meant to have been concluded, the lack of something so elementary as a map indicated how fragile the proposals were. Oslo had come full circle and the Declaration of Principles had led to a proposal for another such declaration. Important movement had taken place, however. Israel had accepted that there would be a Palestinian state, that the Palestinian refugees would have the right to return to it and that Jerusalem could be a shared city. Since 1949 Israel had at various times indicated that between 60,000 and 100,000 refugees could return to Israel itself under a family reunification program, and this offer seems to have been renewed. With these parameters Bill Clinton and Dennis Ross had undoubtedly attempted to rescue something out of a doomed diplomatic initiative.

The problem for the Americans was that neither Palestinians nor Israelis were amenable to genuine talks, and both were too weak politically to make concessions. Arafat had been offered such a weak state with so many restrictions on its powers that he would have been ridiculed by his critics. After all Arafat the leader who had done most to restore Palestinian identity through the armed struggle would have to defend a Palestinian state where Israel would have permanent bases, be granted an unlimited right to enter and initially would be patrolling its borders. That would have seemed a humiliating denouement for a Palestinian President who liked to be seen in military uniform. Arafat was also engaged in internal struggles within Fatah over the direction of his strategy; and Fatah faced competition with an increasingly powerful Hamas opposition.

Barak, however, seemed to have approached Camp David with low expectations. In an interview with Benny Morris in June 2002, Barak argued that the real aim of the Palestinians was for "a state in all of Palestine." He assessed that the old two-stage approach to the liberation of Palestine was still in play. He argued that in the short term this would be difficult to achieve because "Israel is too strong," but "their game plan is to establish a Palestinian state while leaving an opening for further 'legitimate' demands down the road."[37] He outlined his view of this strategy in the following way:

They will exploit the tolerance and democracy of Israel first to turn it into "a state for all its citizens," as demanded by the extreme nationalist wing of Israel's Arabs and extremist left-wing Jewish Israelis. Then they will push for a binational state and then, demography and attrition will lead to a state with a Muslim majority and a Jewish minority. This would not necessarily involve kicking out all the Jews. But it would mean the destruction of Israel as a Jewish state. This, I believe is their vision.[38]

As a result Barak did not relate to Arafat as a partner negotiating in good faith. Not only did the Palestinians hide their true political program but, he believed, they were mired in a culture of deception:

They are products of a culture in which to tell a lie...creates no dissonance. They don't suffer from the problem of telling lies that exists in Judeo-Christian culture. Truth is seen as an irrelevant category. There is only that which serves your purpose and that which doesn't. They see themselves as emissaries of a national movement for whom everything is permissible. There is no such thing as "the truth."[39]

Working within this crude Orientalist imagery it would seem improbable that Barak could have held any meaningful discussions with Arafat or indeed any Palestinian. This no doubt explained his suspicions of the Oslo process and his abstention on the interim agreement in 1995. Barak appeared to suggest that the years of secret and then open talks which hammered out all those detailed documents was on the part of the Palestinians just a ruse; the first stage towards the destruction of Israel. Barak seemed to have thought of Camp David as a test to see whether Arafat "would rise to the occasion" and overcome his inherent nature. As he thought that that was entirely unlikely the purpose of the conference, for Barak, appeared to have been to unmask Arafat before the international public. This attitude could explain why Barak did not arrive at Camp David with any particular settlement in mind except the demand that there should be an "end of conflict" agreement. How this stance was to expose Arafat's true nature remains unclear. This was especially so as the Clinton parameters were to be portrayed as the Israeli "generous offer." It would seem contradictory that Barak would want to be associated with such an offer which could have provided Arafat with part of his alleged strategy which would have liquidated Israel. As Arafat rejected Clinton's proposals Barak's account of Camp David seems curious. He appeared to want us to believe that if Arafat had accepted the parameters that would have been evidence of deception and if he rejected them it would prove that the Palestinians were unwilling to compromise. What was starkly revealing in Morris' interview was Barak's racist attitude toward Palestinians – and toward Arabs and Muslims in general. He was probably not alone in the Israeli government in harboring such views. As we have seen at other points in the conflict politics was to take second place to ideological fealties and racial stereotypes.

While both leaders returned home the members of the negotiating teams did continue talking. The Clinton parameters offered a basis for some very serious and interesting discussions. Significant progress was made but they took place against the background of the outbreak of the second *intifada* in September 2000, sparked by a provocative visit by Ariel Sharon, the then leader of the Likud opposition, to Temple Mount.[40] The *intifada* began as a protest against his visit and soon spread into violent confrontations between Palestinians and the IDF in the occupied territories. As the intensity and the scale of the clashes grew the talks appeared less and less connected with events on the ground. Barak began to respond by military incursions into area A and so even the meager results of the Oslo redeployments were rolled back. The talks ended in February 2001 when Ariel Sharon was elected Prime Minister. Sharon was to complete Barak's military policy and effectively to re-conquer the West Bank. When George W. Bush succeeded Clinton US involvement in the Middle East peace process became much more remote.

At first Ariel Sharon's government pursued an almost entirely military response to the *intifada*. This included full-scale attacks on Palestinian cities and towns, and Israeli troops were active in areas nominally under exclusive Palestinian control. In Ramallah President Arafat's compound was held under siege by Israeli forces. The President remained at his post as electricity was cut off and the surrounding area was reduced to rubble. Sharon and many in the Israeli political establishment held Arafat personally responsible for the *intifada*. Barak strongly agreed with this assessment and took the view that Arafat had planned the *intifada*; it was "preplanned, pre-prepared. I don't mean that Arafat knew that [it would begin] on a certain day in September but it was definitely on the level of planning, of a grand plan."[41] Israeli forces were to surround the *Muqata* (Arafat's headquarters) for weeks. This was not to make a moral point about Arafat's alleged responsibility. Holding Arafat hostage was part of a wider Sharon policy to demonstrate that Arafat held responsibility for the breakdown of talks and that he did not have the capacity at any level to be a partner for peace. Negotiations with such a patron of violence, the line went, was quite impossible; the peace process with the Palestinians was declared to be over.

The defining moment at the beginning of the twenty-first century was the September 11, 2001, al-Qa'ida attacks on the World Trade Center and the Pentagon. The impact on the Palestinian–Israeli conflict was quite immediate as Ariel Sharon responded by placing Israel in the frontline of the "war on terror." Arafat, the Fatah-sponsored al-Aqsa Martyrs Brigade and the Hamas militias were lined up alongside Osama bin Laden and al-Qa'ida. Sharon wanted to stress that all were terror organizations and that they used the same methods. The Palestinian groups were equally a threat to civilization; they too targeted civilians, they acted irrationally and like al-Qa'ida they could not be negotiated with. This stance chimed well with many in the Bush administration. Thus despite the fact that Arafat had denounced the September 11 attacks (and even publicly donated blood for the people of New York) he was to be portrayed as a comrade in arms of Osama bin Laden. The use of suicide bombing by Hamas and the al-Aqsa Martyrs Brigade was offered as further evidence that the United States and Israel were facing the same enemy.[42]

Sharon's main policy aim was to convince the United States and the international community that the Oslo agreements were now dead and that they had been killed by the Palestinian leadership. His account of the situation was similar to that of Barak. The PLO was said to have been revealed as an untrustworthy partner, one that had not negotiated in good faith but had been biding its time to build up its forces so that it could return to the armed struggle. The negotiations had been used to facilitate the relocation of the PLO leadership and military forces from Tunis to Ramallah so that it could confront Israel from a more favorable position. For Sharon the *intifada* had confirmed this strategy.

While Sharon had been successful in convincing the Bush administration that Arafat was part of the international terrorist threat, the US President was also under pressure to produce a strategic response to the deepening Palestinian–Israeli conflict. September 11 had been a humanitarian disaster for the United States, but the real targets of al-Qa'ida and other militant Islamist groups were the regimes within the Islamic world which were regarded as collaborators with the West. In the new political situation the Bush administration – and others in the West – sought to shore up support for these governments who were to be regarded as allies in the war on terror. Chief amongst them was Saudi Arabia which had had close political and economic relations with the United States for many decades. Within the Arab world the unresolved conflict over Palestine and the USA's perceived support for Israel often undermined the effectiveness of US policy. Within a month of September 11 President Bush had announced that the creation of a Palestinian state had always been part of US policy. In June 2002 Bush was more forthcoming with the details as he announced that his vision was a Palestinian state living alongside Israel. However, bold as this statement was Bush elaborated this policy by referring to the creation of a "provisional Palestinian state" and one which would have new leaders and new institutions. This neatly bridged the gap between the Arab needs for greater US support for Palestine and Israeli demands to isolate Arafat. It was support for some form of Palestinian state but minus Arafat.

While Bush was developing his Palestinian policies the Arab world was debating its attitude to Israel. As a result in March 2002 the Arab League meeting in Beirut adopted a policy for a two-state solution to the Palestinian–Israeli conflict. The proposal which was initiated by then Prince (now King) Abdullah of Saudi Arabia was a highly significant development. The plan was based on the principle that "a military solution to the conflict will not achieve peace or provide security for the parties." This marked a fundamental change in the Arab position. As the League had been committed to the military option since 1946 this was an important declaration that this policy was decisively at an end. The Arab League Council then called for Israel to adopt a similar position and declared that "a just peace is a strategic option." It then addressed a series of obligations which it asked Israel to accept:

(a) Full Israeli withdrawal from all the territories occupied since 1967, including the Syrian Golan Heights to the lines of June 4 1967 as well as the remaining territories in the south of Lebanon.

(b) Achieve a just solution to the Palestinian Refugee problem to be agreed upon in accordance with UN General Assembly Resolution 194.

(c) The acceptance of the establishment of a Sovereign Independent Palestinian State on the Palestinian Territories occupied since

4th of June 1967 in the West Bank and the Gaza strip, with East Jerusalem as its capital.[43]

In exchange for Israel meeting these obligations, Arab countries would:

(a) Consider the Conflict ended, and enter into a peace agreement with Israel, and provide security for all the states of the region.
(b) Establish normal relations with Israel in the context of this comprehensive peace.[44]

These proposals completely transformed the political and legal narratives of the Arab League since its inception. The new policy incorporated the logic of several previous Arab diplomatic initiatives but the bold and open culmination of that logic was decisive. It was all the more poignant that the statement was issued in Beirut, the Arab city which had suffered so much at the hands of Israel – and while Sharon had been Minister of Defense. In March 2002 the Arab states were to accept Israel within borders much more expansive than those that the same body had so vehemently opposed in 1947. The Arab League's acceptance of partition was on terms much less favorable to the Palestinians than the UN had proposed 55 years before. It was also significant that the plan included an "end of conflict" clause, something which Barak had demanded at Camp David. Sharon's government rather sidestepped this new opportunity by claiming that Israel could not accept the clause on refugees as this referred to General Assembly resolution 194. Although as we have seen this resolution was highly conditional on the right to return and in any event the Arab League's formulation required agreement by all the parties on its meaning. The historic significance of the movement by the Arab League was not grasped by the Israeli government – as it had another altogether different plan.

Much of 2002 was overshadowed by the lead up to the Iraq war during which there was much talk of "regime change." Once in the air, regime change increasingly became grafted to the discussion of Palestine. Within the United States and Israel in particular it seemed to offer a new legal and political option with which to address the Palestine question. The Palestinian people were portrayed as victims not of Israeli occupation but of their own leadership. The miseries of life in the occupied territories had been brought about due to the policies of the Arafat leadership which had turned to violence rather than accept the "generous offer" of Camp David. Removing

Arafat was projected as the key to rescuing the Palestinian people. Regime change was the answer.

During 2002 a strange quartet of the United Nations, the USA, Russia and the European Union began to meet to hammer out a new international initiative which was to take shape in the form of the "roadmap." Entitled "a performance-based roadmap to a permanent two-state solution to the Israeli–Palestinian conflict" it announced that the destination was "a final and comprehensive settlement" by 2005.[45] The performance aspect of the roadmap applied particularly to the Palestinians and the central project was the re-building of Palestinian institutions. The roadmap was divided into three phases. In the first both sides were to end violence and Israel was to withdraw its forces to the positions they had occupied in September 2000 at the outbreak of the *intifada*. At the same time Palestinians should begin major institutional reform. In the second phase these reforms would continue and end with a Palestinian state with provisional borders which would be established by December 2003. Finally, over the next two years Israel and the Palestinians would resolve all outstanding issues – in particular the final borders between the two states.

The reform of Palestinian institutions included proposals that were in fact partial regime change. One of the requirements was that there had to be "immediate action" to draft a constitution for the Palestinian state that would be "based on strong parliamentary democracy and cabinet with empowered prime minister." This was a not too subtle formula for sidelining Arafat. The intention in making the new Prime Minister "empowered" was that the center of power would move from the presidency to the Prime Minister. The authors of the roadmap were so insistent on this development that the Palestinians were not to wait for the niceties of drafting the proposed new constitution before appointing "an interim prime minister or cabinet with empowered executive authority/decision-making powers."[46] And just to underline the character of these powers the text continues that cabinet ministers should be appointed who are "empowered to undertake fundamental reform." Thus Israeli and US policy on Arafat's alleged inadequacies had been largely accepted by the international community in the new plan. While placing emphasis on democracy and the rule of law, the roadmap demanded that Palestinians should ignore the existing legal framework, appoint a new government by fiat and ensure the exclusion from power of the democratically elected President.

The roadmap was hailed as a program that would rapidly end the conflict. In its grand sweep there were to be international conferences that would consecrate the main stages. However, the plan assumed that the Palestinians would be prepared to agree to the establishment of the state with provisional borders. This was a dubious proposition given the failure of Oslo and clear reluctance of Israel to remove its settlements. The document required that Israel would freeze settlement building and remove "outposts" – settlements illegal even by Israeli standards. Israel had previously promised to dismantle the outposts but had failed to do so. The state with provisional borders would have meant essentially a fragmented territory comprising of about 40 percent of the West Bank and 70 percent of Gaza. There were then to be two years of further negotiations. Palestinians would find themselves in much the same borders that Netanyahu had proposed in 1993 except that these areas would be designated as a "provisional state." Israel would retain the initiative on withdrawal, as it had done under Oslo, and under much less pressure from the international community as it could claim it had already conceded the creation of a Palestinian state. In addition given the security aspects of the roadmap – a term that only seemed to apply to Israel – Palestinians would have found themselves confined within the patchwork of Bantustan-like plots of land still encircled with checkpoints. The negotiations would take place with an Israeli government with a policy to retain most of the settlements and the Jordan Valley. Such a plan was difficult for the Palestinian leadership to accept. It was also hardly a recipe to weaken the resolve of militant organizations which rejected the peace option. While the roadmap might have had the potential to deliver a genuine state its convoluted formulas and emphasis on Israeli security rather than Palestinian freedom put that outcome in some doubt. It put the onus on the Palestinians to carry out major institutional reform while effectively remaining under the Israeli occupation.

Despite the dire situation that it found itself in the Palestinian leadership did take steps to conform to the roadmap and launched a major program of administrative, judicial and security reform. This included revising the existing Basic Law of the Palestinian Authority and creating the office of Prime Minister. These steps, often aided by governments and NGOs, indicated the capacity of sections of the Fatah leadership to adapt to the international climate. Some important changes were brought about and were achieved under the contradictory conditions of creating institutions based on the rule of law while living under the law of occupation.

In the roadmap Sharon had scored a major diplomatic coup as it cast Arafat precisely in the light that he had wanted. The roadmap shifted responsibility for the situation from Israel and placed it instead on the Palestinians. Israel was not required to change its leadership or reform its institutions or policies, whereas the Palestinians were. The international community had now given its *imprimatur* to Sharon's policy of sidelining Arafat.

It was against this background that Sharon began to take a bold new initiative, albeit one carefully choreographed with the Bush administration. When the Palestinians created the office of Prime Minister it first went to Mahmoud Abbas. Sharon, however, having declared Arafat too evil to act as a partner in negotiations, now denounced Abbas as too weak. Either way there was no possibility of negotiations. Sharon now revealed his unilateral disengagement plan. Both Sharon and Bush were at pains to claim that disengagement was entirely consistent with the roadmap.

In April 2004 the United States and Israel published an exchange of letters between President Bush and Prime Minister Sharon which heralded that both countries had decided to impose a solution on the Palestinians. Under the plan Israel would remove all its settlers and military bases from Gaza, dismantle four settlements in the northern part of the West Bank and accelerate the building of its separation wall. The wall represented physical separation, and disengagement was Sharon's political project for separating Israel from Palestine. Sharon was embarking on a scheme to create by fiat the small Palestinian state that he found so advantageous in the mid 1990s. While Israelis would leave the entire Gaza Strip it soon became clear that Israel aimed to annex large sections of the West Bank. The wall's route at the time would have left some 15 percent of Palestinian land on its western side. During this period there were also discussions about building another such wall through the Jordan Valley to the east. Sharon clearly had in mind not merely a small Palestinian state but one which was effectively caged – and surrounded by Israel. However, in April 2004 all attention was on the proposal to leave Gaza and in the process uproot the 8,000 Israeli settlers.

In his letter to Bush, Sharon outlined his view that the existing Palestinian leadership was in breach of its international commitments due to its continued support for terrorism. The Palestinians would never be able to obtain a state "created by terror." Rather there had to be "serious efforts to institute true reform and real democracy and liberty, including new leaders not compromised by terror."[47] With an explicit reference to the roadmap which both Palestinians and Israelis had formally agreed to, he continued:

> The Palestinian Authority under its current leadership has taken no action to meet its responsibilities under the roadmap. Terror has not ceased, reform of the Palestinian security services has not been undertaken and real institutional reforms have not taken place.[48]

Sharon thus neatly weaved his plan into the pattern of the roadmap. He posed as a disappointed supporter of the roadmap; the Palestinians had simply not lived up to their commitments. He made no reference to Israeli obligations such as the dismantling of the doubly illegal outpost settlements. The roadmap's architecture had provided the basis for his arguments to appear coherent to the international community. The main obligations were reasonably placed on the Palestinians. George Bush took the same view and regarded the proposals as consistent with the roadmap and his June 2002 "vision" speech which envisaged a two-state solution. In his reply he went further than any other US President had done in explicitly supporting the annexation of Israeli settlements. "In the light of new realities on the ground," he wrote,

> including already existing major Israeli population centers, it is unrealistic to expect that the outcome of the final status negotiations will be a full return to the armistice lines of 1949... It is realistic to expect that any final status agreement will only be achieved on the basis of mutually agreed changes that reflect these realities.[49]

Bush was thus quite explicit. He also knew that while disengagement was the headline the reality was annexation. Bush's use of the term "major Israeli population centers" instead of settlements was a major gift of legitimacy to Sharon. The Israeli policy of colonizing the West Bank since 1967 would not result in gaining the whole area but was to accrue permanent gains in terms of territory. However, Bush was perhaps rather more sensitive than Sharon might have liked as he did suggest that such results must be "mutually agreed." Even this though was rather abstract in the context of a plan that was premised on the inability to negotiate with the Palestinians.

When reflecting on the discussions with the Americans a year later, it appeared that Sharon had in a perverse way replaced Palestinian with American negotiators. When asked in interview by a *Jerusalem Post* reporter why disengagement had not been discussed with the Palestinian leadership, he replied: "I made an agreement with the Americans... I place more faith in an agreement with the Americans than with an agreement with the Palestinians."[50]

In Israel and the occupied territories the settler movement and its backers such as the National Religious Party began to organize a political campaign in opposition to what they regarded as Sharon's betrayal of the Gaza settlements. There were major tensions within Likud and the rank and file members voted against the plan. Sharon with a significant section of the political right had made a strategic choice to abandon any project of a Jewish state in all of Palestine and to adopt a partition plan of their own. Sharon was forced to split Likud and create Kadima, a new centrist formation which was to include some prominent Labor politicians including (the now President) Shimon Peres.

Many on the Israeli left thought that Sharon would not force through the removal of the Gaza settlers. But in August 2005 he began to execute this part of the plan and drafted in tens of thousands of troops and police to ensure that all the settlers left. Despite some histrionic reactions from some settlers and supporters the operation went ahead. By the end of September no settlers or military bases remained. Sharon had shown his well-known toughness but this time in the face of his erstwhile supporters. The whole affair was a setback for the settlement project. Sharon was soon to be incapacitated and so his next moves were never to be revealed.

Disengagement had a profound effect on Israeli politics. It created a sense of inevitability that Israel would leave most of the occupied territories and that there would be a Palestinian state. In the 2006 elections two-thirds of the Knesset was elected on platforms that supported the creation of a Palestinian state. A policy which only a decade earlier would have been confined to the political fringes had become a mainstream idea. Prime Minister Ehud Olmert and Foreign Minister Zipi Livni – previously two members of the right-wing elite who had once dreamt of a Jewish state on both banks of the Jordan – now subscribed to a Palestinian state to its west. A disengagement law was enacted to provide for the compensation and relocation of the settlers who had moved from their homes. This created a new legal and administrative framework for ending settlements and bringing settlers within the Green Line. Politically it had also

212 PARTITIONING PALESTINE

been established that an Israeli politician showing leadership could confront the settlers and their political backers and win.

In the Palestinian territories the unilateral character of disengagement was to prove highly damaging to politicians who supported the peace process. The second Palestinian legislative elections were to lead to a victory for the Hamas-led electoral alliance "Reform and Change." While the Israeli departure from Gaza could have had positive results for Palestinians[51] the manner of leaving was highly problematic. The lack of any negotiations with the Palestinian Authority over the handover allowed Hamas to claim that it was its armed attacks that had forced Israel to leave – indeed it has been a retreat under fire. This recalled Hezbollah's similar claim when Israel had unilaterally withdrawn from Lebanon in 2000. In both cases the Israeli refusal to negotiate the terms and modalities of the withdrawal with the respective governments allowed armed groups to trumpet a victory. Sharon's policy of sidelining the Palestinian leadership had in effect allowed Hamas to appear more central. This boosted the organization just in the run-up to the elections.

The Hamas alliance which won about 46 percent of the vote (and a large parliamentary majority) had campaigned for honest, efficient and transparent government. The elections had not been fought over relations with Israel. Nonetheless the Palestinian administration that took office was composed in the main of people opposed to Israel's existence and who subscribed to the anti-Israel Hamas Charter. The election results posed serious political challenges to Hamas' politics. The organization had refused to participate in the 1996 elections on the grounds that institutions were tainted by collaboration as they were the results of negotiations with Israel. As a result, Hamas effectively found itself running the Palestinian Authority, an institution which not only owed its existence, but also its day-to-day survival, to Israel. Israel and the international community chose to ignore this contradiction and responded to the election as if the Palestinian electorate had endorsed Hamas' anti-Semitic charter and had voted for Israel's destruction. As a consequence Israel, the European Union and the United States took a series of steps to isolate the Palestinian Authority. The financial aspect of this policy was to plunge Palestine into a humanitarian and economic crisis.

While Israel had removed itself from Gaza, disengagement had not been a military withdrawal. Under the plan Israel was to keep full security control over the land, sea borders and the airspace. This meant that Israel remained in effective control and legally its occupation had not ended. The population although freed from settlers and checkpoints inside Gaza was surrounded by Israel and dependent on it. As Israel continued to build the wall in the West Bank Gaza had already been secured behind an electrified fence. This fostered a sense of isolation among the population and rendered Gaza's economy fragile. These conditions nourished support for Hamas. From its perspective however it had won the battle to free the Strip from Israel's presence; the next stage was to remove Israel's grip on the borders.

The Hamas-led government under Ismael Haniyyeh as Prime Minister had to coexist with the Fatah President Mahmoud Abbas which led to an uneasy struggle over the demarcations of power. The international community and Israel which had so assiduously worked for regime change by institutional means now had to deal with Hamas occupying the post of the "empowered Prime Minister," which had been so prominent in the roadmap. While there was little doubt that the elections had been free and fair the international community insisted that the new government make three public commitments: to renounce violence, to recognize Israel and to stand by all Palestinian–Israeli agreements. Haniyyeh refused. The international community's response was to cut direct financial support for the Palestinian Authority on the grounds that it was now led by a terrorist organization. Israel stopped handing over the VAT receipts. Without donor financial aid and the receipts the Authority became increasingly unable to fund services or pay regular salaries. Unemployment and poverty rates rose alongside lawlessness and violence. As the international community demanded political and legal reform it adopted policies that plunged Palestinian society into chaos.

These were not conditions in which any peace process could be nurtured. Inside and outside Palestine various efforts were made to bring about a unity government between Hamas and Fatah. This process was made all the more difficult as Fatah had rejected such a proposal made by Hamas immediately after the elections. In June 2007 Hamas organized a coup in Gaza to remove the Fatah-controlled security forces and in the process brought its own government down. It effectively turned its back on its democratic mandate. President Abbas formed an emergency government in Ramallah and Palestine found itself divided further. It was ironic that at a time when intellectuals in Palestine and beyond began to argue in favor of a one-state solution, Arab Palestine itself was divided into two distinct entities.

In Annapolis in November 2007 George W. Bush convened yet another Middle East peace conference. President Abbas and Prime Minister Olmert were joined by many representatives from the Arab world. It initiated a new round of direct negotiations and had the aim of producing a two-state settlement of the conflict by the end of the Bush presidency in January 2009. As with so many deadlines in the past this one also passed without any substantive movement. Expectations had been low; however, one positive result was the regular direct contact between the Palestinian and Israeli leaderships. There were some concrete discussions and for the first time there were serious attempts to negotiate a map of the two states. The main interlocutors were two politicians who were in a weaker position than Arafat and Barak were in 2000. Abbas' government only controlled the West Bank and Olmert had been mired in corruption allegations that led to his forced resignation. However, perhaps because the expectations had been so low progress was made as both sides had been under less public pressure than on previous occasions. It was as if the bleak prospects offered a more conducive atmosphere for success.

As the talks proceeded the Israeli cabinet discussed an evacuation and compensation law for West Bank settlers. At the meeting which discussed the new law Prime Minister Olmert explained the political choices Israel faced by reflecting on his own changing positions:

> Greater Israel is over. There is no such thing. Anyone who talks that way is deluding themselves. I thought that the land from the Jordan River through to the sea was all ours, but ultimately, after a long and tortured process, I arrived at the conclusion that we must share with those we live with if we do not want to be a bi-national state.[52]

He seemed to have accepted that the precedent set in Gaza in 2005 could be followed in the West Bank. At the same cabinet meeting, Vice-Premier Haim Ramon said "the evacuation of the residents of Judea and Samaria [the West Bank] is an unavoidable step for those who believe in two states for two peoples – and that includes most of the Israeli public."[53] That these views had been expressed in the Israeli cabinet and reported to the public marked a major change from the critical period of Oslo in 1995–96 when no such honesty was expressed. It represented the abandonment of political and legal attachments that had undermined all negotiations since 1993.

In September 2008 when President Mahmoud Abbas had expressed the view that an agreement by January 2009 was unlikely he had nonetheless indicated a degree of optimism. He could not have known that that anniversary would in fact be marked by the devastating Israeli war in Gaza during which 1,200 Palestinians were to lose their lives. This made all the more extraordinary Abbas' generous assessment of Olmert's positive contribution to the Annapolis process. He also expressed some frustration that there has been no agreement but at the same time articulated his enduring commitment to one:

> It's unbelievable, it's beyond any imagination that we haven't succeeded in reaching an agreement until now. But even today, I'm convinced that I would have signed the Oslo Accords. I risked my life for peace and if I have to pay for it with my life, that's a negligible price... Twenty years before the agreement I believed in peace with the Israelis, and I still believe in it.[54]

The situation today is more complicated than 20 years ago. The Palestinian national movement is now more deeply divided; the Israeli settlements are more entrenched, and Israeli politics is more unpredictable. The parties to the conflict can surely not be left for another 20 years to continue to fight it out. Led by the Obama leadership, the international community signaling a significant change to past practice, to use political power to change the dynamics and take steps that could result in enforcing a settlement. Pressures on the Netanyahu government to make a clear commitment on a two-state solution have had some success.[55] This has been the result mainly of the reinvigoration of American policy on the conflict. This also appears to have been coordinated with the European Union whose former foreign policy chief suggested imposing "a fixed deadline."[56] In 1947 the United Nations lacked the will to enforce its partition plan. The result has been a humanitarian disaster. In the past the United Nations General Assembly and Human Rights Council have too often been used to promote posture politics rather than address a genuine solution. In order to discharge its duties to Palestinians and Israelis, the international community will have to implement, with force if necessary, the policy of partition of Palestine.

International lawyers also have a responsibility to help to change the environment. There are no fundamental roots of international law that result in one side or the other having a monopoly of justice or blame. Zionism and Palestinian nationalism are equally legitimate. International law must be used to foster dialogue and contact on the basis of equality, self-determination and human rights. In this context tough action will have to be taken to address the Israeli colonial settlements, the rights of refugees to return to the Palestinian state and ending both state violence and terrorism. Partitioning Palestine remains the only viable way of ending the conflict. It must be achieved by creating two states that provide security for both peoples. All those who insist on recycling the old narratives will delay the decolonizing of Palestine and lay the basis for the next war. International law should be deployed, not to censor either side but to provide the means for peace and reconciliation.

Notes

INTRODUCTION

1. See: Rosalyn Higgins, *Problems and Process: International Law and How We Use It* (Oxford: Clarendon, 1994).
2. Legal Consequences of the Construction of a Wall in the Occupied Palestinian Territory, International Courts of Justice, General List No. 131, July 9, 2004.
3. See: Separate Opinion of Judge Higgins at: http://www.icj-cij.org/docket/files/131/1681.pdf (last visited October 10, 2008).
4. UNGA A/Res/ES-10/14 (A/ES-10L.16), December 8, 2003.
5. See for example: John Quigley, *The Case for Palestine* (Durham and London: Duke University Press, 2005) and Alan Dershowitz, *The Case for Israel* (Hoboken: John Wiley and Sons, 2003).
6. Legal Consequences, paragraph 67.
7. Ibid., paragraph 78.
8. Edward W. Said, *Orientalism: Western Conceptions of the Orient* (London: Penguin Books, 1991); Edward W. Said, *Culture and Imperialism* (London: Chatto and Windus, 1993).
9. See the discussion in Chapters 3 and 4.

CHAPTER 1

1. Known as the "'Urabi Revolt" after Colonel Ahmed 'Urabi who initiated an insurrection against foreign influence in Egypt in 1879. As a result the country remained unstable for a number of years and led to the British intervention in 1882.
2. Viscount Palmerston, 1784–1865; Prime Minister 1855–58 and 1859–65.
3. Quoted in: Sir William Hayter, *Recent Constitutional Developments in Egypt* (Cambridge: Cambridge University Press, 1924), 6.
4. Mark Sykes, 1879–1919, was a British politician and official who was a specialist on the Middle East and became Secretary to the British war cabinet.
5. Georges Picot, 1870–1951, was a senior French diplomat.
6. See: David Fromkin, *A Peace to End all Peace: Creating the Modern Middle East 1914–1922* (London: Andre Deutsch, 1989), 188–96.
7. For the classical account of the emergence of Arab nationalism, see: George Antonious, *The Arab Awakening: The Story of the Arab National Movement* (London: Hamish Hamilton, 1938).
8. As quoted in Bassam Tibi, *Arab Nationalism: A Critical Enquiry*, edited and translated by Marion Farouk-Sluglette and Peter Sluglette (London and Basingstoke: Macmillan Press, 1981), 79.
9. As quoted in Elie Kedourie, *Arab Political Memoirs and Other Studies* (London: Frank Cass, 1979), 122.

10. See generally: Zeine E. Zeine, *Arab–Turkish Relations and the Emergence of Arab Nationalism* (Beirut: Khayat, 1958) and Bernard Lewis, *Semites and Anti-Semites* (London: Phoenix Giant, 1997), 173–4.

11. Farid Kassab, *Le Nouvel Empire Arab: la curie romaine et le pretendu peril juif universal* (1906); see Lewis, *Semites and Anti-Semites*, 174.

12. See for example: Hazem Zaki Nuseibeh, *The Ideas of Arab Nationalism* (Ithaca: Cornell University Press, 1956), 37.

13. See for example: Zeine, *Arab–Turkish Relations and the Emergence of Arab Nationalism*, 73.

14. c. 1838–1897. He was a journalist and publicist who is often referred to as the founder of Islamic modernism.

15. 1849–1905. Egyptian theologian and philosopher who was a student of Afghani.

16. See: Basheer M. Nafi, *Arabism, Islamism and the Palestine Question 1908–1941* (Reading: Ithaca Press, 1998), 19–20.

17. Walter Laqueur, *A History of Zionism* (London: Tauris Parke Paperbacks, 2003), 222–3.

18. Ibid., 225.

19. Hussein Ibn Ali, 1852–1931, was Sherif and Emir of Mecca 1908–17 when he declared himself King of Hejaz, a position he held until defeated by Ibn Saud in 1924. He died in exile in Transjordan which at the time was ruled by his son Abdullah.

20. 1881–1955. A British Foreign Office official who was working in Egypt at the time – was later to become the Governor of Jerusalem in 1917.

21. See: Storrs, *Orientations* (London: Ivor Nicholson, 1937), 122–3. Zeine, *Arab–Turkish Relations and the Emergence of Arab Nationalism*, 100.

22. Lord Kitchener, 1850–1916, had a long career in the colonies in the military and as an administrator and spent much time in the Middle East. He was Secretary of State for War 1914–16.

23. Henry McMahon, 1862–1949, was High Commissioner in Egypt (1915–17) at the time of the negotiations.

24. Fromkin, *A Peace to End all Peace*, 174.

25. Ibid., 88–105 and 111–15.

26. T.E. Lawrence, 1888–1935. British army officer who served as the liaison officer between the British and the Arab command during the Revolt.

27. See: M.E. Yapp, *The Near East Since the First World War: A History to 1995* (London, New York: Longman, 1996), especially 49–207.

28. This is a quotation from the "Basle Programme" which was adopted by the First Zionist Congress in that city in 1897.

29. See: Nahum Solokow, *History of Zionism 1600–1918* (London: Longmans, 1919).

30. Arthur Herzenberg (ed.), *The Zionist Idea: A Historical Analysis and Reader* (Philadelphia: Jewish Publication Society of America, 1997), 105.

31. Moses Hess, *The Revival of Israel: Rome and Jerusalem: The Last Nationalist Question*, translated by Mayer Waxman (Lincoln and London: University of Nebraska Press, 1995), first published in German as *Rom und Jerusalem, de letzte nationalitatsfrage*, in Leipzig 1862.

32. Herzenberg, *The Zionist Idea*, 121.

33. Leo Pinsker, *Auto-Emancipation: A Call to His People from a Russian Jew* (London: Rita Searl, 1947).

34. Eliezer Ben Yehudah, 1858–1922.
35. Asher Zvi Ginsberg, 1858–1927.
36. See: Steven I. Zipperstein, *Elusive Prophet: Ahad Ha'am and the Origins of Zionism* (Berkeley: University of California Press, 1993).
37. Aliyah comes from the Hebrew "to ascend," and Jewish immigrants thus ascend to the national home.
38. Theodor Herzl, 1860–1904.
39. The trial of Alfred Dreyfus (a French military officer and a Jew) for treason took place in 1894 in Paris. The trial took place in an anti-Semitic atmosphere. He was initially convicted but eventually released from prison and finally exonerated in 1906.
40. Theodor Herzl, *Der Judenstaat* (Leipzig und Vien: M. Britebenstein Verlags-Buchhandlung, 1896).
41. Theodor Herzl, *The Jewish State* (New York: Dover Publications, 1988), 145.
42. Joseph Chamberlain, 1836–1914. He was Colonial Secretary between 1895 and 1903.
43. See generally: Robert G. Weisbord, *African Zion: The Attempt to Establish a Jewish Colony in the East Africa Protectorate 1903–1905* (Philadelphia: The Jewish Publication Society of America, 5728/1968).
44. See: Elizabeth Huxley, *White Man's Country: Lord Delamere and the Making of Kenya* (London: Macmillan and Co., 1935, 2 vols.), Vol. 1, 117.
45. Weisbord, *African Zion*, 253.
46. Chaim Weizmann, 1874–1952, was a major leader of the Zionist movement who served as President of the World Zionist Organization on two occasions, 1921–31 and 1935–46, and was to become the first President of the State of Israel, 1949–52.
47. Quoted in Weisbord, *African Zion*, 255.
48. Richard P. Stevens, *The Settler-Colonial Phenomenon in Africa and the Middle East* (Khartoum: Khartoum University Press, 1976), 9–10.
49. See: Chaim Shur, *Shromrim in the Land of Apartheid: The History of Hashomer Hatzair in South Africa 1935–1970* (Kibbutz Dalia: Yad Yaari-Givat Haviva, 1998), 71–2.
50. See: Weisbord, *African Zion*, 126–7.
51. Solokow, *History of Zionism 1600–1918*, Vol. I, 298.
52. See: Baruch Kimmerling and Joel S. Migdal, *The Palestinian People: A History* (Cambridge, London: Harvard University Press, 2003), 39.
53. See: ibid., 6–14.
54. See: Rashid Khalidi, *Palestinian Identity: The Construction of Modern National Consciousness* (New York: Columbia University Press, 1997).
55. Ibid., 126–7.
56. Justin McCarthy, *The Population of Palestine: Population History and Statistics in the Late Ottoman Period and the Mandate* (New York: Columbia University Press 1990).
57. Recorded in: Bernard Wasserstein, *Israel and Palestine: Why They Fight and Can They Stop?* (London: Profile Books, 2003), 9–10.
58. See: Martin Gilbert, *Israel: A History* (Uxbridge: Black Swan, 1999), 30.
59. The British had granted 10,000 Palestinian Jews asylum in Egypt in 1915 alone, see: Martin Sicker, *The Middle East in the Twentieth Century* (Westport CT: Greenwood Press, 2001), 25.

60. See: Ilan Pappé, *A Modern History of Palestine: One Land, Two Peoples* (Cambridge: Cambridge University Press, 2004), 62–4.

61. Ibid., 73.

62. David Ben-Gurion, 1886–1973, Chairman of the Executive Committee of the Jewish Agency 1935–48; Prime Minister of Israel, 1948–54 and 1955–63.

63. See: Gertrude Samuels, *B-G: Fighter of Goliaths, The Story of Ben-Gurion* (Lincoln NE: Authors Guild Backprint, 2000), 44–54.

64. Arthur Balfour, 1848–1930, was a conservative politician who held many cabinet positions from the late 1880s including as Prime Minister 1902–05. He was Foreign Secretary from 1916 to 1919.

65. Chaim Weizmann, *Trial and Error* (London: East West Library, 1950), 235.

66. Ibid., 238.

67. Ibid.

68. Ibid., 239.

69. Ibid., 256.

70. Nahum Sokolow, 1859–1936, was Secretary of the World Zionist Organization 1907–09. In 1911 he became responsible in the WZO for coordinating efforts to win support for Zionism in the United States and Britain. He headed the Zionist delegation at the Versailles peace conference in 1919 and served as President of the World Zionist Congress 1931–35.

71. Quoted in Leonard Stein, *The Balfour Declaration* (London, Jerusalem: Magnes Press, 1983), 466.

72. Quoted in ibid., 466.

73. Quoted in ibid., 466.

74. Quoted in ibid., 644.

75. Chaim Weizmann, "Introduction," in Harry Sacher (ed.), *Zionism and the Jewish Future* (London: John Murray, 1916), 7–8.

76. Ibid., 8.

77. Norman Bentwich, 1883–1971, was legal secretary to the British Administration in Palestine 1918–22, and the Attorney-General until 1929. He had worked in the Ministry of Justice in Cairo from 1912 to 1915.

78. Norman Bentwich, "The Future of Palestine," in Sacher (ed.), *Zionism and the Jewish Future*, 196–209, 204.

79. Bentwich in ibid., 204–5.

80. Bentwich in ibid., 206.

81. See for example: Nur Masalha, *A Land without a People: Israel, Transfer and the Palestinians 1949–1996* (London: Faber and Faber, 1997).

82. See for example: Avi Shlaim, *The Iron Wall: Israel and the Arab World* (London: Penguin, 2000), especially 1–27.

83. Quoted in Stein, *The Balfour Declaration*, 512.

84. Alfred, Viscount Milner, 1854–1925, was Minister without Portfolio and was a leading member of the war cabinet at the time. Milner knew the Middle East well as he had been Under-secretary for Finance in Egypt between 1889 and 1892.

85. Leo Amery, 1873–1955, was Under-secretary to the war cabinet and regarded Milner as his mentor.

86. Edwin Montagu, 1879–1924, entered the cabinet in 1915 and was Secretary of State for India 1917–22.

87. Tahseen Basheer (ed.), *The Arab League, Edwin Montagu and the Balfour Declaration* (New York: Arab League Office, 1967), 13–14.

88. Ibid., 9.
89. Ibid., 10.
90. Quoted in Stein, 1983, 527.
91. Stein, *The Balfour Declaration*, 507.
92. Walter, Lord Rothschild, 1868–1937, Liberal Member of Parliament 1899–1910 and a leader of the British Jewish community in 1917.
93. See: Fromkin, *A Peace to End all Peace*, 441, 504–5.
94. See: J.C. Smuts, *The League of Nations: A Practical Suggestion* (London: Hodder and Stoughton, 1918), 7–30.
95. Ibid., 11.
96. Ibid., 4.
97. Ibid., 15.
98. Antony Anghie, *Imperialism, Sovereignty and the Making of International Law* (Cambridge: Cambridge University Press, 2005), 146.
99. Smuts, *The League of Nations*, 15.
100. Walter Phillimore, 1845–1929, served as a judge and was active in international law circles particularly after World War I.
101. Edward Mandell House, 1858–1938. He used "colonel" as a nickname and did not hold a military rank.
102. See: Frederick L. Shuman, *International Politics* (New York, Toronto, London: McGraw Hill, 1948), 299–326.
103. See: Anghie, *Imperialism, Sovereignty and the Making of International Law*, 115–95.

CHAPTER 2

1. See: Baruch Kimerling and Joel S. Migdal, *The Palestinian People: A History* (Cambridge: Harvard University Press, 2003), 76–93.
2. See: Rashid Khalidi, *Palestinian Identity: The Construction of Modern National Consciousness* (New York: Columbia University Press, 1997), 162–75.
3. Musa Kazim Al Husseini, 1850–1944, was Mayor of Jerusalem 1918–20 and President of the Arab Executive 1920–28.
4. As quoted in Khalidi, *Palestinian Identity*, 165.
5. Mandate for Palestine, League of Nations, C.529.M314. 1922, VI. August 12, 1922.
6. Herbert Samuel, 1870–1963, was a member of the cabinet in 1909–16 and again in 1931–32. He was High Commissioner for Palestine in 1920–25 and led the Liberal Party between 1931 and 1935.
7. Palestine: Correspondence with the Palestine Arab Delegation and the Zionist Organization, Cmd. 1700 (1922).
8. Tom Segev, *One Palestine Complete: Jews and Arabs under the British Mandate* (London: Little Brown, 2000), 128.
9. David Fromkin, *A Peace to End all Peace: Creating the Middle East 1914–1922* (London: Andre Deutsch, 1989), 517–18. According to Fromkin a Muslim Electoral College nominated three candidates from which Samuel should have chosen but due to "intrigue by a violently Anti-Zionist official Ernest T Richmond," Amin Al Husseini's name was added.
10. Palestine: Correspondence, Letter 1, February 21, 1922.

11. See for example: Ghadi Kami, *Married to Another Man: Israel's Dilemma in Palestine* (London: Pluto Press, 2007).

12. Arab Palestine Congress, message to US Secretary of State, May 8, 1921, quoted in Lawrence Davidson, *America's Palestine: Popular and Official Perceptions from Balfour to Israeli Statehood* (Gainesville: University Press of Florida, 2001), 54.

13. See: Walter Laqueur, *A History of Zionism* (London: Tauris Parke Paperbacks, 2003), 209.

14. Quoted in David Fromkin, *A Peace to End all Peace*, 516.

15. See Chapter 5.

16. Palestine: Correspondence, Letter 1, February 21, 1922.

17. See: Peter Fitzpatrick, *Modernism and the Grounds of Law* (Cambridge: Cambridge University Press, 2001), 146–82.

18. John Shuckburgh, 1877–1953.

19. Palestine: Correspondence, Letter 2, March 1, 1922.

20. Ibid.

21. Ibid.

22. Ibid.

23. See: Fromkin, *A Peace to End all Peace*, 173–87.

24. Quoted in: Palestine: Correspondence, Letter 3, March 16, 1922.

25. Ibid., Letter 4, April 11, 1922.

26. Samuel, June 3, 1921, quoted in: ibid., Letter 2. March 1, 1922.

27. This statement was included as an enclosure in the letter to the Zionist Organization (Letter 5) on June 3, 1922.

28. Quoted in ibid.

29. Ibid.

30. Ibid.

31. See: Frederick L. Schuman, *International Politics* (New York, London, Toronto: McGraw-Hill, 1948), 448–9.

32. Palestine: Correspondence, Letter 5.

33. See generally: Deborah S. Bernstein, *Constructing Boundaries: Jewish and Arab Workers in Mandatory Palestine* (Albany: State University of New York Press, 2000).

34. Correspondence, Letter 3.

35. Ibid., Letter 6, June 17, 1922.

36. Ibid.

37. See: Abigail Jacobson, Alternative Voices in late Ottoman Palestine: Jews and Arabs on the Evolving National Conflict, paper given at a PASSIA meeting May 24, 2004 at: http://passia.org/meetings/2004/May-24-Late-Ottoman-Palestine.htm (last visited July 2007).

38. Palestine: Correspondence, Letter 6.

39. Norman Bentwich, *England in Palestine* (London: Kegan Paul, Trench, Tubner, 1932), 88–9.

40. Ibid., 239.

41. Frederic M. Goadby, *Introduction to the Study of Law: A Handbook for the Use of Egyptian Students* (London: Butterworths, 1910). A second edition appeared in 1914.

42. Frederic M. Goadby, *Introduction to Law: A Handbook for the Use of Students in Egypt and Palestine* (London: Butterworths, 1921).

43. See: John Strawson, "Orientalism and Legal Education in the Middle East: Reading Frederic Goadby's *Introduction to the Study of Law*," *Legal Studies*, vol. 21, no. 4 (2001), 663–78.

44. For the most incisive account of law during the British Mandate, see: Assaf Likhosvski, *Law and Identity in Mandate Palestine* (Chapel Hill: University of North Carolina Press, 2006).

45. Jacob Stoyanovsky, *The Mandate for Palestine: A Contribution to the Theory and Practice of International Mandates* (London, New York, Toronto: Longmans, Green and Co., 1928).

46. Ibid., 42–3.

47. Norman Bentwich, *The Mandates System* (London, New York, Toronto: Longmans, Green and Co., 1930), v.

48. Ibid., v–vi.

49. Ibid., 17.

50. Ibid., 13.

51. Ibid., 21.

52. Ibid., 23.

53. W.F. Boustany, *The Palestine Mandate: Invalid and Impractical* (Beirut: American Press, 1936).

54. Ibid., 18.

55. Ibid., 32–3.

CHAPTER 3

1. See: Palestine: Statement of Policy Cmd 6019, May 1939. It stated that the Jewish National Home had been completed, introduced strict controls on Jewish immigration and contained a ten-year plan to bring the mandate to an end.

2. The party adopted a declaration calling for a Jewish state in Palestine and for the forced removal of the Palestinians, much to the discomfort of the Zionist leadership, see: Yosef Gorni, *The British Labour Movement and Zionism 1917–1948* (London: Routledge, 1983), 179–84.

3. Elizabeth Monroe, *Britain's Moment in the Middle East 1914–1971* (London: Chatto and Windus, 1981), 168.

4. The United Nations was first formed not as an international organization but as a military alliance led by the USA, UK and the USSR when they and 23 other states signed the Declaration of the United Nations in January 1942.

5. See: Walter Laqueur, *The History of Zionism* (London, New York: Tauris Parke Paperbacks, 2003), 545–9.

6. As Matthias Kuntzel argues, this had been carefully encouraged by the German government in Egypt in the mid 1930s. See: Matthias Kuntzel, *Jihad and Jew-Hatred: Islamism, Nazism and the Roots of 9/11*, translated by Colin Meade (New York: Telos Press, 2007), 18–31.

7. Arab relations with the Nazis were part of the public consciousness during the war, see: Pierre van Passen, *The Forgotten Ally* (New York: Dial Press, 1943), 175–236.

8. See generally: Robert Satloff, *Among the Righteous: Lost Stories from the Holocaust's Long Reach into Arab Lands* (New York: Public Affairs, 2006).

9. See: Joseph B. Schechtman, *The Mufti and the Fuehrer: The Rise and Fall of Haj Amin e-Husseini* (New York, London: Thomas Yoseloff, 1965), 127–8.

In addition Schechtman records that the Mufti was actively involved in preventing Jews from escaping Nazism to Palestine, see: pp. 154–66.

10. Quoted in ibid., 140.
11. Quoted in ibid., 139.
12. UNGA A/C.1/PV.48 (May 7, 1947).
13. Ibid.
14. Ibid.
15. Ibid.
16. In Baghdad several Palestinian leaders worked with Germans, amongst them Akram Zu'tar, Abd al-Qader al-Husseini and Mu'in al-Madi. See: Hillel Cohen, *Army of Shadows: Palestinian Collaboration with Zionism, 1917–1948*, translated by Haim Watzman (Berkeley, Los Angeles, London: University of California Press, 2008), 203.
17. See: Schechtman, *The Mufti and the Fuehrer*, 108–15.
18. See: Matthias Kuntzel, "National Socialism and Anti-Semitism in the Arab World," *Jewish Political Studies Review*, vol. 17, nos. 1–2 (2005).
19. Irgun (Etzel) or National Military Organization of the Land of Israel, the organization had broken with Ben-Gurion's position and began operations against the British in 1944.
20. Lehi, Fighters for the Freedom of Israel, known by the British as the "Stern Gang" after its leader.
21. The Haganah ("defense") was the main militia of the *Yishuv* and was to become the nucleus of the Israeli Defense Force, the armed forces of the State of Israel.
22. For a contemporary account of Jewish illegal immigration, see: Daphne Trevor, *Under the White Paper: Some Aspects of British Administration of Palestine from 1939–1947* (Jerusalem: the Jerusalem Press, 1948), 177–341.
23. See: Benny Morris, *Righteous Victims: A History of the Zionist–Arab Conflict 1881–1999* (New York: Alfred A. Knopf, 1999), 168–9.
24. See: Yosef Gorny, *From Binational Society to Jewish State: Federal Concepts in Zionist Political Thought, 1920–1990, and the Jewish People* (Leiden and Boston: Brill, 2006), 111.
25. Supplement to A Survey of Palestine: Notes compiled for the Information of the UNSCOP (Jerusalem: Government Printer, June 1947), 15.
26. See: Gorny, *From Binational Society to Jewish State*, 109.
27. Ibid., 116.
28. Ibid., 176.
29. See: UNGA A/364 paragraph 18.
30. UNGA A/2/PV.79 (May 15, 1947).
31. UNGA A/2/PV.78 (May 14, 1947).
32. Ibid.
33. Ibid.
34. Ibid.
35. This theory is historically untenable as Judaism was adopted as an official religion by the Khazars in the late eighth century and was practiced by the aristocracy only. Even this section of society appeared to return to Orthodox Christianity by the tenth century.
36. UNGA A/2/PV.78 (May 14, 1947).
37. UNGA A/2/PV.77 (May 14, 1947).
38. Ibid.

39. Ibid.

40. It is important to correct the false impression that the Arab voice was not heard by UNSCOP as erroneous implications can then be drawn. See for example: Ilan Pappé, *The Ethnic Cleansing of Palestine* (Oxford: Oneworld, 2006), 31. He claims that the Zionists stepped into this "vacuum" when no such vacuum existed.

41. See: Avi Shlaim, *The Politics of Partition: King Abdullah, the Zionists and Palestine 1921–1951* (Oxford: Oxford University Press, 1990), 92–100.

42. Efraim Karsh, *Fabricating Israeli History: The "New Historians"* (London, Portland: Frank Cass, 1997), 69–108.

43. UNGA A/PV.126 (November 28, 1947).

44. UNGA A/364 (September 3, 1947), United Nations Special Committee on Palestine, Report to the General Assembly (subsequently cited as UNSCOP), chapter II, paragraph 117.

45. Ibid.

46. UNSCOP, chapter II, para. 118.

47. See: Martin Gilbert, *Israel: A History* (Uxbridge: Black Swan, 1999), 145.

48. UNSCOP, chapter II, para. 119.

49. UNSCOP, chapter II, para. 120.

50. Ibid.

51. See: Benny Morris, *1948: A History of the First Arab–Israeli War* (New Haven and London: Yale University Press, 2008), 68.

52. UNSCOP, chapter II, para. 121.

53. Ibid.

54. UNSCOP, chapter II, para. 122.

55. Ibid.

56. Ibid.

57. UNSCOP, chapter II, para. 127.

58. UNSCOP, chapter II, para. 131.

59. UNSCOP, chapter II, para. 141.

60. UNSCOP, chapter II, para. 145.

61. UNSCOP, chapter II, para. 146.

62. UNSCOP, chapter II, para. 147.

63. UNSCOP, chapter II, para. 157.

64. UNSCOP, chapter II, para. 159.

65. See: UNSCOP, chapter II, paras. 160, 161.

66. UNSCOP, chapter II, para. 163.

67. UNSCOP, chapter II, para. 170.

68. UNSCOP, chapter II, para. 173.

69. UNSCOP, chapter II, para. 177.

70. UNSCOP, chapter II, para. 179.

71. This would not be surprising as the American Council of Judaism had been established by a group of Reform Rabbis to oppose Zionism in 1942. See: Thomas A. Kolsky, *Jews Against Zionism: The American Council for Judaism, 1942–1948* (Philadelphia PA: Temple University Press, 1992).

72. This had been adopted at the 22nd Zionist Congress held in Basle in 1946.

73. UNSCOP, chapter IV, paras. 9 and 10.

74. UNSCOP, chapter IV, para. 11.

75. Ibid.

76. Ibid.

77. Institute of Palestine Studies, *The Partition of Palestine*, Monograph Series 9 (Beirut, 1967), 42.
78. Ibid.
79. Ibid.
80. See for example: Hussein Abu Hussein and Fiona McKay, *Access Denied: Palestinian Land Rights in Israel* (London, New York: Zed Press, 2003).
81. UNSCOP, chapter IV, para. 13.
82. UNSCOP, chapter V, para. 2.
83. Ibid.
84. UNSCOP, chapter V, para. 3.
85. Ibid.
86. UNSCOP, chapter V, recommendation II.
87. UNSCOP, chapter V, recommendation IV.
88. UNSCOP, chapter V, recommendation VI.
89. Ibid.
90. UNSCOP, chapter VII, recommendation VIII (4).
91. Ibid.
92. UNSCOP, chapter VI, part I, para. 1.
93. UNSCOP, chapter VI, part I, para. 2.
94. UNSCOP, chapter VI, part I, para. 3.
95. UNSCOP, chapter VI, part I, paras. 4, 5, 6 and 7.
96. UNSCOP, chapter VI, part I, para. 9.
97. Ibid.
98. UNSCOP, chapter VI, part I, para. 10.
99. The UN Economic and Social Council is one of the principal organs of the United Nations with humanitarian responsibilities (see the UN Charter chapter X).
100. The Trusteeship Council is a UN principal organ which had responsibility for some "non-self-governing territories" (see UN Charter chapters XI, XII and XIII).
101. UNSCOP, chapter VI, recommendation A, section B, para. 4.
102. Ibid.
103. Ibid.
104. UNSCOP, chapter VI, Recommendations (II) commentary of partition.
105. Ibid.
106. Ibid.
107. Ibid.

CHAPTER 4

1. UNGA A/C.1/PV.48 (May 7, 1947).
2. See: David Tal, *The War in Palestine 1948: Strategy and Diplomacy* (London and New York: Routledge, 2004), 8.
3. Ibid., 9.
4. As quoted in: ibid., 10.
5. See: Yoav Gelber, *Palestine 1948: War Escape and the Emergence of the Palestinian Refugee Problem* (Brighton and Portland: Sussex Academic Press, 2006), 45.
6. The Arab Case for Palestine: Evidence submitted by the Arab Office to the Anglo-American Committee of Inquiry, March 1946, in Walter Laqueur (ed.),

The Israel–Arab Reader: A Documentary History of the Middle East Conflict (Harmondsworth: Penguin Books, 1970), 122–34, 123.

7. UNGA A/PV.124 (November 26, 1947).
8. See: Jean Allain, *International law in the Middle East: Closer to Power than Justice* (Aldershot and Burlington: Ashgate, 2004), 86–7.
9. See: Rosalyn Higgins, *Problems and Process: International Law and How We Use It* (Oxford: Clarendon, 1994), 111–28.
10. See: International Committee of Jurists, The Aaland Island Case, LNOJ, Special Supplement 3 (1920), 5.
11. UNGA resolution 1514 (1960); 1541 (1960) and 2625 (1970).
12. UNGA A/PV. 124 (November 26, 1947).
13. Ibid.
14. Ibid.
15. Ibid.
16. Ibid.
17. Ibid.
18. Ibid.
19. Ibid.
20. UNGA A/PV. 125 (November 26, 1947).
21. Ibid.
22. Ibid.
23. Ibid.
24. Ibid.
25. Arslan inaccurately refers to *Races of Mankind* as a book; it is in fact a 32-page pamphlet published in New York by the Public Affairs committee in 1943. It is a sustained argument against all forms of racism and the quotation needs to be read in that light. The authors make a distinction between races and nations, as is clear when they write "Aryan, Italians and Jews are not races." See: Ruth Benedict, *Race: Science and Politics* (Westport: Greenwood Press, 1982), 167–93, at 177. This volume contains *Races of Mankind* based on a 1945 edition.
26. UNGA A/PV.125 (November 26, 1947).
27. Ibid.
28. Ibid.
29. Ibid.
30. Ibid.
31. Ibid.
32. Ibid.
33. Ibid.
34. Ibid.
35. Ibid. This view that Zionism is essentially expansionist has been frequently repeated. The 1967 war is often given as proof. However, the subsequent withdrawal from the Sinai might have put a question mark over that view. Nonetheless, such developments have not prevented some continuing to make the claim. See: Ralph Schoenman, *The Hidden History of Zionism* (Santa Barbara: Veritas Press, 1988), 134.
36. UNGA A/PV. 126 (November 28, 1947).
37. Ibid.
38. Ibid.
39. UNGA A/PV. 128 (November 29, 1947).

40. UNGA A/PV. 124 (November 26, 1947).
41. Ibid.
42. Ibid.
43. UNGA A/2/PV.77 (May 14, 1947).
44. UNGA A/PV.125 (November 26, 1947).
45. Ibid.
46. Ibid.
47. Ibid.
48. UNGA A/PV. 128 (November 29, 1947).
49. Ibid.
50. See: Chaim Weizmann, *Trial and Error* (London: East and West Library, 1950), 554–63.
51. UNGA A/PV. 128 (November 29, 1947).
52. Ibid.
53. Ibid.
54. Ibid.
55. CIA, The Consequences of the Partition of Palestine (ORE 55), November 28, 1947.
56. Ibid., 1.
57. Ibid.
58. Ibid., 2.
59. Ibid., 9.
60. Gelber, *Palestine 1948*, 34.
61. Ibid., 63.
62. See: Yigal Allon, *The Making of Israel's Army* (New York: Universe Books, 1970), 31–2.
63. Arab League Declaration on the Invasion of Palestine, May 15, 1947 at http://www.jewishvirtuallibrary.or/jsource/history/arab_invasion.htm (last visited August 28, 2008).

CHAPTER 5

1. See generally: Allis Radosh and Ronald Radosh, *A Safe Haven: Harry S. Truman and the Founding of Israel* (New York: HarperCollins, 2009).
2. David Tal, *War in Palestine 1948: Strategy and Diplomacy* (London, New York: Routledge, 2004), 34.
3. Ibid., 183.
4. Ibid., 285.
5. Tal, *War in Palestine 1948*, 3.
6. Martin Gilbert, *Israel: A History* (London: Black Swan, 1999), 189.
7. See: Tal, *War in Palestine 1948*, 29–34.
8. Gilbert, *Israel*, 191.
9. The English text of the Declaration of the Establishment of the State of Israel, May 14, 1948 can be found at: http://www.mfa.gov.il/MFA (last visited August 28, 2008).
10. Quoted in Avi Shlaim, "The Rise and Fall of the All-Palestine Government in Gaza," *Journal of Palestine Studies*, vol. 20, no. 1 (1990), 37–53.
11. Ibid., 43.
12. Ibid., 50.

13. See: ibid. and Yoav Gelber, *Palestine 1948: War, Escape and the Emergence of the Palestinian Refugee Problem* (Brighton: Sussex Academic Press, 2006), 180–1.

14. Benny Morris, *The Birth of the Palestinian Refugee Problem 1947–1949* (Cambridge: Cambridge University Press, 1987), 1.

15. Ibid., xiv–xviii.

16. See: Ahmad H. Sa'di and Lila Abu-Lughod (eds.), *Nakba: Palestine 1948, and the Claims of Memory* (New York: Columbia University Press, 2007).

17. See: Nur Masalha, *A Land Without a People: Israel, Transfer and the Palestinians 1949–1996* (London: Faber and Faber, 1997); and see below at note 18.

18. See: Ilan Pappé, *The Ethnic Cleansing of Palestine* (Oxford: Oneworld, 2006).

19. Nur Masalha,, *The Politics of Denial: Israel and the Palestinian Refugee Problem* (London, Sterling: Pluto Press, 2003), 28.

20. Benny Morris, *The Birth of the Palestinian Refugee Problem Revisited* (Cambridge: Cambridge University Press, 2004), 39–64.

21. See: Walter Laqueur, *The History of Zionism* (London, New York: Tauris Parke Paperbacks, 2003), 210–11.

22. Ibid., 218.

23. See: Israel Zangwill, *The Voice of Jerusalem* (London: William Heinemann, 1920), 103–10. And for an account of how his views were received, see: Redcliffe N. Salaman, *Palestine Reclaimed: Letters from a Jewish Officer in Palestine* (London, New York: George Routledge and Sons, 1920), 175–6, n. 1. The author comments on Zangwill's idea, "It is radically wrong to suggest the removal of the Arab."

24. Nur Masalha, *Expulsion of the Palestinians: The Concept of Transfer in Zionist Thought 1882–1948* (Washington: Institute for Palestine Studies, 1992), 14.

25. This becomes clear in Nur Masalha's study of the topic cited in note 24. With the exception of Zangwill and Weitz, Masalha is forced to base his arguments mainly on the Zionist leadership's reaction to the Peel Commission and then to non-Jewish schemes such as the Labour Party Conference resolution in 1944. The latter of course was widely rejected.

26. Laqueur, *The History of Zionism*, 215–17.

27. Ibid., 45.

28. John Bagot Glubb, *A Soldier with the Arabs* (London: Hodder and Stoughton, 1957), 59.

29. See: Masalha, *Expulsion of the Palestinians*, 30–8.

30. Yosef Gorny, *From Binational Society to Jewish State: Federal Concepts in Zionist Political Thought, 1920–1990, and the Jewish People* (Leiden and Boston: Brill, 2006).

31. Ibid., 171.

32. Masalha, *The Politics of Denial*, 17–18.

33. See: Gelber, *Palestine 1948*, 176–7.

34. See: ibid., 85.

35. Morris, *Birth of the Palestinian Refugee Problem 1947–1949*, 286.

36. Morris, *Birth of the Palestinian Refugee Problem Revisited*, 588.

37. Gelber, *Palestine 1948*, 116.

38. Benny Morris, Interview by Ari Shavit, *Haaretz* (English edition), January 9, 2004.

39. Reported in *Akhbar al-Yom*, October 11, 1947, quoted in Jewish Agency for Palestine: Memorandum on Arab Acts of Aggression, submitted to the United Nations (Lake Success, New York, February 2, 1947).

40. See: Tal, *War in Palestine 1948*, 13–14.

41. Pappé, *Ethnic Cleansing of Palestine*, 86–126.

42. Plan Daleth (Plan D) at http://www.mideastweb.org/pland.htm (last visited December 2, 2006).

43. Ibid.

44. Ibid.

45. Ibid.

46. Ibid.

47. Morris, *Birth of the Palestinian Refugee Problem Revisited*, 263.

48. Ze'ev Drory, *The Israel Defence Force and Foundation of Israel: Utopia in Uniform* (London, New York: RoutledgeCurzon, 2005), 57.

49. For an account of the war from an Israeli viewpoint, see: Yigal Allon, *The Making of Israel's Army* (New York: Universe Books, 1970), 30–45.

50. See generally: Alfred-Maurice de Zayas, *A Terrible Revenge: The Ethnic Cleansing of the East European Germans* (New York: Palgrave Macmillan, 2006).

51. Laqueur, *The History of Zionism*, 596.

CHAPTER 6

1. The UN Security Council called a cease fire in resolution 62 (November 16, 1948) which opened the way for talks. The agreements were with Egypt, Lebanon, Jordan and Syria, and Saudi Arabia and Iraq indicated that they would accept the results. See: Shabtai Rosenne, *Israel's Armistice Agreements with the Arab States* (Tel Aviv: International Law Association, Israel Branch, 1951).

2. UNGA Resolution 194 (III), December 11, 1948.

3. By UNGA Resolution 302 (IV), December 8, 1949.

4. The working definition used in 1952. See: Lex Takkenberg, *The Status of Palestinian Refugees in International Law* (Oxford: Clarendon Press, 1998), 72.

5. See: Siraj Sait, "International Refugee Law: Excluding the Palestinians," in John Strawson (ed.), *Law after Ground Zero* (London: GlassHouse/Routledge-Cavendish, 2002), 90–107.

6. John Bagot Glubb, *A Soldier with the Arabs* (London: Hodder and Stoughton, 1957), 59.

7. These were based on the British Defence (Emergency) Regulations of 1945. See: Sabri Jiryis, *The Arabs in Israel*, translated by Inea Bushnaq (New York, London: Monthly Review Press, 1976), 9–35.

8. See: Sami Hadawi, *Bitter Harvest: Palestine 1914–1979* (Delmar, NY: Caravan Books, 1979), 144–55.

9. See: David Kretzmer, *The Legal Status of the Arabs in Israel* (Boulder: Westview Press, 1990), 135–62.

10. Hadawi, *Bitter Harvest: Palestine 1914–1979*, 145.

11. Sabri Jirjis, *The Arabs in Israel*, 75–134.

12. Montesquieu, *The Spirit of Laws*, translated by Anne M. Cohler, Basia Caroline Miller and Harold Samuel Stone (Cambridge: Cambridge University Press, 1989), 561.
13. Hadawi, *Bitter Harvest: Palestine 1914–1979*, 301.
14. Sami Hadawi, *Bitter Harvest: A Modern History of Palestine* (Buckhirst Hill: Scorpion Publishing, 1989), 29.
15. Ibid., 301.
16. Sami Hadawi, *The Realities of Terrorism and Retaliation* (Toronto: Arab Palestine Association). The work has no date but date references in the text end in 1989.
17. Hassan Haddad, "The Biblical Basis for Zionist Colonization," in Ibrahim Abu-Lughod and Baha Abu-Laban (eds.), *Settler Regimes in Africa and the Arab World* (Wilmette, IL: The Medina University Press, 1974), 3–19, 3–4.
18. Ibid., 6.
19. Ibid.
20. Ibid., 9.
21. Sayed Yassin, "Zionism as Racist Ideology," in A.W. Kayyali (ed.), *Zionism, Imperialism and Racism* (London: Croom Helm, 1979), 87–105, 97.
22. Juan Comas, quoted in Hadawi, *Bitter Harvest: Palestine 1914–1979*, 24.
23. See for example: Ghada Karmi, *Married to Another Man: Israel's Dilemma in Palestine* (London, Ann Arbor: Pluto Press, 2007), 65.
24. Chaim Weizmann, *Trial and Error* (London: East and West Library, 1950), 555.
25. Israel-PLO Declaration of Principles on Interim Self-Government Arrangements 1993, preamble.
26. Amal Jamal, *The Palestinian National Movement: Politics of Contention 1967–2005* (Bloomington, Indianapolis: Indiana University Press, 2005), 35.
27. Shlomo Ben Ami, *Scars of War, Wounds of Peace: The Arab–Israeli Tragedy* (London: Phoenix, 2006), 125–7.
28. See: Moshe Shemesh, *The Palestinian Entity 1959–1974* (London: Frank Cass, 1988), 140–52.
29. See: Neri Sybesma-Knol, "Palestine and the United Nations," in Sanford R. Silverburg (ed.), *Palestine and International Law: Essays on Politics and Economics* (Jefferson, London: McFarland, 2002), 271–98.
30. See: Jamal, *The Palestinian National Movement*, 32.
31. See for example: Khalid Kishtainy, *Whither Israel? A Study of Zionist Expansion* (Beirut: PLO Research Center, 1970).
32. See: Gershom Gorenberg, *Accidental Empire: Israel and the Birth of Settlements 1967–1977* (New York: Times Books, 2006).
33. See: Ben Ami, *Scars of War, Wounds of Peace*, 86–141.
34. See: Ideth Zertal and Akiva Eldar, *The Lords of the Land: The War over Israel's Settlements in the Occupied Territories*, translated by Vivian Eden (New York: Nation Books, 2007).
35. Samir A. Mutawi, *Jordan and the 1967 War* (Cambridge: Cambridge University Press, 1987), 181–2.
36. See: Avi Shlaim, *The Iron Wall: Israel and the Arab World* (London: Penguin Books, 2000), 243–6.
37. See: Michael Oren, *Six Days of War: June 1967 and the Making of the Modern Middle East* (Oxford: Oxford University Press, 2002); Tom Segev, *1967,*

Israel, the War and the Year that Transformed the Middle East (London: Little, Brown, 2007).

38. Israel-PLO Recognition: Exchange of Letters between PM Rabin and Chairman Arafat. At http://www.mfa.gov.il/MFA (last visited August 18, 2008).

39. See: Sven Behrendt, *The Secret Israeli–Palestinian Negotiations in Oslo: The Success and Why the Process Ultimately Failed* (London, New York: Routledge, 2007).

40. Itamar Rabinovich, *Waging Peace: Israel and the Arabs 1948–2003* (Princeton: Princeton University Press, 2004), 43.

41. Declaration of Principles on Interim Self-Government Arrangements, September 13, 1993 at http://www.mfa.gov.il/MFA (last visited August 18, 2008).

42. See: Raja Shehadeh, "The Weight of Legal History: Constraints and Hopes in the Search for a Sovereign Legal Language," in Eugene Cotran and Chibli Mallat (eds.), *The Arab–Israeli Accords: Legal Perspectives* (London, The Hague, Boston: Kluwer Law International, 1996), 3–20.

43. Declaration, 1993, article 1.

44. UNSC resolution 242 (1967).

45. See: Sydney Bailey, *The Making of Resolution 242* (Dordrecht: Martinus Nijhoff, 1985), 150–6. Meir Rosenne argues that there is a principle of international law that if there is doubt about the authoritative language of a text the original language of the text is to be used. As resolution 141 was drafted by Lord Caradon, the British representative, that language was English. See: Meir Rosenne, "Legal Interpretations of UNSC 242," in Washington Institute for the Near East, *UN Security Council Resolution 242: The Building Block of Peacemaking* (Washington: A Washington Institute Monograph, 1993), 29–34.

46. For an Israeli position on this question, see: Yehuda Z. Blum, *Secure Boundaries and the Middle East* (Jerusalem: Hebrew University of Jerusalem, Institute for Legislative Research and Comparative Law, 1971).

47. See generally: Allan Gerson, *Israel, the West Bank and International Law* (London: Frank Cass, 1978).

48. Declaration, 1993, article 4.

49. Declaration, 1993, article 5(3).

50. See: Shehadeh, "The Weight of Legal History."

51. See: F. Boyle and J. Crawford, "Forum: The Creation of the State of Palestine," *European Journal of International Law*, vol. 1, no. 1/2 (1990), 301–13.

52. Moshe Shemesh, *The Palestinian Entity 1959–1974: Arab Politics and the PLO* (London: Frank Cass, 1988), 7–8.

53. Ibid., 8–14.

54. Ibid., 242.

55. Israel-PLO Recognition – Exchange of Letters, September 9, 1993.

56. UNGA resolution 3379 (XXX), the resolution had defined Zionism as a form of racism.

57. Declaration, 1993, article 6(2).

58. Edward W. Said, *Peace and Its Discontents: Gaza-Jericho 1993–1995* (London: Vintage, 1995), 2.

59. See generally: ibid.

60. Agreement on the Gaza Strip and the Jericho Area, Cairo, May 4, 1994.

61. Ibid., article IV (3).

62. Ibid., article V 1(b) and I 9(c).
63. Ibid., article V 3(a).
64. Ibid., article VI 2(b).
65. Ibid., article VIII.

CHAPTER 7

1. For an incisive analysis of the occupation see: Neve Gordon, *Israel's Occupation* (Berkeley, Los Angeles, London: University of California Press, 2008).
2. For a study of this period see generally: Nathan J. Brown, *Palestinian Politics after the Oslo Accords: Resuming Arab Palestine* (Berkeley, Los Angeles, London: University of California Press, 2003).
3. On the elections see: As'ad Ghanem, *The Palestinian Regime: A "Partial Democracy"* (Brighton, Portland: Sussex Academic Press, 2002), 87–103.
4. Ibid., 101.
5. On Hamas generally see: Shaul Mishal and Avraham Sela, *The Palestinian Hamas: Vision, Violence and, Coexistence* (New York: Columbia University Press, 2006).
6. Ibid., 32.
7. Interim Agreement, article X (2) and XI (2) d.
8. Interim Agreement, article XI (2) e.
9. Then Minister in the Prime Minister's Office and later one of the architects of the Geneva Accords.
10. Abu Mazen is the *nom de guerre* of Mahmoud Abbas, who succeeded Arafat as Palestine President in 2005.
11. "The Beilin–Abu Mazen Understandings," in Yossi Beilin, *The Road to Geneva: The Quest for a Permanent Agreement, 1996–2004* (New York: RDV Books, 2004), 299–312.
12. John Strawson, "Netanyahu's Oslo: Peace in the Slow Lane," *Soundings*, Issue 8 (1998), 49–60.
13. Galia Golan, *Israel and Palestine: Peace Plans from Oslo to Disengagement* (Princeton: Markus Weiner, 2007), 30.
14. Benjamin Netanyahu, *A Place Amongst the Nations: Israel and the World* (London, New York, Toronto, Sydney, Aukland: Bantam Press, 1993).
15. Ibid., 352.
16. Ibid., 252–353.
17. Ibid., 353.
18. See: "Prime Minister Benjamin Netanyahu, Special Interview on Israeli Television, July 28, 1997," *Journal of Palestine Studies*, vol. 27, no. 1 (Autumn 1997), 150.
19. Address by Prime Minister Benjamin Netanyahu to the Council of Jewish Federations General Assembly in Indianapolis, Prime Minister's Reports, vol. 1, no. 11 (November 19, 1997), Prime Minister's Office, Israel.
20. See: Anita Shapira, *Yigal Allon, Native Son: A Biography*, translated by Evelyn Able (Philadelphia: University of Pennsylvania Press, 2008), 312–16.
21. Declaration of Principles, article V(4).
22. Cairo Agreement, article XIII (3).
23. Interim Agreement, article XXXI (6).
24. Interim Agreement, article, XXXI (7).

25. Stephen Schwebel, American international lawyer and scholar who was to serve as a Justice of the International Court of Justice from 1981 to 2000.

26. Quoted in: Yehuda Z. Blum, *For Zion's Sake* (New York: Cornwall Books, 1987), 111.

27. An Islamic legal land category which approximates public land and is designated in the Ottoman Land Code of 1858 which is still in force in a modified form in the West Bank. See: Raja Shehadeh, *The Law of the Land* (Jerusalem: PASSIA, 1993).

28. See: Carol Farhi, "On the Legal Status of the Gaza Strip," in Meir Shamgar (ed.), *Military Government in the Territories Administered by Israel 1967–1980: The Legal Aspects*, Volume I (Jerusalem: Hebrew University of Jerusalem, 1982), 61–83.

29. Mahmoud Abbas, *Through Secret Channels* (Reading: Garnet Publishers, 1995), 220.

30. See: Ghanem, *The Palestinian Regime*, 129–35.

31. See: Dennis Ross, *The Missing Peace* (New York: Farrar, Straus and Giroux, 2004), 801–5 and Beilin, *The Road to Geneva*, 321–35. Both contain the text that was issued on December 23, 2000. There are some slight differences between the versions, but the overall shape of the plan is the same.

32. Ross, *The Missing Peace*, 801.

33. Ibid.

34. See: Benny Morris, "Camp David and After: An Exchange" (an interview with Ehud Barak), *New York Review of Books*, vol. 49, no. 10 (June 13, 2002). In the interview Morris writes: "Barak says that Palestinians were promised a continuous piece of sovereign territory except for a razor thin Israeli wedge running from Jerusalem through Maale Adumin to the Jordan River."

35. Ross, *The Missing Peace*, 804–5.

36. Ibid., 805.

37. Morris, "Camp David and After."

38. Ibid.

39. Ibid.

40. Sharon insisted on visiting the area where the Dome of the Rock and al-Aqsa Mosques stand above the Western Wall. He was insisting that it was the right of Jews to visit the areas where the Temple had once been. The Jewish religious authorities have forbidden Jews from visiting Temple Mount and Sharon's actions were widely seen as a nationalist statement to boost his popularity in the coming elections.

41. Morris, "Camp David and After."

42. See: Rafiq Latta, "Palestine/Israel: Conflict at the Crossroads," in John Strawson (ed.), *Law after Ground Zero* (London: GlassHouse Press/ Routledge-Cavendish, 2002), 170–86.

43. Arab Peace Initiative, Beirut Summit of the Arab League, March 2002, as quoted in: Golan, *Israel and Palestine*, 186.

44. Ibid.

45. The UN Security Council endorsed the roadmap in resolution 1515 (2003).

46. Quoted in Golan, *Israel and Palestine*, 193.

47. Exchange of Letters between PM Sharon and President Bush, April 14, 2004.

48. Ibid.

49. Ibid.

50. David Horowitz and Herb Kienon, "Prime Minister speaks to 'the Post,'" *The Jerusalem Post*, April 22, 2005.
51. For example, see: David Makovsky, *Engagement through Disengagement: Gaza and the Potential for Renewed Israeli–Palestinian Peacemaking* (Washington DC: The Washington Institute for Near East Policy, 2005).
52. Barak Ravid, "Olmert: There's no such thing as 'Greater Israel' anymore," *Haaretz* (English edition), September 14, 2008, at http://www/haartez.com.
53. Ibid.
54. Akiva Eldar and Avi Issacharoff, "Abbas to Haaretz: We Will Compromise on Refugees," *Haaretz* (English edition), September 14, 2008.
55. See: Speech by PM Netanyahu at Special Knesset Session, July 22, 2009. At: http://www.mfa.gov.il/MFA/Government/Speeches+by+Israeli+leaders/2009/Speech_PM_Netanyahu_special_Knesset_session_22-Jul-2009.htm (last visited July 29, 2009).
56. See: Javier Solana, "Europe's Global Role – What Next Steps?" Ditchley Foundation Lecture, London, July 11, 2009.

Bibliography

Abbas, Mahmoud, *Through Secret Channels* (Reading: Garnet Publishers, 1995).

Abu Hussein, Hussein and Fiona McKay, *Access Denied: Palestinian Land Rights in Israel* (London, New York: Zed Press, 2003).

Allain, Jean, *International Law in the Middle East: Closer to Power than Justice* (Aldershot, Burlington: Ashgate, 2004).

Allon, Yigal, *The Making of Israel's Army* (New York: Universe Books, 1970).

Anghie, Antony, *Imperialism, Sovereignty and the Making of International Law* (Cambridge: Cambridge University Press, 2005).

Antonious, George, *The Arab Awakening: The Story of the Arab National Movement* (London: Hamish Hamilton, 1938).

Bailey, Sydney, *The Making of Resolution 242* (Dordrecht: Martinus Nijhoff, 1985).

Basheer, Tahseen (ed.), *The Arab League, Edwin Montagu and the Balfour Declaration* (New York: Arab League Office, 1967).

Behrendt, Sven, *The Secret Israeli–Palestinian Negotiations in Oslo: The Success and Why the Process Ultimately Failed* (London, New York: Routledge, 2007).

Beilin, Yossi, *The Road to Geneva: The Quest for a Permanent Agreement 1996–2004* (New York: RDV books, 2004).

Ben Ami, Shlomo, *Scars of War, Wounds of Peace: The Arab–Israeli Tragedy* (London: Phoenix, 2006).

Benedict, Ruth, *Race: Science and Politics* (Westport CT: Greenwood Press, 1982).

Bentwich, Norman, "The Future of Palestine," in Harry Sacher (ed.), *Zionism and the Jewish Future* (London: John Murray, 1916), 196–209.

Bentwich, Norman, *England in Palestine* (London: Kegan Paul, Trench, Tubner, 1932).

Bentwich, Norman, *The Mandates System* (London, New York, Toronto: Longmans and Co., 1930).

Bernstein, Deborah, *Constructing Boundaries: Jewish and Arab Workers in Mandatory Palestine* (Albany NY: State University of New York Press, 2000).

Blum, Yehuda Z., *For Zion's Sake* (New York: Cornwall Books, 1987).

Blum, Yehuda Z., *Secure Boundaries and the Middle East* (Jerusalem: Hebrew University of Jerusalem, Institute for Legislative Research and Comparative Law, 1971).

Boustany, W.F., *The Palestine Mandate: Invalid and Impractical* (Beirut: American Press, 1936).

Boyle, F. and J. Crawford, "Forum: The Creation of the State of Palestine," *European Journal of International Law*, vol. 1. nos. 1/2 (1990), 301–13.

Brown, Nathan J., *Palestinian Politics after the Oslo Accords: Resuming Arab Palestine* (Berkeley, Los Angeles, London: University of California Press, 2003).

Cohen, Hillel, *Army of Shadows: Palestinian Collaboration with Zionism 1917–1948*, translated by Haim Watzman (Berkeley, Los Angeles, London: University of California Press, 2008).

Daphne Trevor, *Under the White Paper: Some Aspects of British Administration of Palestine, 1939–1947* (Jerusalem: the Jerusalem Press, 1948).

Davidson, Lawrence, *America's Palestine: Popular and Official Perceptions from Balfour to Israeli Statehood* (Gainesville FL: University Press of Florida, 2001).

Dershowitz, Alan, *The Case for Israel* (Hoboken: John Wiley and Sons, 2003).

Drory, Ze'ev, *The Israel Defence Force and the Foundation of Israel: Utopia in Uniform* (London, New York: RoutledgeCurzon, 2005).

Eldar, Akiva and Avi Issacharoff, "Abbas to Haaretz: We Will Compromise on Refugees," *Haaretz* (English edition), September 14, 2008.

Farhi, Carol, "On the Legal Status of the Gaza Strip," in Meir Shamgar (ed.), *Military Government in the Territories Administered by Israel 1967–1980: Legal Aspects*, Volume I (Jerusalem: Hebrew University of Jerusalem, 1982), 61–83.

Fitzpatrick, Peter, *Modernism and the Grounds of Law* (Cambridge: Cambridge University Press, 2001).

Fromkin, David, *A Peace to End all Peace: Creating the Modern Middle East 1914–1922* (London: Andrew Deutsch, 1989).

Gelber, Yoav, *Palestine 1948: War Escape and the Emergence of the Palestinian Refugee Problem* (Brighton: Sussex Academic Press, 2006).

Gerson, Allan, *Israel, the West Bank and International Law* (London: Frank Cass, 1978).

Ghanem, As'ad, *The Palestinian Regime: A "Partial Democracy"* (Brighton: Sussex Academic Press, 2002).

Gilbert, Martin, *Israel: A History* (Uxbridge: Black Swan, 1999).

Glubb, John Bagot, *A Soldier with the Arabs* (London: Hodder and Stoughton, 1957).

Goadby, Frederic M., *Introduction to the Study of Law: A Handbook for the Use of Egyptian Students* (London: Butterworths, 1910).

Goadby, Frederic M., *Introduction to the Study of Law: A Handbook for the Use of Students in Egypt and Palestine* (London: Butterworths, 1921).

Golan, Galia, *Israel and Palestine: Peace Plans from Oslo to Disengagement* (Princeton: Markus Weiner, 2007).

Gordon, Neve, *Israel's Occupation* (Berkeley, Los Angeles, London: University of California Press, 2008).

Gorenberg, Gershom, *Accidental Empire: Israel and the Birth of Settlements 1967–1977* (New York: Times Books, 2006).

Gorny Josef, *From Binational Society to Jewish State: Federal Concepts in Zionist Political Thought, 1920–1990, and the Jewish People* (Leiden, Boston: Brill, 2006).

Gorny, Joseph, *The British Labour Movement and Zionism* (London: Routledge, 1983).

Hadawi, Sami, *Bitter Harvest: A Modern History of Palestine* (Buckhurst Hill: Scorpion Publishing, 1989).

Hadawi, Sami, *Bitter Harvest: Palestine 1914–1979* (Delmar NY: Caravan Books, 1979).

Hadawi, Sami, *The Realities of Terrorism and Retaliation* (Toronto: Arab Palestine Association, n.d. – date references in the text end in 1989).

Haddad, Hassan, "The Biblical Bases for Zionist Colonization," in Ibrahim Abu-Lughod and Baha Abu-Laban (eds.), *Settler Regimes in Africa and the Arab World* (Wilmette IL: The Medina University Press, 1974), 3–19.

Hayter, Sir William, *Recent Constitutional Developments in Egypt* (Cambridge: Cambridge University Press, 1924).

Herzenberg, Arthur (ed.), *The Zionist Idea: A Historical Analysis and Reader* (Philadelphia: Jewish Publication Society of America, 1997).

Herzl, Theodor, *Der Judenstaat* (Leipzig und Vien: M. Britebrnstein Verlas-Buch-handlung, 1896).

Herzl, Theodor, *The Jewish State* (New York: Dover Publications, 1988).

Hess, Moses, *The Revival of Israel: Rome and Jerusalem: The Last Nationalist Question*, translated by Mayer Waxman (Lincoln, London: University of Nebraska Press, 1995).

Higgins, Rosalyn, *Problems and Process: International Law and How We Use It* (Oxford: Clarendon, 1994).

Horowitz, David and Herb Kienon, "The Prime Minister speaks to 'the Post,'" *The Jerusalem Post*, April 22, 2005.

Huxley, Elizabeth, *A White Man's Country: Lord Delamere and the Making of Kenya* (London: Macmillan and Co., 1935, 2 vols.).

Institute of Palestine Studies, *The Partition of Palestine*, Monograph Series 9 (Beirut, 1967).

Jacobson, Abigail, "Alternative Voices in Late Ottoman Palestine: Jews and Arabs and the Evolving National Conflict," paper given at a PASSIA meeting May 24, 2004. http://passia.org/meetings/2004/May-24-Late-Ottoman-Palestine.htm (last visited July 20, 2007).

Jamal, Amal, *The Palestine National Movement: Politics of Contention 1967–2005* (Bloomington: Indiana University Press 2005).

Jiryis, Sabri, *The Arabs in Israel*, translated by Inea Bushnaq (New York, London: Monthly Review Press, 1976).

Karmi, Ghada, *Married to Another Man: Israel's Dilemma in Palestine* (London: Pluto Press, 2007).

Karsh, Efraim, *Fabricating Israeli History: The "New Historians"* (London, Portland: Frank Cass, 1997).

Kedourie, Elie, *Arab Political Memoirs and Other Studies* (London: Frank Cass, 1979).

Khalidi, Rashid, *Palestinian Identity: The Construction of Modern National Consciousness* (New York: Columbia University Press, 1997).

Kimmerling, Baruch and Joel S. Migdal, *The Palestinian People: A History* (Cambridge MA, London: Harvard University Press, 2003).

Kishtainy, Khalid, *Wither Israel? A Study of Zionist Expansion* (Beirut: PLO Research Center, 1970).

Kolsky, Thomas A., *Jews against Zionism: The American Council for Judaism 1942–1948* (Philadelphia PA: Temple University Press, 1992).

Kretzmer, David, *The Legal Status of the Arabs in Israel* (Boulder: Westview Press, 1990).

Kuntzel, Matthias, "National Socialism and Anti-Semitism in the Arab World," *Jewish Political Studies Review*, vol. 17, nos. 1–2 (2005).

Kuntzel, Matthias, *Jihad and Jew-Hatred: Islamism, Nazism and the Roots of 9/11*, translated by Colin Meade (New York: Telos Press, 2007).

Laqueur, Walter (ed.), *The Arab–Israeli Reader: A Documentary History of the Middle East Conflict* (Harmondsworth: Penguin Books, 1970).

Laqueur, Walter, *A History of Zionism* (London: Tauris Parke Paperbacks, 2003).

Latta, Rafiq, "Palestine/Israel: Conflict at the Crossroads," in John Strawson (ed.), *Law after Ground Zero* (London: GlassHouse Press/Routledge-Cavendish, 2002), 170–86.

Lewis, Bernard, *Semites and Anti-Semites* (London: Phoenix Giant, 1977).

Likhovski, Assaf, *Law and Identity in Mandate Palestine* (Chapel Hill: University of North Carolina Press, 2006).

Makovsky, David, *Engagement through Disengagement: Gaza and the Potential for Renewed Israeli–Palestinian Peacemaking* (Washington DC: The Washington Institute for Near East Policy, 2005).

Masalha, Nur, *A Land without a People: Israel, Transfer and the Palestinians 1949-1996* (London: Faber and Faber, 1997).

Masalha, Nur, *The Politics of Denial: Israel and the Palestinian Refugee Problem* (London, Sterling: Pluto Press, 2003).

McCarthy, Justin, *The Population of Palestine: Population History and Statistics in the Late Ottoman Period and the Mandate* (New York: Columbia University Press, 1990).

Mishal, Shaul and Avraham Sela, *The Palestinian Hamas: Vision, Violence and Co-existence* (New York: Columbia University Press, 2006).

Monroe, Elizabeth, *Britain's Moment in the Middle East 1914–1971* (London: Chatto and Windus, 1981).

Montesquieu, Charles de Secondat, baron de, *Spirit of Laws*, translated by Anne M. Cohler, Basia Caroline Miller and Harold Samuel Stone (Cambridge: Cambridge University Press, 1989).

Morris, Benny, "Camp David and After: An Exchange" (an interview with Ehud Barak), *New York Review of Books*, vol. 49, no. 10 (June 13, 2002).

Morris, Benny, *1948: A History of the First Arab–Israeli War* (New Haven, London: Yale University Press, 2008).

Morris, Benny, Interview with Ari Shavit, *Haaretz* (English edition), January 9, 2004.

Morris, Benny, *Righteous Victims: A History of the Zionist–Arab Conflict 1881–1999* (New York: Alfred A. Knopf, 1999).

Morris, Benny, *The Birth of the Palestinian Refugee Problem 1947–1949* (Cambridge: Cambridge University Press, 1987).

Morris, Benny, *The Birth of the Palestinian Refugee Problem Revisited* (Cambridge: Cambridge University Press, 2004).

Mutawi, Samir A., *Jordan and the 1967 War* (Cambridge: Cambridge University Press, 1987).

Nafi, Basheer M., *Arabism, Islamism and the Palestine Question 1908–1941* (Reading: Ithaca Press, 1998).

Netanyahu, Benjamin, "Prime Minister Benjamin Netanyahu, Special Interview on Israeli Television July 28, 1997," *Journal of Palestinian Studies*, vol. 27, no. 1 (Autumn 1997), 149–50.

Netanyahu, Benjamin, *A Place Amongst the Nations: Israel and the World* (London, New York, Toronto, Sydney, Auckland: Bantam Press, 1993).

Netanyahu, Benjamin, Address by Prime Minister Benjamin Netanyahu to the Council of Jewish Federations General Assembly in Indianapolis, Prime Minister's Reports, vol. 1, no. 11 (November 19, 1997), Prime Minister's Office, Israel.

Nuseibeh, Hazem Zaki, *The Ideas of Arab Nationalism* (Ithaca: Cornell University Press, 1956).

Oren, Michael, *Six Days of War: June 1967 and the Making of the Modern Middle East* (Oxford: Oxford University Press, 2002).

Pappé, Ilan, *A Modern History of Palestine: One Land, Two Peoples* (Cambridge: Cambridge University Press, 2004).

Pappé, Ilan, *The Ethnic Cleansing of Palestine* (Oxford: Oneworld, 2006).

Passen, Pierre van, *The Forgotten Ally* (New York: Dial Press, 1943).

Pinsker, *Auto-Emancipation: A Call to His People from a Russian Jew* (London: Rita Searl, 1947).

Quigley, John, *The Case for Palestine* (Durham, London: Duke University Press, 2005).

Rabinovich, Itamar, *Waging Peace: Israel and the Arabs 1948–2003* (Princeton: Princeton University Press, 2004).

Raddosh, Allis and Ronald Radosh, *A Safe Haven: Harry S. Truman and the Founding of Israel* (New York: HarperCollins, 2009).

Ravid, Barak, "Olmert: There's no such thing as 'Greater Israel' anymore," *Haaretz* (English edition), September 14, 2008.

Rosenne, Meir, "Legal Interpretations of UNSC 242," in Washington Institute for the Near East, *UN Security Council Resolution 242: The Building Block of Peacemaking* (Washington DC: A Washington Institute Monograph, 1993).

Ross, Dennis, *The Missing Peace* (New York: Farrar, Straus and Giroux, 2004).

Rossenne, Shabtai, *Israel's Armistice Agreements with the Arab States* (Tel Aviv: International Law Association, Israel Branch, 1951).

Sa'di, Ahmad H. and Lila Abu-Lughod (eds.), *Nakba: Palestine 1948, and the Claims of Memory* (New York: Columbia University Press, 2007).

Said, Edward W., *Culture and Imperialism* (London: Chatto and Windus, 1993).

Said, Edward W., *Orientalism: Western Conceptions of the Orient* (London: Penguin Books, 1991).

Said, Edward W., *Peace and Its Discontents: Gaza and Jericho 1993–1995* (London: Vintage, 1995).

Sait, Siraj, "International Refugee Law: Excluding the Palestinians," in John Strawson (ed.), *Law after Ground Zero* (London: GlassHouse/Routledge-Cavendish, 2002), 90–107.

Salaman, Redcliffe N., *Palestine Reclaimed: Letters from a Jewish Officer in Palestine* (London, New York: George Routledge and Sons, 1920).

Samuels, Gertrude, *B-G: Fighter of Goliaths, The Story of Ben-Gurion* (Lincoln NE: Authors Guild Backprint, 2000).

Satloff, Robert, *Among the Righteous: Lost Stories from the Holocaust's Long Reach into Arab Lands* (New York: Public Affairs, 2006).

Schechtman, Joseph B., *The Mufti and the Fuehrer: The Rise and Fall of Haj Amin-e-Husseini* (New York, London: Thomas Yoseloff, 1965).

Schoenman, Ralph, *The Hidden History of Zionism* (Santa Barbara: Veritas Press, 1988).

Segev, Tom, *1967, Israel, the War and the Year that Transformed the Middle East* (London: Little Brown, 2007).

Segev, Tom, *One Palestine Complete: Jews and Arabs under the British Mandate* (London: Little Brown, 2000).

Shapira, Anita, *Yigal Allon, Native Son: A Biography*, translated by Evelyn Able (Philadelphia: University of Pennsylvania Press, 2008).

Shehadeh, Raja, "The Weight of Legal History: Constraints and Hopes in the Search for a Sovereign Legal Language," in Eugene Cotran and Chibli Mallat (eds.), *The Arab–Israel Accords: Legal Perspectives* (London, The Hague, Boston: Kluwer Law International, 1996).

Shehadeh, Raja, *The Law of the Land: Settlements and Land Issues Under Israeli Military Occupation* (Jerusalem: PASSIA, 1993).

Shemesh, Moshe, *The Palestinian Entity 1959–1974* (London: Frank Cass, 1988).

Shlaim, Avi, "The Rise and Fall of the All-Palestine Government in Gaza," *Journal of Palestine Studies*, vol. 20, no. 1 (1990), 37–53.

Shlaim, Avi, *The Iron Wall: Israel and the Arab World* (London: Penguin, 2000).

Shlaim, Avi, *The Politics of Partition: King Abdullah, the Zionists and Palestine, 1921–1951* (Oxford: Oxford University Press, 1990).

Shuman, Frederick L., *International Politics* (New York, Toronto, London: McGraw Hill, 1948).

Shur, Chaim, *Shomrim in the Land of Apartheid: The History of Hashomer Hatzair in South Africa 1935–1970* (Kibbutz Dalia: Yad Yaari-Givat Haviva, 1998).

Sicker, Martin, *The Middle East in the Twentieth Century* (Westport CT: Greenwood Press, 2001).

Smuts, J.C., *The League of Nations: A Practical Suggestion* (London: Hodder and Stoughton, 1918).

Solokow, Nahum, *History of Zionism 1600–1918* (London: Longmans, 1919).

Stein, Leonard, *The Balfour Declaration* (London, Jerusalem: Magnes Press, 1983).

Stevens, Richard P., *The Settler-Colonial Phenomenon in Africa and the Middle East* (Khartoum: Khartoum University Press, 1976).

Stoyanovsky, Jacob, *The Mandate for Palestine: A Contribution to the Theory and Practice of International Mandates* (London, New York, Toronto: Longmans, Green and Co., 1928).

Strawson, John, "Netanyahu's Oslo: Peace in the Slow Lane," *Soundings*, Issue 8 (1998), 49–60.

Strawson, John, "Orientalism and Legal Education in the Middle East: Reading Frederic Goadby's *Introduction to the Study of Law*," *Legal Studies*, vol. 21, no. 4 (2001), 663–78.

Sybesma-Knol, Neri, "Palestine and the United Nations," in Sanford R. Silverburg (ed.), *Palestine and International Law: Essays on Politics and Economics* (Jefferson NC, London: McFarland, 2002).

Takkenberg, Lex, *The Status of the Palestinian Refugees in International Law* (Oxford: Clarendon Press, 1998).

Tal, David, *The War in Palestine 1948: Strategy and Diplomacy* (London, New York: Routledge, 2004).

Tibi, Bassam, *Arab Nationalism: A Critical Enquiry*, edited and translated by Marion Farouk-Sluglette and Peter Sluglette (London, Basingstoke: Macmillan Press, 1981).

Wasserstein, Bernard, *Israel and Palestine: Why They Fight and Can They Stop?* (London: Profile Books, 2003).

Weisbord, Robert G., *African Zion: The Attempt to Establish a Jewish Colony in the East Africa Protectorate 1903–1905* (Philadelphia: The Jewish Publication Society of America, 5728/1968).

Weizmann, Chaim, "Introduction," in Harry Sacher (ed.), *Zionism and the Jewish Future* (London: John Murray, 1916).

Weizmann, Chaim, *Trial and Error* (London: East West Library, 1950).

Yapp, M.E., *The Near East Since the First World War: A History to 1995* (London, New York: Longman, 1996).

Yassin, Sayed, "Zionism as Racist Ideology," in A.W. Kayyali (ed.), *Zionism, Imperialism and Racism* (London: Croom Helm, 1979).

Zangwill, Israel, *The Voice of Jerusalem* (London: William Heinemann, 1920).

Zayas, Alfred-Maurice de, *A Terrible Revenge: The Ethnic Cleansing of the East European Germans* (New York: Palgrave Macmillan, 2006).

Zeine, Zeine E., *Arab–Turkish Relations and the Emergence of Arab Nationalism* (Beirut: Khayat, 1958).

Zertal, Ideth and Akiva Eldar, *The Lords of the Land: Israel's Settlements in the Occupied Territories*, translated by Vivian Eden (New York: Nation Books, 2007).

Zipperstein, Steven I., *Elusive Prophet: Ahad Ha'am and the Origins of Zionism* (Berkeley, Los Angeles: University of California Press, 1993).

Index

Compiled by Sue Carlton